Dependency and Development

Dependency and Development

An Introduction to the Third World

Ted C. Lewellen

BERGIN & GARVEY
Westport, Connecticut • London

Library of Congress Cataloging-in-Publication Data

Lewellen, Ted. C.
Dependency and development : an introduction to the Third World / Ted
C. Lewellen.
p.   cm.
Includes bibliographical references and index.
ISBN 0–89789–399–9. — ISBN 0–89789–400–6 (pbk.)
1. Developing countries—Dependency on foreign countries.
2. Sustainable development—Developing countries. 3. Developing
countries—Politics and government. I. Title.
HC59.7.L4172   1995
337'.09172'4—dc20   94–39193

British Library Cataloguing in Publication Data is available.

Library of Congress Catalog Card Number: 94–39193
ISBN: 0–89789–399–9
       0–89789–400–6 (pbk.)

First published in 1995

Bergin & Garvey, 88 Post Road West, Westport, CT 06881
An imprint of Greenwood Publishing Group, Inc.

Printed in the United States of America

The paper used in this book complies with the
Permanent Paper Standard issued by the National
Information Standards Organization (Z39.48–1984).

10 9 8 7 6 5 4

Contents

Illustrations

Preface

An interdisciplinary overview of the Third World is comparable with a guided tour through the entire Metropolitan Museum. One gets tantalizing glimpses while passing by at a heady pace, though now and then it is possible to pay special attention to a captivating exhibit before proceeding. On reaching the exit, the individual should feel frustrated, rather than sated, and look forward to a later visit with the time to really observe, to analyze, and to ponder, focusing perhaps on only one display of special interest. That return trip will be much easier and much more edifying, because the visitor will have a mental map of the place, a feeling for what is there, a respect for the complexity of it all, and a knowledge of how the various parts relate to the whole.

This analogy can be stretched, but it does suggest the value of the wide view, often repudiated by an academia that is by nature segmented within tight disciplines. At a crucial point in my own studies, the more sweeping vista would have been very useful. Though I am suspicious of the term "expert," it is possible that I might have qualified as an expert on about four square miles of Peru at one brief point in time. My anthropological field work among the Aymara Indians on an island in Lake Titicaca gave me many fascinating insights into the life of one community; I learned a lot about their labor migration, their religion and rituals, their social interactions, and so forth. However, looking back a decade and a half later, I cannot help but wish that Eric Wolf's *Europe and the People Without History* (1982) had been available at the time. This seminal book, which situates indigenous cultures within the world-system, offers a panoramic viewpoint that might have given my analysis a very different turn. I would have been more aware of how these isolated Indians fit within historical patterns common to peasants across the globe.

Truly interdisciplinary classes on the Third World may be a wave of the future, but the reality today is that the subject is taught in a multitude of discipline-specific classes, especially in the fields of economics,

cultural geography, and political science. A book such as this might be
valuable to such courses in two ways. First, it links one discipline to
other disciplines and provides a broad context for focused studies.
Political science, for example, might well consider the demographic
transition in relation to state power. Similarly, an expanded awareness
of ecological constraints is of value to the economic point of view.
Second, teachers of such courses might benefit from an easily accessible
introduction to other disciplinary perspectives to augment their own
bases of knowledge.

Though I hope this book will find its place in the classroom, I prefer
to think of it as an analytical overview, rather than as a textbook.
Textbooks try to cover their material thoroughly; this is impossible with
a subject as expansive and complex as the Third World. A reasonable
approximation might be accomplished in 2,000 pages or so, but the
result would be a reference work rather than a book to be read and
enjoyed. Textbooks aim for at least the illusion of objectivity. There is,
however, virtually nothing about the Third World that is not controversial, and there are usually a multitude of scholarly opinions rather
than just two or three. While trying to be fair and factual, I have chosen
to take a stand to avid bogging down in endless quibbling. Needless to
say, I come to the project with certain convictions, and others have
evolved naturally out of the research and writing. It will be obvious that
I have little sympathy for one-size-fits-all economic prescriptions for
development that are based on idealized mathematical models that
ignore history, individual culture, and the different stages of development of different nations. Also, I made no attempt to gloss over the
lamentable human rights record of the United States during the period
of the Cold War, a subject that has been of particular interest to me for
some years. Readers will, without doubt, recognize such biases and
evaluate them according to their own knowledge and understandings.

Finally, textbooks try to be self-contained, whereas I see this volume
as background for more focused studies of individual nations, peoples,
and issues. The book might be assigned at the beginning of a course as
an overview of the subject, to be supplemented by case studies and
analyses of particular issues, or its ten chapters can be used along with
appropriate readings to provide the structure for a semester-long
course. I also hope the book finds an audience outside the classroom;
the subject will be of interest to the casual reader who wants a better
understanding of the non-Western world.

The book is truly interdisciplinary. Though the author is a cultural
anthropologist, information and theories have been drawn from almost
every division of the social sciences, from economics and demographics
to human ecology. I tackled this project only after ten years of teaching
a course titled "Dependency and Development: An Introduction to the
Third World" at the University of Richmond. The course is interdisciplinary, taught as part of the International Studies program. At first, I

was highly intimidated by the sheer amount of material available, and I was hardly unaware of the hubris of venturing out of my own field into the lions' dens of other disciplines. What I found was that the various perspectives fit together rather nicely and constantly reinforced each other. History led easily and naturally into political science, which in its turn inevitably involved economics, human rights, and urban studies. The world is of a piece, and the process of dividing it arbitrarily according to discipline seems increasingly artificial. Nevertheless, writing the book was a humbling experience. The bibliography includes a minute fraction of the available material on a subject this vast. It is inevitable that there are large areas left uncovered. For example, ideally there might be chapters on the richness of Third World cultures and religions, and on the many brilliant writers, artists, scientists, and statesmen who have emerged from these countries. Alas, one must always choose — and take the responsibility for one's choices.

Acknowledgments

I thank Professor Jonathan Wight, who read drafts of the two chapters on economics and offered valuable insights, which found their way into the finished product. The University of Richmond provided the sabbatical and research grant that made the project possible. Finally, I thank each of my sources, without whom a book like this would not even be conceivable.

1

Does the Third World Exist?

Yousri, a dark and handsome young man from southern Egypt, feels trapped in the teeming city of Cairo. Yousri's father, a caretaker at a city mosque, believed that education would allow his seven children to rise higher than he had himself, and Yousri stayed in school. His fluent Hebrew and English earned him a radio-room job eavesdropping on the Israelis during his mandatory military service. Afterward, despite his education and a talent for languages, Egypt offered few job opportunities. Like tens of thousands of others of his generation, he tried working in the oil-rich countries of Saudi Arabia and Kuwait, but the loneliness and the contempt afforded imported labor were unbearable. Back in Cairo, at the age of thirty he finds himself still living with his parents and working the night shift at a hotel. Though a part of Egypt's enviable "middle class," he seems to have attained the limits of his prospects. Marriage is as desirable as it is impossible; he would need his own apartment, furniture, and some savings. He can only dream, with little real hope, of escape to America or Europe (Horwitz 1991:96–102).

Alicia, an Aymara Indian, lives in a complex of three thatch-roofed mud rooms that enclose a small courtyard near Lake Titicaca in southern Peru. In her entire thirty-five years she has never been farther than Ilave, only forty miles away. She and her husband Cirilo together own nine small plots of land, upon which they grow barley, beans, quinoa, and several varieties of potatoes. The land will be inherited equally by their three children (two others died in their first year). This continual division of the land, combined with population growth, renders it impossible for even a relatively well-off family to survive any longer on its own produce. Twice a year, for two months each during planting and harvest, Cirilo travels several hundred miles to work for meager wages in the rice fields on the coast. These wages have purchased a foot-treadle sewing machine and a portable radio (although they can seldom afford batteries, and, of course, there is no electricity, any more than there is running water). In many ways, life goes on much as it always has for Alicia. Though nominally Catholic, she still believes in the ghosts and spirits of the old pre-Inca religion and would not think of celebrating a major event, such as the roofing of a house, without chewing coca with the local shaman and perhaps burying a llama fetus in the corner of the courtyard to protect against evil. She will probably die of tuberculosis or typhoid before the age of fifty (Lewellen 1978).

Chung Lee is an elderly businessman in Indonesia. As a child he had emigrated with his family from Java, where he was born, to China. There, the terrors of the Japanese occupation were followed by the chaos of civil war and the triumph of the Communists. Originally a supporter of Mao Zedong's armies against the corrupt Koumintang nationalists, young Lee became repelled by the increasing repression of the revolutionary government. He escaped through Hong Kong to join his father, who had already resettled in Jakarta. After working for his father's construction company for a while, he started a dress shop with his wife. Ethnic tension grew increasingly violent between the Indonesians and the elite Chinese, a mere 10 percent of the population that held almost 90 percent of all businesses. During a period of economic depression, local Indonesian youths beleaguered the shop, demanding "protection" money and ultimately driving Lee out of business. With the emergence of a new, more stable government, Lee and his wife opened a beauty salon and beautician school, which became quite successful. Though of retirement age, the couple still puts in long hours at their trade and are considered leading lights in the Jakarta business community. They live in a large house with several servants (Williams 1991:77–83).

Desperate for food, Agnes Shabalala arrived at the township of Alexandra, South Africa, from rural Natal. Two months later, she finds herself standing in line at a soup kitchen with her two young children. Decades of apartheid coupled with a four-year recession fiercely affected rural areas, where tens of thousands of blacks lived on land insufficient to feed themselves at even barest subsistence levels. Shabalala's husband was killed two years earlier in factional fighting, and drought ruined what crops she could raise herself, forcing her migration to the city. The township, which abuts a wealthy white residential area, had grown into a huge shantytown as it burgeoned from 80,000 residents in the late 1980s to over 300,000 in 1993. Shabalala moved to the township in the hopes that her relatives already there could take her in, but they had no room, nor could she find a job. She lives in a tiny lean-to with her children, dependent on charity for merest survival (Taylor 1993).

About the only thing that Yousri, Alicia, Lee, and Shabalala have in common is that they all live in the Third World. Although none might be considered typical, neither are they atypical. They are worthy of mention for two reasons. First, taken together, they give at least a rough impression of the vast diversity that can be found in the Third World. Second, it is important to be reminded at the outset that the Third World is not a statistical abstraction nor a set of political or economic principles; it is, first and foremost, *people* — men, women, and children, each with his or her own peculiar intelligence and emotions, tragedies and successes, pleasures and suffering, realities and dreams. The human dimension is easily forgotten amid the sea of statistics, generalities, theories, and ideologies that pervade any discussion of such an immense and diffuse concept as the Third World. This is not to promote a psychological reductionism that views societies and nations as nothing more than multiple individual actions taken together; a broad general perspective is not only legitimate, it is also absolutely essential if we are to understand the structural underpinnings of social systems. Population growth, for example, looks very different when charted on a national or world level than it does to the individual couple engaged in the intensely personal decision whether or not to have another child. However, ultimately, of course, it is that couple who are the source and object of all our theorizing. Social science may periodically need to forget that its study is about real people, but it should not forget for long.

THE THIRD WORLD — AN "ARBITRARY, PEJORATIVE, AND IRRITATING" TERM

The meaning of the term "Third World" has been in a continual state of evolution since the phrase was first coined in France in 1952. On August 14 of that year it was prominently used in an article in *L'Observateur* by French demographer Alfred Sauvy to refer to the *tiers état* — the poor, powerless, and marginalized — in France prior to the 1789 revolution. Such a useful concept would not be confined long to the history of one country. It was quickly widened to include countries that were marginalized in the international system.

What started as an economic and social concept became increasingly political as the Cold War continued to heat up and the United States attempted to force all nations into a Procrustes Bed that had room only for capitalists, communists, or fellow travelers. In an attempt to escape such restrictive definitions, and all that was implied in terms of aid and intervention by the great powers, the poorer countries came together in a Non-Aligned Movement in 1961 and a "neutral" Group of seventy-seven in 1964. The mass media handled such movements as a third way between capitalism and communism, though most of the "neutral" countries were really allied with either the United States or the Soviet Union. The Third World, thus, assumed a pastiche of political and economic meanings that never made a whole lot of sense (Worsley 1984:307; Bissio 1984:7).

The First World is a fairly coherent entity consisting of the industrialized capitalist countries, including the United States, Canada, the countries of western Europe, Australia, and Japan. These countries have much in common besides capitalism. All are democracies. Per capita income is relatively high, and although the distribution of wealth and income is often extreme, the larger part of their citizenry are middle class. With a few notable exceptions, these countries have been politically stable at least since the end of World War II, and political repression seems to be relatively low (though, as we shall see, some of them have supported severe repression in their colonies or client states). There are borderline cases. Israel and South Africa, for example, seem First World in some respects and Third World in others, and Portugal is usually considered First World by dint of its geographic placement in western Europe, although its per capita income is less than that of South Korea.

The Second World no longer exists — its components are either in transition to the First World or to the Third World — but until about 1989 it was also a coherent group, consisting of the industrialized socialist countries, namely, the Soviet Union and eastern Europe. The classification presented minor problems — Romania and Albania (included) were not much more "developed" than Cuba (excluded) — but there was little argument about the nature of the Second World.

The Third World was — and increasingly *is* — more problematic. Such a wide range of nations are encompassed in this nebulous concept that perhaps the only definition that truly fits is simply: not First World and not Second World (and even then there are many borderline cases) (Figure 1.1). The term includes both socialist and capitalist economies, and many variations of the two. It includes the poorest nations of the earth, such as Tanzania and Afghanistan, and the richest, such as the United Arab Emirates and Kuwait. It includes the most populous countries in the world such as China (over a billion people) and the least populous such as the island nation of Tonga (less than 200,000). Why use the term at all?

The alternative seems to be to employ some variation of "development" — less developed countries (LDCs), underdeveloped countries (UDCs), or developing nations. One problem here is that many of these countries — those sometimes referred to as the Fourth World — are not developing and are not going to develop in the foreseeable future. A more fundamental difficulty is that the concept of development is itself ambiguous. The term is usually used in reference to the industrialization and consumerism of the First World, but some countries might wisely choose a different track. It is questionable whether all countries should be held up to a standard, defined by the West, to which most can never really aspire. For this reason, it might be argued that any variation of "development" is both condescending and ethnocentric (though it is virtually impossible to escape such usage).

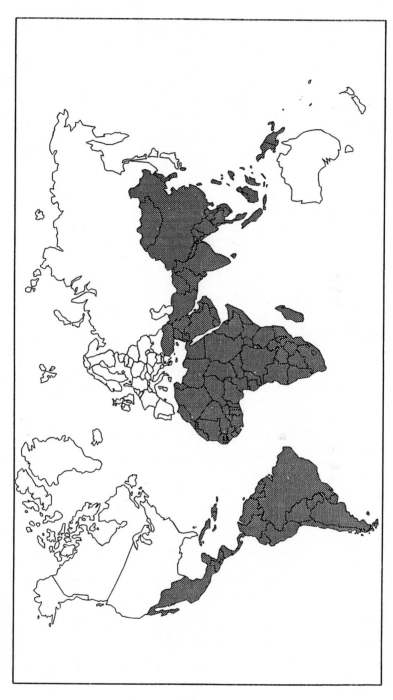

FIGURE 1.1
The Third World

One sometimes encounters the term "South" to refer to the Third World and "North" to the industrialized nations (Brandt 1980). There is a very rough geographical logic to this, at least for Europe, Africa, and the Americas. When one reaches Asia and the Pacific, however, the rich-North/poor-South distinction falls apart. Australia (rich) is below the equator and China (poor) extends well north of Japan (very rich). The North/South distinction also suggests a geographical determinism — tropics create poverty while temperate and cold climates are conducive todevelopment — that is difficult to defend historically. The first states evolved in tropical settings such as Mesopotamia, Egypt, Peru, and Mesoamerica. Great civilizations have thrived in most of the regions now considered the Third World. Another term one often encounters is "periphery." This term derives from a world-system perspective that views the industrialized countries as the "core." The term conjures images of satellites orbiting a nucleus, which many find offensive, and, indeed, the term strongly suggests dependency theory, which many scholars do not accept.

What it amounts to is that no term is truly adequate, but all are useful and, to some extent, unavoidable, depending on what aspect one is emphasizing. In this book, I will employ "South," "periphery," and the variations of "developing" as need be, though conscious of their limitations.

The phrase "Third World" will find few ardent defenders — especially now that the disappearance of the Second World makes it flatly misleading — but we may be stuck with it because it has gained a place in the common vocabulary of nations. Many scholars and laymen in both the First and Third Worlds consider the term to be derogatory, but many others accept it as simply descriptive. Mao Zedong used a variant of the three-worlds classification, seeing the First World as the superpowers — the United States and the Soviet Union — the Second World as the clients of the superpowers, and the Third World as the rest. A prominent journal, *The Third World Quarterly*, has many scholars from Third World countries on its editorial board, and the *Third World Guide* is originally published in Uruguay and represents the views of the periphery. One might ultimately find oneself agreeing with Australian scholar Donald Denoon (1985:856) who holds that "Third World" is an "arbitrary, pejorative, and thoroughly irritating term" but that, unfortunately, "the conditions it describes are . . . profoundly entrenched in the political, social and economic structure of the contemporary world."

DEPENDENCY AND DEVELOPMENT: COMMON FEATURES OF THE THIRD WORLD

The Third World is too vast to encompass a neatly coherent collection of traits. There will be many exceptions to any generalization made about over 100 large and small nations. This must be constantly kept in mind, because any book such as this is forced to make such generalizations, and endless disclaimers get readily tiresome. This said, there are a number of overlapping features that these countries do hold in common. In fact, a majority of Third World countries will have *all* of the following traits. Each will be discussed in more detail in subsequent chapters.

Poverty

There are many problems with using such levelling statistics as per capita income or gross domestic product (GDP) to measure poverty. Measuring by income alone does not tell the whole story. A family is not necessarily "poor" even if it has very little money income as long as its culture is intact and it owns sufficient land to feed itself. Such a situation, common only a few decades ago, is increasingly rare, because throughout the world indigenous cultures have collapsed and former subsistence producers have been pushed off their land or have been brought into the market economy. The main objection to the use of per capita statistics, however, is that they do not measure income or wealth distribution. Brazil is rated among the wealthiest of Third World countries by the World Bank (1992), but the lowest 60 percent of the people receive only 19 percent of national income; the top decile receives almost 50 percent. Brazil is an extreme case, but it does reveal a common pattern: a small segment of the population — in some cases, less than 1 percent — is extremely wealthy, while a vast majority is exceedingly poor.

If these caveats are kept in mind, per capita income can be used as a very rough measure for ranking countries. By this measure, the countries of the First World, with approximately 20 percent of the global population, exist as islands in a sea of poverty. From 800 million to 1 billion people are considered to be living in "absolute poverty," unable to provide even the basic necessities of life. Mozambique, with a per capita GDP of $80, is the poorest country in the world. China and India, which together comprise 38 percent of the world's population, have per capita GDPs of less than $400 (though, as we will see, purchasing power, income distribution, and social welfare are vastly different in the two countries).

Poverty is total; it is not just economic. Poverty means poor health because one cannot afford sufficient calories or proper nutrition. It means disease and little access to modern medicine. It means lack of education. It means constantly searching for employment, and it means the psychological consequences of hopelessness and insecurity. It may mean familial violence, broken homes, and crime. Where jobs exist, it can mean backbreaking labor for long hours and exposure to toxic chemicals that are banned in First World countries. It may mean that any protest against such conditions will result in arrest, torture, perhaps even death.

Lack of Industrialization, or Sectoral Development

The large majority of Third World countries lack big industry, and, thus, the agricultural sector, often grossly inefficient, must account for most of the national wealth. Many countries have the capability for industry — large labor forces, natural resources — but lack the infrastructure to attract investment. Without good roads, railroads, ports, hydroelectric dams, and so forth, many countries are unable to develop their potentials. If most of the people are poor, there is insufficient domestic demand for the produce of industry, nor is there sufficient capital to finance it. Often a country can import manufactured goods more cheaply and of better quality than it can make. Traditionally, multinational corporations have tended to invest in agriculture and mining rather than than industry.

Where heavy industry has taken root, it is not distributed throughout the country, as in the United States, but may be concentrated in a single port city, such as Lima, Peru, or Jakarta, Indonesia. The result is that one sector of the country may thrive while the rest is stagnant or in decline.

There is an increasing tendency for multinational companies to shift labor-intensive industry to Third World countries, because of the low labor costs. The norm, however, is still that industry remains capital-intensive, that is, based on assembly lines and machinery, providing few jobs relative to the money invested. The result is that jobs in industry have not been able to keep up with population growth, and in many countries, only a minuscule percent of working adults have jobs in industry.

Dependency

Virtually every country of the Third World is a former colony of one of the European powers. The structures of dependency were embedded over decades or even centuries and did not disappear with the end of colonialism. In country after country, subsistence or domestic agriculture was shifted to export crops. Minerals were exported on a massive scale. Even oil-rich countries, wealthy enough to control their own industries, such as Saudi Arabia, are dependent on multinational corporations for processing and distribution. Many of the countries are monocultures, utterly reliant on only one or two products for most of their export earnings. They have little room to negotiate prices and scant flexibility to sustain a drop in world demand for their product.

The desperate need for foreign investment pits countries with the same product against each other in providing the best investment climate for multinational corporations (which usually means the lowest taxes and the most generous corporate laws). A country often must negotiate with a corporation many times wealthier than itself.

Some countries are heavily dependent on foreign aid, and a threatened cutoff can be a potent means of control. Often there are requirements that foreign aid (mostly guaranteed loans) must be spent within the host country. When factory equipment, tractors, and trucks are purchased from a single source, the recipient country can become utterly dependent on that source for replacement parts.

Over the past twenty years or so, a new form of dependency has been developing — debt dependency. Deeply in debt to the World Bank, foreign governments, and private banks and unable to pay even the interest on their loans, some countries virtually have had to turn over their economies to the International Monetary Fund (IMF) in order to get short-term loans and maintain their credit.

Dependency is not only economic. The massive military aid conferred by both the United States and the former Soviet Union conveys enormous power over the armed forces of Third World countries. This method of gaining influence by creating military-aid dependency has been especially effective in countries where the security forces are autonomous — that is, not under the control of the civilian government — or have actually formed the government.

Dependency is a two-way street. The United States and Japan are equally dependent on the Third World for raw materials, cheap labor, and markets. The First World, however, is dependent from a position of power. If Chile decides to nationalize its copper mines, the United States, and the multinationals centered there, have many alternatives: an embargo to destroy the heavily dependent Chilean economy, a cutoff of foreign loans and aid, manipulation of world copper prices, a shift of purchasing to another copper-producing country such as Zaire, or even the secret destabilization of the government (all of these were used against Chile between 1970 and 1973). A Third World country, on the other hand, has little power to support its demands.

Population Growth

All First World countries and most former Second World countries have stabilized their populations (we will examine the reasons later). This means that virtually all of the enormous growth in global population is taking place in the Third World, and it is generally the poorest countries that have the most rapid rates of growth. Just to stay even, a country that doubles its population in twenty years must in the same period double its employment opportunities, its health facilities, its teachers and schoolrooms, its industrial output, its agricultural production, and its exports and imports. It must do this while paying off a huge international debt. Little wonder that many countries are backsliding economically. A 2 percent growth in gross national product (GNP) coupled with a 3 percent growth in population effectively means a 1 percent economic decline.

Population growth should not be taken as the most important cause of poverty. As we will see, the severity of the problem depends on many factors, most importantly, the nature of the economy. Some countries handle population growth better than others. Also, some countries have been successful at reducing the rate of population growth, while others seem impotent to do so or have yet to recognize population as a problem.

Urbanization

Population growth is one of many factors giving rise to rapid urbanization. On the one hand, peasants are pushed into cities by the reduction in available land per family, by mechanization of agriculture, or by the expansion of large landholdings. On the other hand, cities act as magnets, drawing people from rural areas and small towns with the promise of jobs, better education for their children, and better health services. In addition, natural urban population growth rates can be quite high. Few Third World cities have been able to absorb such increases, with the result that slums and squatter settlements have grown apace. Mexico City and São Paulo, Brazil, are already the two largest cities in the world (though the Tokyo-Yokohama area remains the largest metropolitan complex). In such situations, unemployment — in the sense of lacking a steady full-time job — may be so severe that the concept is virtually meaningless. Everybody does something for a living. Massive *under*employment may be the norm; a thirty-five-year-old man supporting a family by selling chewing gum in an open market will be listed in employment statistics as engaged in "commerce."

Authoritarianism and the Soft State

In few countries in the Third World has democracy really taken root. There are countries, such as most of those in the Middle East, that have never had a democracy, but even in those countries with such experience, democracy may not yet have achieved complete legitimacy. In a country like Bolivia, which has alternated democracy and dictatorship for a century, one form of government may seem just as tenable as another. Even when a democracy exists, it may be unwieldy and ineffective because of a multitude of contending political parties, it may mask an oligarchy of special interests, or it may be a mere front for military rule.

Though there has been a promising trend toward democracy in the 1990s, repressive dictatorships remain the norm in many countries. Political imprisonment, the routine use of torture, and political killing by uniformed security forces or by "death squads" (usually security forces in civilian clothes) remain common means of propping up dictatorial regimes.

Except in those rare cases of true revolution — an actual change in the political and economic structures of society — neither dictators nor democratically elected presidents replace the bureaucracy of their predecessors. To do so would add to unemployment and create unnecessary enemies. One of the fundamental powers of government is the ability to buy friends with jobs. Instead of firing the old bureaucracy, a new layer of supporters is added, like the layers of an onion. The tertiary sector — government jobs — is used not only as a payoff for political support but also as a sort of employment program. The inevitable overlegislation, inefficiency, duplication of effort, and outright corruption create what Swedish economist Gunnar Myrdal (1970) calls the "soft state."

A Lack of National Integration

Nation-building is a long and difficult process, and many of the countries of Africa, the Middle East, and Asia have been at it only since the collapse of colonialism in the 1950s and 1960s. The physical boundaries of the countries of Africa are notoriously artificial, with often antagonistic tribes united by a strange logic known only to the colonizing European powers of the past century.

In the United States, Australia, Japan, and most of the countries of Europe, there is a "referent culture" to which most ethnic groups aspire, at least in the second or third generations (Spindler and Spindler 1990). Lacking this, a nation may be no more than a patchwork quilt of conflicting cultures and loyalties. Even in the longer-established countries of Latin America and Asia, the state must make national claims on a multitude of ethnic groups and subcultures. Generating a national identity that overrides tribal or ethnic loyalties is difficult in the best of circumstances, but the process may be further impeded by the existence of dominant and subordinate groups. When one restrictive group — often a minority — holds the bulk of political and economic power, there is little stimulus for others to acquiesce in their own repression and subservience by identifying with the state.

Lack of national integration may be exacerbated by a country's geography. Because of the enormous cost of road building, Peru has few paved roads leading down the eastern side of the Andes to the jungles that comprise a third of the country. Peoples of mountains and of deserts may be so vastly different in their adaptations, developed over thousands of years, that they may have little in common with each other; their cultures, needs, and interests may be in conflict.

Poverty, dependency, lack of industrialization, authoritarianism, disunity, and rapid population growth are not autonomous factors; each may be closely related to the others in a complex system. The nature of government, for example, might be tied to wealth distribution and the existence of a powerful elite maintained from outside the country by foreign aid, multinational corporations, and a real or imagined military threat. Stemming population growth might depend on industrialization and on the provision of social services.

Proposed solutions to Third World problems are often of the simplistic "if only" type. If only they had a more open free-market economy; if only they were socialist; if only they were democratic; if only they would cut their population; if only they would encourage multinational investment; if only they would disengage from the world capitalist system; and so forth. Given the complexity of the interrelated factors and the uniqueness of each individual country, such solutions are seldom effective.

A (VERY) ROUGH CLASSIFICATION OF THIRD WORLD COUNTRIES

Although emphasizing the diversity of the Third World at the outset, it can now be understood why we have waited to attempt even a rough classification. Though originally defined economically, and then politically in relation to the Cold War, in reality, the concept of the Third World includes a multitude of factors. The existence of overlapping economic, demographic, social, and political structures makes meaningful classification difficult, if not impossible. Selecting out any single factor — such as political type — will lump together a host of countries with little else in common. Ultimately one is forced to give up the project altogether or to fall back on the tried (but hardly true) method of economic ranking.

A major problem with using economic ranking is shown in Table 1.1. The World Bank classification based on GNP per person reveals a country's standing in relation to other nations but says little about purchasing power within the country itself (Kidron and Segal 1991:110–117). Because basic necessities are subsidized or paid for by the state in China, a "dollar" goes a lot farther there than in Haiti, although the two countries are equivalent ($370 per year) in the World Bank classification. GNP per capita for Sri Lanka is $470, but per person purchasing power is $2,050. Also, we do not have even reasonable approximations of GNP or purchasing power for most communist countries and for countries in extended crisis, such as Somalia. Such difficulties render any classification rather subjective as well as somewhat distorting. The Third World is not amenable to ideal types. Countries slip and slide between divisions, refuse to be placed in neat little categories. Where do we put Libya, which has its own form of economy, neither communist nor capitalist? In South Africa, the 17 percent of the population that is white lives in First World conditions, while most of the 70 percent that is black lives in extreme poverty.

Despite such reservations, a classification may be justified if it emphasizes not only the similarities but also the immense differences between countries. In the typology below, I have considered not only GNP and purchasing power but also such factors as income distribution and level of industrialization.

The Fourth World

In this category we might include countries with per capita GNPs and per capita purchasing power under $1,000 a year. These countries tend to be predominantly agricultural and have relatively little industrialization. These are also often the countries with the highest population growth rates. Their potential for significant economic development is, at this time, minimal. Politically, these countries range from military or one-party dictatorships to fragile democracies, and many suffer civil war or low-scale internal violence at any given time. All should be considered unstable because of their poverty. Included in this group would be a number of countries in sub-Saharan Africa — Tanzania, Zaire, Burundi, Mali, among others — plus such countries as Afghanistan, Bangladesh, and Haiti.

Lower Middle Income

This category includes a wide range of countries with combined per capita GNP/purchasing power of, roughly, $1,000 to $2,500. The major difference from the previous category is that these show more promise of development. Agriculture remains the dominant occupation, but in India, Egypt, the Philippines, and Guatemala there is substantial industry, as well as strong export sectors. However, industry is invariably confined to one or a few areas of the country, so that the benefits of modernization are limited; industrial cities may even drain resources from the rest of the country. Relative to their populations, their middle classes are small. Because of the severe maldistribution of wealth, absolute poverty — malnutrition, little access to health care, homelessness — is a critical problem. Although *average* purchasing power per capita may seem relatively high in countries like Bolivia ($1,380) and El Salvador ($1,730), income is so unequally distributed that the large majority of people really live in the Fourth World.

Upper Middle Income — Highly Unequal

These countries are distinguished by strong industrial sectors and significant middle classes. They have large, modern cities, and their

TABLE 1.1
Two Ways of Classifying Third World Countries

GNP Per Capita

Low Income (to $600 per year)

Tanzania	110	Benin	360
Ethiopia	120	China	370
Malawi	200	Haiti	370
Bangladesh	210	Kenya	370
Burundi	210	Pakistan	380
Zaire	220	Ghana	390
Uganda	220	Zambia	420
Sierra Leone	240	Sri Lanka	470
Mali	270	Indonesia	570
Nigeria	290	Honduras	590
Rwanda	310	Egypt	600
India	350		

Lower Middle Income ($600 to $2,400 per year)

Bolivia	630	Columbia	1,260
Zimbabwe	640	Turkey	1,630
Philippines	730	Panama	1,830
Guatemala	900	Costa Rica	1,900
Ecuador	980	Botswana	2,040
El Salvador	1,110	Algeria	2,060
Paraguay	1,110	Argentina	2,370
Peru	1,160		
Jordan	1,240		

Purchasing Power Per Capita

Zaire	220	Nigeria	670
Tanzania	410	Benin	670
Ethiopia	450	Zambia	720
Burundi	450	Haiti	780
Malawi	480	Kenya	790
Ghana	480	Bangladesh	880
Sierra Leone	480	India	1,050
Uganda	510	Honduras	1,120
Mali	540	Zimbabwe	1,180
Rwanda	570		

		Egypt	1,360
		Bolivia	1,380
		Pakistan	1,590
		Indonesia	1,660
		El Salvador	1,730
		Philippines	1,880
		Guatemala	1,960
		Sri Lanka	2,050
		China	2,120

14

Upper Middle Income ($2,500 to $7,500 per year)

Mexico	2,490
South Africa	2,530
Venezuela	2,560
Uruguay	2,560
Brazil	2,680
South Korea	5,400

Botswana	2,500
Paraguay	2,80
Algeria	2,630
Ecuador	2,690
Peru	3,130
Jordan	3,160
Columbia	3,520
Costa Rica	3,760
Turkey	3,780
Malaysia	3,850

Panama	4,010
Venezuela	4,310
Brazil	4,310
Mexico	4,620
Argentina	4,650
South Korea	4,830
Chile	4,860
South Africa	4,980
Uruguay	5,060

Upper Income (above $7,500 per year)

Israel	10,920
Singapore	11,160
United Arab Emirates	19,860

Israel	9,180
United Arab Emirates	12,190
Singapore	12,790

United States (for reference) — 21,790

United States (for reference) — 17,600

Note: Classification of Third World countries based on GNP per person can distort the actual living conditions of the people. The figures on the left are from the World Bank and roughly show income as though it were being spent in the international economy. The reality is that prices, especially for such necessities as food, health, and housing, vary greatly from country to country. The figures on the right show estimated purchasing power. Note some major discrepancies: China is listed in GNP per capita terms as "low income" at $370 a year, but in terms of purchasing power it appears at the higher end of the "lower middle income" range with $2,120. The situation is similar for Egypt, India, and Honduras, among others. There are far more countries in the "upper middle" range when purchasing power is considered.

Sources: World Bank, *World Development Report 1992* (Oxford: Oxford University Press, 1992), pp. 218–19; Kidron, Michael, *The New State of the World Atlas*, 4th ed. (London: Simon and Schuster, 1991), pp. 110–17.

economies are less reliant on agriculture. Though many of their economies have stagnated or declined because of international debt and the worldwide recession of the 1980s, they show strong promise of development. They have relatively high levels of education. Many are either stable democracies or in the transition to democracy. However, massive discrepancies of income mean that there remain large marginalized sectors of society — impoverished peasants and poor shantytown dwellers. Unemployment and underemployment are severe problems. In this category would be included Brazil, Argentina, Chile, Venezuela, Mexico, Turkey, and South Africa.

Upper Middle Income — More Equal

This category is often combined with the preceding one under the phrase "newly industrializing countries," but the two groups are really quite different. This is a very small, elite group of capitalist countries in which the populations *as a whole* have benefited from development. They are characterized by large middle classes, few slums, and relatively little real poverty or unemployment. These are Third World countries in transition to the First World. This category includes South Korea, Taiwan, Singapore, and, perhaps, Costa Rica (Hong Kong is often included, though it is not really a country so much as a city-state that is about to become a province of China). Malaysia seems to be moving into this category, and a case could be made for Uruguay. Israel, with a per capita income and purchasing power almost double any of these countries, is in a class by itself, already First World in many ways.

The Communist Countries

Centrally planned Marxist economies require a separate classification. Because the state subsidizes basic needs — food, health, education, housing — per capita GNP and purchasing power do not mean quite the same things as they do in capitalist societies. Relative to capitalist societies, income and wealth are more equally distributed, though powerful elites may have numerous privileges that are difficult to measure in purely economic terms. Although China and North Korea are poor in terms of per capita GNP, they have attained high levels of education, health, and longevity. All of these countries are one-party dictatorships, often quite repressive (though it should be remembered that repression is a characteristic of the Third World in general, not just one type of economy). These countries range from the extremely poor (Ethiopia, Vietnam) to the relatively well-off (Cuba until about 1991). A handful of countries that embraced socialism during the Cold War, such as Angola and South Yemen, have become capitalist with the collapse of the Soviet Union, which was their mentor, protector, and financier.

The Wealthy Oil Producers

This category includes some of the richest countries in the world, such as Saudi Arabia, Kuwait, Oman, Bahrain, Qatar, and the United Arab Emirates (excluded are less-wealthy, mixed-economy oil producers such as Syria, Iran, Mexico, and Venezuela). These are Middle Eastern traditional hereditary sheikdoms. Standards of living are quite high, and the government may provide cradle-to-grave health, education, and pension benefits. The highly educated citizenry works in business and service occupations, often at high wages, so that there is a need to hire large numbers of laborers from surrounding countries. Labor immigrants may make up a substantial proportion of the population. These countries are quite conservative, with little in the way of industrialization or democratization. Their Islamic religion motivates a rejection of Western influence, and their wealth allows them to keep such influence at bay.

ONE WORLD — OR TWO?

The Second World has already ceased to exist, and several countries of the Third World will claim their place among the developed nations within the next decade or two. Will the Third World then disappear also? The answer is simply and emphatically, No! Not only are the First the Third Worlds not coming together in terms of GNP or per capita income, but, rather, the gap is widening at a rapid rate. There are those who argue convincingly that the very structure of the world system assures the marginalization of huge numbers of people.

However, in many ways, we are already one world, bound together by mutual dependence on the trade of goods and services and by a vast network of communications and intercultural exchanges. The United States is involved economically in virtually every country and has a military presence, either overt or covert, in a great many of them. Western culture, if only in the form of Coca Cola and action movies, reaches into the most remote towns of Africa, Asia, and Latin America. By the same token, one can hardly open a newspaper or watch the evening news without being confronted with stories about Nicaragua or Rwanda or Indonesia. The luxury of ignorance of the Third World is a thing of the past. The Third World is a reality increasingly demanding acknowledgment and understanding.

SUGGESTED READINGS

Brandt, Willy, *North-South: A Programme for Survival* (Cambridge, Mass.: MIT Press, 1980). Though dated, this report of an independent investigation by a group of international statesmen and leaders not only provides a good overview of the problems of the Third World but also offers solutions. Their long-term recommendations include a new approach to international finance.

Kidron, Michael, and Ronald Segal, *The New State of the World Atlas*, 4th Ed. (New York: Simon and Schuster, 1991). Double-page world maps provide a colorful visual examination of national income, energy production, religious beliefs, and just about anything else of which one can think (including off-the-wall categories such as number of business schools). A "World Table" at the end gives per country statistics on population, purchasing power, GNP, and so forth.

Rohr, Janelle, ed., *The Third World: Opposing Viewpoints* (San Diego: Greenhaven Press, 1989). Short essays by important scholars give different views on such subjects as "Why is the Third World Poor?," "Does US Foreign Aid Benefit the Third World," "What Policies Would Promote Third World Development." An excellent reader for stimulating thought and discussion.

World Bank, *World Development Report* (Oxford: Oxford University Press, Annual). Each year this ongoing series tackles another issue in depth, such as health, the environment, population, and economic development. The theories and data are supported by numerous full-color charts and maps. Each issue contains an appendix of more than thirty tables giving the latest country-by-country statistics on everything from life expectancy to balance of payments. A standard reference work that also deserves to be closely read.

Worsley, Peter, *The Three Worlds: Culture and World Development* (Chicago: University of Chicago Press, 1984). As a Marxist sociologist Worsley places his emphasis on the underclasses — peasants, laborers, ethnic groups — rather than the elites. The book, already something of a classic, analyzes the nature of rural and urban poverty and the structural interrelations among the three worlds.

2

The Creation of the Third World:
A Brief History

Early analysts of the Third World tended to view underdevelopment as a primary condition, an initial stage through which all countries must pass on their journeys toward modernization. Poorer countries merely lacked those qualities that had evolved in richer nations — industrial technology, investment capital, high levels of education, and the entrepreneurial ethic.

A second look, however, reveals that the characteristics that define the Third World are in no way primal or natural. Poverty certainly has a long history, but the destitution of urban shantytown dwellers and of peasants pushed off their land by the expansion of export agriculture is very different from the feudal poverty of the past. Neocolonial economic dependency, extremely rapid population growth, bloated militaries supplied by a vast international arms market, and governments striving to provide attractive investment climates to huge multinational corporations — none of this suggests some innate condition that will soon be outgrown. In many ways, the term "Third World" designates not a place so much as a relationship, specifically, a relationship with the First World.

One does not think of India as "underdeveloped" during the early Mughal Empire or Peru during the reign of the Incas. Even a hunting-gathering culture, such as the Bushmen of the Kalahari Desert of southern Africa, could hardly be considered underdeveloped when their culture was intact and their food sources ample. India became underdeveloped in relation to its British colonizers; Peru became underdeveloped after conquest by the Spanish; the Bushmen became underdeveloped only when they were forcibly integrated into the national economy of South Africa. Far from being an original condition, Third Worldism evolved out of the military, political, and economic expansion of Western Europe beginning in the fifteenth century.

THE GROWTH OF A WORLD ECONOMIC SYSTEM

Although 1492 is remembered for Columbus's "discovery" of America, significantly, it was also the year that the Muslims, who had occupied Spain for almost nine centuries, were expelled, and the country was finally united under King Ferdinand and Queen Isabella. Although still incipient, the emergence of unified nation-states in Western Europe would come to have a profound impact on the entire world.

In the late fifteenth century, Europe remained divided into feudal kingdoms or city-states, only nebulously united as countries under weak monarchs. In much of the rest of the world, on the other hand, large and powerful empires held sway over millions. In the Middle East, the vast Byzantine empire had been conquered by the expanding Ottoman Turks. Though in retreat in Europe, Islam was on the move elsewhere, spreading south across the Sahara desert to connect with the African commercial kingdoms of Mali and Songhai and expanding north into Turkistan and east into India. In eastern China, the vast Ming Dynasty ruled. In the New World, though the ancient Mayan culture was in decline, the mighty Aztecs dominated central Mexico, and in South America, the Incas administered a territory three thousand miles in length along the Andes and the western coast. That these would all fall, soon or late, under European domination attests to some remarkable changes that were taking place in the latter fifteenth century.

The near millennium-long Medieval Period in Europe, characterized by great religious architecture but relatively little economic or technological progress, slowly gave way to a period of artistic florescence, religious factionalism, scientific inquiry, nation building, and maritime exploration. In the political sphere, a new breed of rulers declared themselves free of the papacy and united larger and larger areas through warfare, intimidation, and political marriages, creating true states out of areas previously united by little more than common language. Economically, Europe remained largely agricultural, but during the later Middle Ages, towns became increasingly important. A nascent capitalism emerged in those towns, where merchant elites developed around craft guilds and commercial fairs. Fortunes built on burgeoning trade provided the wealth for large banking houses that flourished in the Italian republics and, later, in Holland and England. Feudalism — in which serfs, bound to their estates, produced for the benefit of landlords — began to decay. Originally, rent was paid in labor, but by the fifteenth century, money-rents were already well established in some areas, providing taxes for state development and investment capital. State bureaucracies emerged where previously there had been only royal courts or personalistic patron-client rule.

Meanwhile, coastal navigation was being transformed into true seagoing shipping. The Portuguese took full advantage of such inventions as the compass and "Jacob's staff," used to fix position at sea. The Chinese invention of gunpowder was adapted to shipboard cannon. By the time of Columbus's first voyage, the Portuguese had mapped out the entire coast of Africa, and only six years later, Vasco de Gama reached India by sea.

Despite these increases in accessibility to previously uncharted areas of the world, the first region to be brought into the Western European orbit as a dependency — and thus, in retrospect, the earliest to assume the status of Third World — was the landlocked countries of Eastern Europe. This trade, dominated by Holland, established a system in which an underdeveloped periphery exported raw materials to a wealthy center at low cost and imported finished goods at high cost. Poland and Lithuania provided rye, cattle, furs, timber; Hungary exported cattle and copper. In return, these Eastern European countries received textiles, hardware, and other manufactures. The Americas would be the next to assume this pattern, as Spain first plundered its newfound continent of gold and silver and then turned indigenous economies to producing agricultural goods for the mother country.

The Rise of Capitalism

Along with the emergence of the European nation-state as the primary unit of international economic power, there grew the doctrine of mercantilism. Fundamental to mercantilist philosophy was the simple principle: collect wealth, but don't give it out, or, in the words of seventeenth-century French economist Montchretien, "We must have money, and if we have none from our own productions, then we must have some from foreigners" (quoted in Beaud 1983:37). Significantly, it was the state, not individuals, that got most of the money and that also controlled expenditures, through, for example, passing laws to limit imports and to prohibit the departure of precious metals. Money had to be spent, of course, but at home, on armies and ships that would expand the potential for gaining wealth abroad. Gold and silver was most highly valued (so much was brought from the New World to Spain that these riches helped cause century-long inflation), but the policy also encouraged other imports. Previously, overseas trade had been in spices and fine silks for the noble classes; now the emphasis was on agricultural commodities and raw materials for manufacture.

Capitalism — the competitive drive for profit by individuals or privately owned companies — grew up alongside and, in many ways, out of mercantilism. Although such an economy had been developing among town merchants, under mercantilism, the state remained the focus of investment and profit internationally. The Spanish conquerors of the Americas functioned under state authority and claimed lands for the crown; a "royal fifth" of all gold and silver went directly into state coffers. However, state bureaucracies had neither the wealth nor the competence for the degree of expansion that as inevitable once the processes of conquest and colonization were set in motion. Although states made every attempt to control overseas expansion and trade, they increasingly did so by granting monopolistic royal charters to individuals and to joint stock companies, such as England's East India Company. Mercantilism, in many places, blended into a sort of state capitalism.

In the overseas dominions, both mercantilism and early capitalism implied tributary production; natives were compelled to produce for the benefit of Europeans but did not work for wages. The means by which the natives were obliged to produce varied; in some cases, the Europeans owned or controlled a critical part of the production process, such as the land or the irrigation works. In other cases, it was a matter of military force or of building up a dependency on European manufactured goods. The pattern in Latin America was based on the *encomienda*, a large land grant that included the right to the labor of the natives who lived there. In India, peasants were already accustomed to being taxed a substantial part of their production, but in many areas, the English introduced a landlord system based on English law that brought peasants under more complete domination. The slave trade, which decimated large parts of Africa for more than four centuries, provided mass labor for single-crop plantations in America and the West Indies. Though tributary systems took many forms, the result was invariably that production for domestic use was turned to production for export to Europe, and this had a profound effect on every aspect of the cultures that were touched.

A fully capitalist mode of production — based on the buying and selling of human labor by elites who owned the means of production — did not emerge until the state was transformed from a manager and collector of tributary production to a structure of support for private enterprise. From this point of view, capitalism's first real break with mercantilism emerged only in the latter half of the eighteenth century with the development of mechanized industry in England. Though wage labor had long existed on a small scale, with the industrial revolution, it gradually became normative throughout the world. European factories had the capacity to turn out hundreds of times the goods of individual craftsmen. These factories needed to be supplied with raw materials, such as cotton for textiles, and the end products required markets. Factory production gave rise to vicious competition among entrepreneurs, breaking the system of state-sanctioned monopolies. The state no longer was the focus of economic progress. Its function became the protection and encouragement of private capitalism. The state's job now was to create the infrastructure that capitalists would use to make and move goods and to provide armies to safeguard markets, displace recalcitrant natives, and coerce laborers to produce at subsistence wages. New laws had to be written to enforce labor contracts and protect private property.

A second industrial revolution, starting in the mid-nineteenth century, greatly amplified world trade and investment, which increased over 400 percent in the century and a half after 1850 (Open University 1983:34–35). The replacement of coal by steel, new sources of power — including electricity — and major advances in medicine and chemicals helped spread industry at a hitherto unknown rate. Among the global effects was the destruction of handicrafts, which were replaced by machine-made goods manufactured in Europe or in local industrial enclaves. Steam transportation and the opening of the Suez Canal provided faster and cheaper access to markets. The pace of agricultural transformation also increased, with the introduction of South American crops, such as cocoa and rubber, into Asia and the conversion of large areas of subsistence lands to plantation production for European consumption.

Colonialism and Anticolonialism

Distinctions must be made between three overlapping concepts: colonization, colonialism, and imperialism. *Colonization* is the creation of permanent communities in foreign lands. *Colonialism* is the establishment of full state sovereignty over another country or region. Often the process of expansion began with colonization and ended with full colonialism. On the other hand, much colonialism in Central Africa and parts of Asia included relatively little colonization by Europeans; entire regions were administered through native officials under European control. *Imperialism* is the act of extending a state's political domination over another territory, either directly or indirectly, in order to establish military bases, to protect trade, or for other interests. Imperialism, without colonization or colonialism, became the policy of the United States in the early twentieth century, for example, in Central America and the islands of the Caribbean where U.S. troops invaded and occupied at will, without establishing permanent settlements or creating colonial governments.

Despite Europe's loss of most of the colonial Americas by the 1830s, the industrial revolution stimulated a new spate of European expansion, especially in Africa. In the early 1700s, the possessions of Europe included only 10 percent of the world's land area and 2 percent of the world's people; by 1914, 56 percent of the land was under European colonial rule and 34 percent of the people (Open University 1983:28–36).

Colonialism was stimulated by multiple motives: the search for raw materials and markets, religious and cultural ideologies of bringing

Christianity or civilization to backward peoples, the need for strategic control of trade routes or critical waterways, and the desire to gain national prestige. England led the way; it was true that "the sun never set" on the British Empire that came to include multiple African colonies, India, Hong Kong, and Australia. By the late 1800s, the French empire encompassed Indochina, Algeria, Tunisia, and much of Subsaharan Africa. Other countries in the competition for empire were the Portuguese, Dutch, Spanish, Belgians, Russians, Germans, Japanese, and Americans.

One of the crucial results of colonialism was the creation of new countries. Few if any of the colonies were nation-states at the advent of colonial expansion. Europeans needed clearly defined borders, even if those borders made little cultural sense. One of the unanticipated effects was to create the basis for nationalism that would ultimately become a primary factor in the demise of the colonial system after World War II. Throughout the colonial period, ethnic uprisings and wars of national liberation erupted throughout Africa and Asia.

The collapse of the colonial system was, however, much more peaceful than anyone might have imagined. With some dramatic exceptions — such as the French in Indochina and Algeria — the European powers, exhausted by five years of total war, relinquished their colonies with relatively little bloodshed. From 1947 through the 1960s, the colonies of Asia and Africa gained their freedom, often only to soon collapse into internecine conflict and dictatorship.

With the end of colonialism, over one hundred new states took their places on the international scene. However, the structures of colonialism did not disappear overnight; the former colonies continued to provide raw materials and cheap labor to feed the consumer cultures of Europe and North America. The economic, political, and cultural domination of the now-sovereign states of the Third World by the First World continued as *neocolonialism*. The new system would be maintained less by the deliberate efforts of conquering governments (though military power would, as always, remain a crucial factor) than by the inherent logic of a world marketplace in which the rich could control the terms of trade for goods and services.

In the decades since independence, many countries have found their own voice. The first leaders of the new states, who emerged from elites created by the colonizers, have died off or been pushed out of power. Several formerly impoverished countries have established themselves as strong participants, rather than passive pawns, in international affairs. Far from being totally subservient to the dynamics of international trade, most countries have developed unique internal structures that must be taken into account. Thus, it is questionable whether neocolonialism — in its simplistic form as an extension of colonialism — is as useful an explanation of Third World poverty as it once was. Nevertheless, the system in which one quarter of the world's population utilizes over 80 percent of the world's resources — a system with its origins in the fifteenth century — has not only persisted but also intensified.

LATIN AMERICA — FROM CONQUEST TO DEPENDENCY

Geography is often cited as a reason for underdevelopment, and there is a certain truth to this. Much of the western coast of South America is arid and lifeless; the Atacama Desert between Chile and Peru has experienced no precipitation in recorded times. The rugged Andes that stretch the length of the continent rise to above 22,000 feet and, in places, are over three hundred miles wide. On the eastern side of these formidable mountains, the Amazonian rain forest stretches thousands of miles to the Atlantic Ocean. Roads and railroads are difficult and expensive to construct, causing a lack of integration not only of regions but also of countries. Deserts and jungles are not habitable for large populations. There are relatively few "breadbasket" areas, such as the Great Plains of the United States, where modern intensive agriculture can be practiced, and those that exist are unevenly distributed among the more than twenty nations that make up modern Latin America.

However, these geographical barriers were no obstacle to the indigenous cultures of the region. More than 1,000 years before Columbus, civilizations were evolving in the alluvial deltas along the Pacific Coast of present-day Peru and in the mountains, culminating in the Inca empire. Now-collapsed but still visible terraces testify to the remarkable agricultural sophistication of these people, who are justifiably famous for their cities, fortresses, and roads. Nor were the jungles of the Amazon and Orinoco River basins obstacles to such tribes as the Yanomomo, who knew how to get the most from their environment without destroying it. To people whose cultures evolved in symbiotic interaction with mountains, deserts, and jungles, geography was no barrier. It was only with the alien development patterns transported from across the sea that geography became an enemy to be conquered.

This conflict between the *organic* development of indigenous peoples and the *imposed* development of European conquerors is a universal theme of the Third World but is seldom as blatantly evident as in Latin America. Where people produced for their own use, now they labor to supply the wealthy citizens of countries thousands of miles away; where populations were relatively small and widely distributed, now millions crowd the shantytowns of a handful of coastal port cities; where tribal Indians practiced small-scale slash-and-burn horticulture, now ranchers permanently destroy hundreds of thousands of acres of rainforest every year.

A World to Gain

When "discovered" by Spain, Latin America was not only fully occupied, it was also home to two empires that were the rivals of any in the world at the time. The great Mayan civilization, which had existed for two thousand years, was already in decline, but the Aztec of Mexico and the Inca of Peru were at their apex. Surprisingly, perhaps, it was these two societies, which were organized into powerful states, that were easiest to conquer. Tribal Indians were either inaccessible in the jungle or sufficiently mobile that they could escape from European armies; the Auricanians of Chile still fought guerrilla battles well into the nineteenth century. Farmers, however, could not run away, and states, with their cities and top-heavy bureaucracies, could be decapitated.

The Aztec capital of Tenochtitlan, built on an island in a lake where Mexico City now sits, was one of the most beautiful cities in the world and, with a population of over a quarter million, was larger than any city in Europe at the time. From there the Aztec armies ruled over subject nations from the Atlantic to the Pacific coasts and as far south as Guatemala. The Aztecs, who built on previous civilizations, were only a century out of barbarism. Their religion required great numbers of human sacrifices every year, which were supplied in tribute and through ritual "flower wars" that the conquered tribes were forced to fight.

In 1519, Hernán Cortés sailed from Cuba for Mexico with 550 men, 16 horses, and a few cannon. He burned his ships on the coast, so there would be no temptation to turn back, and marched inland, fighting as he went and making allies with enemies of the Aztec. The conquest of Tenochtitlan would take two years of some of the bloodiest warfare the New World would ever see; the final assault on the city would cost 240,000 native lives.

Eleven years after the conquest of Mexico, Francisco Pizarro with 180 men set foot in Peru and ascended into the Andes. At that time the century-old Inca empire stretched from present-day Ecuador into Chile. The Incas were brilliant administrators and engineers who ruled with a forceful beneficence. By an enormous stroke of luck, Pizarro marched into a civil war between the forces of two sons of the recently deceased emperor. Atahualpa had just defeated his brother's army in battle. Pizarro invited the now-unchallenged ruler to parlay in the small, walled town of Cajamarca and, in a half hour, slaughtered Atahualpa's retinue of five thousand and took him captive. The prisoner was held for a ransom of 2 rooms full of gold and silver and, when the ransom was paid, was burned at the stake. Pizarro installed a puppet emperor, Manco, and marched south to the Inca capital of Cuzco. Manco escaped to join the Inca forces and rebelled against his foreign masters, burning his own sacred city to the ground around them. The Spanish, against enormous odds, would miraculously prevail.

In a mere two decades, a region six thousand miles long — from the Rio Grande to Tierra del Fuego — had been effectively conquered by the technology of steel, by horses (which were previously unknown in the Americas), by battle tactics perfected in the Moorish wars, and by the rapacious will and brutality of men with nothing to lose and a world to gain.

God, Gold, and Glory

Native Americans were treated differently in each of the conquered regions of the New World. The French in Canada came to barter for furs, and they treated the Indians respectfully as trading partners. The English, in what is today the United States, came to settle and farm with their families. For them, the Indians were a nuisance — like the forest — to be removed as rapidly and as thoroughly as possible. Those who were not killed by disease, starvation, and warfare were pushed west and settled on reservations that were sometimes little more than concentration camps.

The pattern in Latin America was very different. Motivated by "God, Gold, and Glory," the conquistadores came to plunder and convert the natives to Catholicism. They did not bring wives or families, because many had little intention of staying. They would get their gold and return wealthy to the old country. Some did get gold — in amounts undreamed of — but others had to be paid off with large land grants called *encomiendas*. The Indians came to be viewed as a labor force to produce agricultural exports or to be conscripted into mining; tens of thousands were virtually worked to death at the great silver mine at Potosí, Bolivia. The Indians — or at least those that survived the European-introduced epidemics that depopulated entire regions — were left in place to labor for the Spanish. This had several major consequences. First, the conquerors took native wives and concubines, thus, creating, over centuries, not only a mixed race but also a mixed culture. Variously termed *mestizo* or *ladino*, this blending of Spanish and Indian became the racial and cultural norm in Latin America. Second, some countries, such as Peru and Guatemala, would enter the twentieth century with large unassimilated Indian populations that would comprise the broad and exploited substratum of a rigid pyramid of classes. Third, as everywhere, production for domestic use would become secondary to supplying Europe. Most major cities of the new era would be deliberately located at natural coastal ports.

During the colonial period, Spanish America was divided into four large viceroyalties, each ruled by a viceroy appointed by the king (in addition, the Viceroyalty of Brazil, belonging to Portugal, was established in 1760) (Figure 2.1). Government was based on patronage to the royal court in Spain. Over the centuries, there grew up a conflict between the *peninsulares* — Spanish-born administrators — and the excluded *creollos*, Europeans born in the New World. From 1810 to 1825, revolution erupted throughout Central and South America. A leading general of the triumphant *creollos*, Simón Bolívar, dreamed of a united continent, but no sooner had independence been achieved than the victors fell to factional and regional fighting. The viceroyalties were broken up into mutually hostile states.

The period from the end of the revolutionary war to about 1880 was the age of the *caudillo*, literally, the man on horseback. Local strongmen, whose fragile power was based on personal charisma and the

FIGURE 2.1
The Colonization of Central and South America

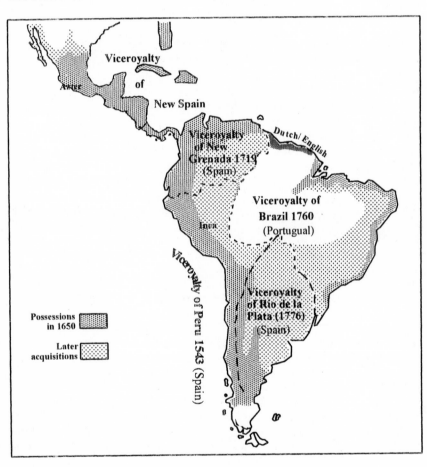

ability to command the machetes of disgruntled peasants and laborers, fought one another. A peculiar breed of dictator would take form during this era — virile, hard-drinking, outgoing, a man of the people (rulers such as Juan Perón and Fidel Castro would carry the *caudillo* mantle into the twentieth century). The *encomiendas* of the colonial period were originally granted only for the lifetime of the owner, but they were passed on from generation to generation, to become the legally titled haciendas of the postcolonial period. Briefly, Latin American agriculture turned away from its export orientation as powerful *hacendados* ran their estates as self-sufficient fiefdoms. Private professional standing armies and police forces were established for the protection of ruling families against the exploited peasantry, a function that security forces would maintain into present times.

The 1880s saw a return to export-led economic growth, under and ideology of "liberalism," which at the time roughly meant laissez-faire international trade. Many haciendas became plantations, in a process sometimes called the "rationalization" of agriculture. Feudal agriculture, no matter how exploitive it might be, implies bonds of mutual dependency between master and peasant, and the peasant has his own meager lands for subsistence crops. Under the capitalist plantation system, in which efficiency and profit are the sole goals, the peasant is only a wage laborer, with no security guarantees whatsoever. The peasant may lose his small plot of subsistence land, so that he is forced to survive on the scant wages that can be earned during the three or four months of planting and harvest. However, export production once more brought the landed gentry into the national economy and politics, creating a modernizing elite.

The period until the Great Depression was one of continued export-import growth that created something of a middle class and saw the development of trade unions but had little effect on the masses. Despite the growth of cities, Latin America remained mainly agrarian and predominantly poor. Prosperity and modernization were confined to small enclaves around mines and ports.

The United States Takes an Interest

U.S. interest in Latin America had been manifested in the Monroe Doctrine of 1823, which announced to Europe that there would be no recolonization of the Americas. From the time of the Spanish-American War in 1898, the United States assumed a much more active role with three decades of gunboat imperialism, during which U.S. forces invaded and occupied the islands and countries of the Caribbean. Cuba, Nicaragua, and Panama became economic and political satellites of the United States. The more overt forms of domination ceased with President Franklin Roosevelt's Good Neighbor Policy, but in the post–World War II period, the Caracas Declaration of 1954 would reiterate the

Monroe Doctrine, warning this time not the Europeans but the communists to stay out of Latin America. Because the definition of "communism" from the 1950s through the 1980s was sufficiently broad to include a wide range of reforms and virtually any attempt to break economic and political dependency on the United States, the Caracas Declaration was enforced with bloody regularity (Pierce 1981).

The Depression destroyed much of Latin America's export market as commodity products, such as coffee and sugar, became luxuries. Many countries, under the pressures of burgeoning populism, would turn inward, protecting their indigenous entrepreneurs and workers against foreign competition with "import substitution" — high tariffs or the outright prohibition of goods that could be produced within the country. The policy of emphasizing exports and minimizing imports would continue long after the Depression, though elites would seldom have much problem accessing foreign luxury goods. After 1960, and especially after the oil shocks of the 1970s — when the Arab cartel sent the price of petroleum spiraling upward — borrowing for development became an international pastime. After two decades of steady but highly distorted growth, the debt-ridden countries fell into a period of stagnation or even deterioration beginning in the 1980s.

A Continent of Contrasts

Latin America carries a mixed bag of blessings and afflictions toward the twenty-first century. Relative to the other Third World continents of Africa and Asia, Latin America is well off. The Southern Cone countries of Uruguay, Argentina, and Chile, with their largely European populations, are modern industrial nations with substantial middle classes. Brazil and Mexico are major industrial powers, though they are also the most debt-ridden countries of the Third World, each owing more than a hundred billion dollars. Although democracy has become the norm, few countries are more than a decade or two away from repressive dictatorship, and in some countries, democracy is little more than a facade on military or oligarchic rule.

With only one or two exceptions, wealth is extremely maldistributed, and the processes of modernization seem to be amplifying the problem rather than closing the gap between the rich and the poor. Because Latin America escaped the social and economic disruptions of both world wars, no other region on earth has such a long continuity of elite rule. Concentrations of land, power, and wealth that were established over five centuries ago continue today. In those few countries, such as Peru, that have enacted land redistribution programs, the old money maintained its power by shifting from agriculture to industry, mining, or fishing. Neither the emergence of new elites nor the rise of populism has much affected the extreme concentration of wealth. In El Salvador — a country with a population of over 5 million — one can still speak of the "fourteen families" (actually now about a hundred families closely interrelated by kinship and marriage).

Despite a great deal of progress in the twentieth century, the conditions that can bring about revolution or dictatorship are still very much present.

ASIA — CONQUEST BY COMMERCE

The Americas after 1519 and Africa after 1885 would fall with great rapidity under European domination, and that domination would be, at least for a time, nearly total. The process in Asia was much more dragged out and was never complete; large areas of China, Afghanistan, and Japan would remain relatively untouched. The sheer size of the region, much of it inaccessible by ship, made conquest difficult. Until the opening of the Suez Canal, even the coastal areas could be reached only by a long and dangerous journey around the tip of Africa. Equally important, unlike in the Americas, the civilizations of the region were not concentrated and top-heavy, and they could not be conquered in quick and bloody wars. There would be great battles, to be sure, but conquest would start with trade and proceed through centuries of negotiation; war would be the last recourse, rather than the first.

Asia boasts two "nuclear areas" — regions where archeologists believe civilizations arose spontaneously, without being influenced by previous civilizations: the Indus Valley of India and western China (the four other nuclear areas of the world are in Iraq, Egypt, Mexico, and Peru). India would experience an incursion of Aryans from the west and would be invaded by the Persians and, later, the Greeks under Alexander. Chinese civilization, isolated by the Himalayan Mountains, the Gobi Desert, and the vast Manchurian Plain, would escape such influences and would continue, relatively untouched, into the twentieth century. China carried on an overland silk trade with Persia and Syria but imported little. Though dynasty followed dynasty, the everyday life of the farmer remained relatively unchanged over centuries and millennia.

Unlike China and India, Southeast Asia — including the large island complexes of Indonesia, Borneo, and the Philippines — developed no common culture or language. In heavily forested areas, which included most of the region, numerous horticultural "tribes" lived in relative isolation from each other. Indian traders settled along the coast, bringing the Hindu and Buddhist religions. In the early seventh century A.D., the powerful Khmer kingdom, with its capital at the huge city of Angkor, was founded in Cambodia; it would last for five hundred years.

By 1450, Islam extended through much of India and down into Malaya and Indonesia. The Muslim Turks under Babur, who claimed direct descent from the Mongol (Mughal) Genghis Khan, invaded the plains south of Afghanistan using the new technology of musket and artillery. The Mughal empire would ultimately cover most of central India from the Arabian Sea to the Bay of Bengal.

European expansion into the Far East might be seen to begin with the travels of Marco Polo, who returned to Venice in 1295 and wrote of his adventures while in prison a few years later. However, although Polo's writings would have an enormous influence on Europe's cultural awareness of Asia and on the development of a limited Italian overland trade in luxury goods, it was not until the Portuguese explorations by ship two centuries later that major interaction between Europe and the Far East became possible. Vasco de Gama's discovery of a sea route to India in 1497 opened the way for extensive trade.

In the sixteenth and seventeenth centuries, not only the Portuguese, but also the Dutch, English, and French, formed their respective East Indian Trading Companies. These companies were a logical development of the wedding of mercantilism and international capitalism. They were independent associations of merchants chartered as monopolies by the mother country. Though there were constant attempts by the various governments to control them, their political and economic strength at home and the distance of their operations from their governments gave them a high degree of independence. The four companies sometimes traded peaceably but often fought each other for trade monopolies and for port settlements. Though spices and other goods were carried back to the mother country, the distances and expenses were so great that much of the most lucrative trade by European ships was among the various ports of Asia itself. Asian empires and city-states existed, but no Asian power learned to redesign its ships to carry heavy cannon; the Europeans remained uncontested at sea.

By the early twentieth century, three European powers would dominate south Asia: the English in India, Burma, Malaya, and Hong Kong; the Dutch in the East Indies; and the French in Indochina (after 1898, one might add the United States in the Philippines) (Figure 2.2).

The British in India

For a while, Portugal, which was more interested in commerce than empire, monopolized trade with India. After they were decisively defeated at sea by the English, the Mughal emperor extended trading rights to Britain in return for the fleet's protection of Muslim pilgrims to Mecca. The colonization of India was accomplished piecemeal over a long period and resulted as much from weaknesses within the Indian social and political systems as from British power. The caste system — of four main castes and hundreds of subcastes — assured that interests and loyalties remained focused on local groups rather than on the

FIGURE 2.2
The Colonization of Asia

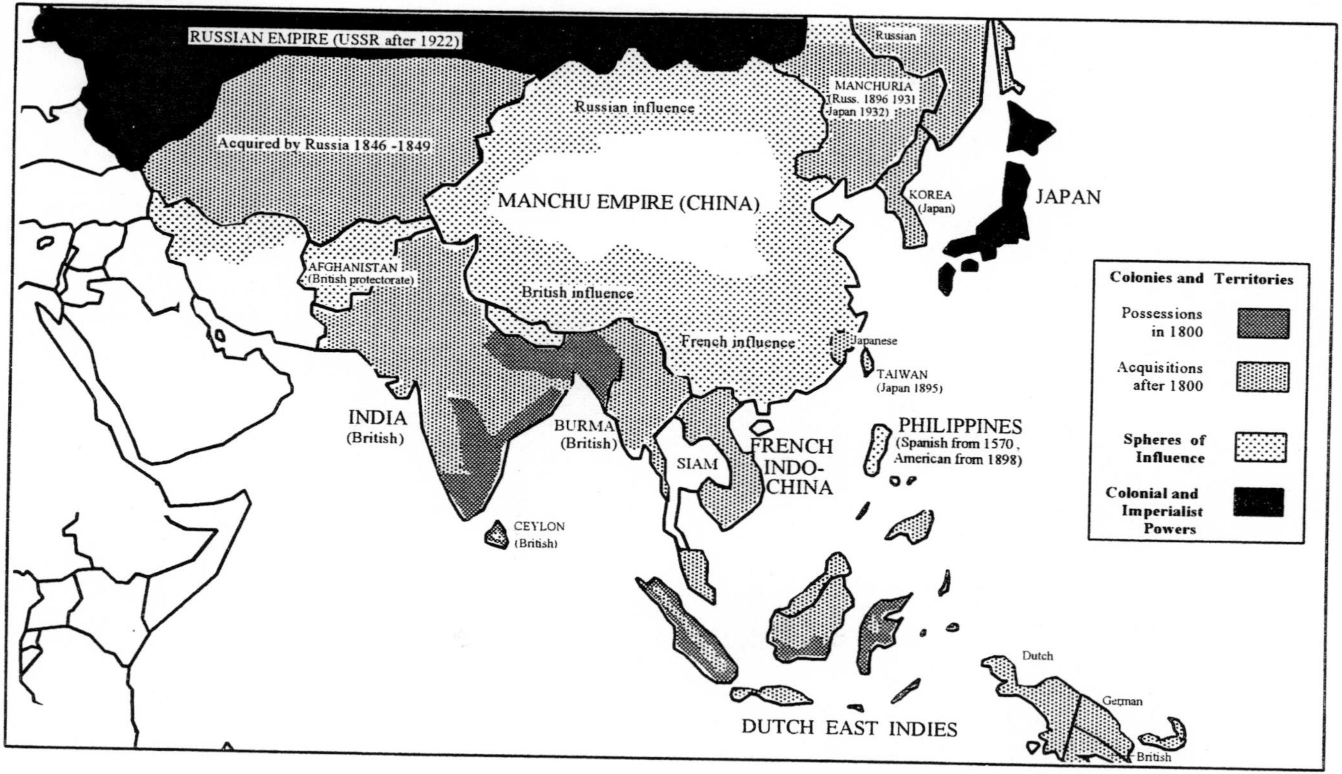

Colonies and Territories

Possessions in 1800

Acquisitions after 1800

Spheres of Influence

Colonial and Imperialist Powers

RUSSIAN EMPIRE (USSR after 1922)

Russian

MANCHURIA
Russ. 1896 1931
(Japan 1932)

KOREA
(Japan)

JAPAN

Russian influence

MANCHU EMPIRE (CHINA)

Acquired by Russia 1846-1849

AFGHANISTAN
(British protectorate)

British influence

French influence

Japanese

TAIWAN
(Japan 1895)

PHILIPPINES
(Spanish from 1570,
American from 1898)

INDIA
(British)

FRENCH INDO-CHINA

SIAM

BURMA
(British)

CEYLON
(British)

DUTCH EAST INDIES

Dutch

German

British

nation. Under the Mughals, the imposition of Muslim rule on a predominantly Hindu country (less than a fifth of the people would be converted to Islam) meant that the majority of subjects felt little common cause with the state or allegiance to it. In the declining years of the Mughal Empire, religious persecution against Hindus led to alienation and open warfare. Finally, in the early 1700s, the empire collapsed; power was assumed increasingly by provincial governors and princes.

By this time, British merchants were well entrenched in Bombay, Madras, and Calcutta and in many other places had established permanent warehouse and port settlements known as "factories." They had developed strong alliances with indigenous commercial elites, who formed a new and powerful capitalist class dependent on East India Company trade. Together, the English and their native allies were able to play off Hindu against Muslim and Moghul against local prince. As imperial power disintegrated into anarchy, the factories became increasingly fortified and defended by native troops, called "sepoys." It was from these fortified settlements and with the use of sepoys that the East India Company gradually extended its rule over southern India and the heavily populated region north along the Ganges from Calcutta. The English ruled much of the rest of the country indirectly through treaties made with ruling princes.

Revolts against British rule were relatively common, but the great Indian Mutiny of 1857–58 — which started with a protest of sepoys and ended as a general rebellion — stimulated the British government to take over from the East India Company. This move established a secretary of state for India in London and a viceroy in India, assisted by an executive council. Below this, the Indian civil service administered the day-to-day activities of government. In 1900 the British, with less than 1 percent of the population, ruled over half a million Indians (Stavrianos 1981:236). India — "the jewel in the crown" — became the base for the colonization of Burma and many of the independent states of Malaya.

China Opens Its Borders

China provided European ships with a booming but largely one-way trade in tea, silks, porcelain, and cotton goods. Unlike India, China resisted further dealings with Europeans. The Manchus, who were at the peak of their power, felt themselves superior to the outsiders and wanted little from them. Exports had to be paid not with imports but with cash. Except for the Portuguese at Macao, Europeans were allowed to trade only at Canton.

Forced to pay for Chinese goods with precious gold and silver, England solved the problem by importing opium from India into China, systematically building up a huge trade based on increasing addiction to the powerful drug. When the emperor, as part of an attempt to wipe out the odious trade, seized and destroyed 20,000 chests of British opium, the English responded by seizing port after port. The two-year Opium War ended in 1842 with the Treaty of Nanking, which gave Britain Hong Kong (later to be negotiated to a ninety-nine year lease) and opened five ports to foreign trade. Similar treaties were quickly concluded, establishing autonomous foreign settlements, administrations, courts, and customs. Though Christian missionaries had little success in mass conversions, their hospitals, orphanages, and, especially, schools would have long-ranging cultural and social influence.

In 1900, the massive Boxer Rebellion against foreigners was successfully put down by European guns, but the outbreak revealed the cost and difficulty of any attempt to colonize or directly rule China. Mutual suspicion among the various European interests also helped prevent colonization. Instead, an "open door policy" was enacted, throwing China's borders wide to the full impact of Western capitalism. Cheap manufactured imports destroyed local crafts, and standards of living dropped. By the turn of the twentieth century, Western influence and internal weakness had brought the 260-year-old Manchu Dynasty to the edge of collapse.

The Twentieth Century

After 1858, the formerly isolationist Japanese deliberately set out to copy Western progress, especially in technology. They proved their success, beyond anyone's wildest dreams, with their decisive defeat of the Russians in the sea battle of Tsushima in 1905. Japan would take advantage of the European powers' preoccupation with fighting each other in World War I to usurp the trade with China and India. In its attempts to build a Great East Asian Co-Prosperity Sphere, Japan overran Manchuria, invaded China, and occupied much of Southeast Asia. They would not be displaced until the end of World War II.

China, meanwhile, was undergoing its own series of revolutions. With the fall of the Manchu Dynasty in 1911, the nation formally became a republic but, in reality, collapsed into virtual anarchy, with local warlords pillaging the countryside. The Koumintang, or Nationalist, Party was formed to unite the country. Under the leadership of General Chiang Kai-shek, the Koumintang armies turned against their rivals for power, the communists. The communists, led by Mao Zedong, escaped extermination only by a six-thousand-mile Long March across the length of China that left them severely decimated. By organizing the peasants, the communists were able to make a comeback. After a brief and uneasy truce with the Koumintang to drive out the Japanese during World War II, the communists took over mainland China in 1949. Many of the Koumintang escaped to the island of Formosa (Taiwan), where they displaced the local elites and established a one party regime that would lead the country in a remarkable process of modernization

Decades of nationalist violence and massive nonviolent protest led by Ghandi resulted in the independence of India in 1947. The partitioning of Pakistan, created for Muslims in 1949, resulted in massacres of religious minorities in both countries; half a million died in riots, while another million fled their own borders for safety. The liberation of India set the pattern for other areas of Asia, though independence often was granted only after violent nationalist uprisings.

France was the lone holdout in Asia, determined to maintain its Indochinese colonies. When the French were forcibly expelled by the communist Vietminh after the bloody battle of Dien Bien Phu, the country was temporarily divided, with communists to the north and former French supporters to the south. A Geneva conference in 1954 arranged for the reunification of the country by vote. In his autobiography, President Eisenhower (1963:372) noted that if the election had been allowed to take place, the communists would have easily won with perhaps 80 percent of the vote. Fearing that surrounding countries would also topple to communism in a falling-domino effect, the United States stepped in, outlawed the Vietminh in the south, and ran a dubious election that established a U.S. puppet in power. The result would be almost two decades of increasing U.S. involvement, culminating in the U.S. defeat in a war that by the early 1970s encompassed Vietnam, Cambodia, Laos, and Thailand.

Common Problems among Great Diversity

Although the "domino theory" of communist expansion proved false, the end of the Cold War found three of the few remaining communist governments situated in Asia. Both China and Vietnam, two of the poorest countries of the world as measured by per capita income, began making overtures for increased economic relations with the West and showed tendencies to introduce limited capitalism. North Korea remained an isolated and hostile holdout of Stalinism.

Among noncommunist countries, postcolonial patterns of development and underdevelopment have shown enormous variation. Crushed into Third World status at the end of World War II, Japan demonstrated an astounding resilience, rising to become one of the major economic powers of the modern world. Taiwan, South Korea, Singapore, and Hong Kong are all moving rapidly into First World Status. Indonesia and Malaysia have shown strong development tendencies. Other countries, such as Cambodia, Pakistan, and Bangladesh, remain poor, badly factionalized, and technologically backward.

Despite their differences, the countries share many of the common problems of the Third World. Even an industrial power like India remains largely agrarian, its modern factories isolated in enclaves while much of the country remains traditional and impoverished. Ethnic and religious rivalries often lead to violent conflict. Asia has the highest population densities in the world combined with population growth rates second only to those in Africa. The challenge of bringing population rates down while raising the standard of living of the masses is already being met by a handful of countries, but the large majority of nations have yet to find an effective strategy of development.

THE MIDDLE EAST — CRUCIBLE OF HISTORY

The physical environment of the Middle East would seem to be so hostile to human habitation that the area would be little contested. Yet, this arid region — which stretches from Israel to the Indian subcontinent — has been a cauldron of conflict for six thousand years. Here the earliest civilization emerged in Mesopotamia, in what is now Iraq, between the fourth and third millennia B.C. Theories of "environmental circumscription" suggest that the first city-states developed because people were confined by desert within narrow riverine valleys and deltas. With nowhere to spread, natural population growth forced greater elaboration of social systems and technology. The creation of complex irrigation systems led to distinct classes, differentiated between those few who controlled the water supply and those who labored, those who ruled and those who served. Egypt experienced a similar pattern of early development. Over the centuries, few areas in the world would be the focus of so much warfare and social change, as kingdom followed kingdom and empire built upon empire.

Europe Stakes an Early Claim

Trade with Europe dates back to the earliest times, but it was Alexander the Great of Greece who first extended European domination to the region in the third century B.C. Little more than a hundred years later, Rome began its long conquest and occupation. Even after the sack of Rome in 476 A.D., European domination continued under the Christian Byzantine Empire, centered in Constantinople.

Centuries of Roman and Christian influence would leave their mark on the landscape, but the more profound influence would be that of Islam. When Mohammed died in 632 A.D., he had already gone a long way toward establishing his religion. After his death, his inspired teachings were collected and written down as the sacred Koran. Spurred by the call to jihad — holy conflict — his followers attacked the Byzantine empire and within ten years had claimed Syria, Palestine, and Egypt. The Muslim armies were often welcomed by the populace, as was the new religion, because Christian rule was unpopular. By 750,

Islam had spread through Mediterranean Africa to the Atlantic, north to Portugal and Spain, and east to India.

Arab Muslims did not interfere with the many Christian pilgrims that journeyed to the sacred city of Jerusalem during Europe's Middle Ages. However, when the Turks conquered the city in 1071, they tortured and killed Christians found there. The Turks moved north against the remains of the Byzantine Empire. In retaliation, the Pope called for a holy war against Islam. The First Crusade recaptured Jerusalem in 1096. For the next 250 years, Crusaders would control much of the region from their great castle fortresses, before finally being expelled.

The Turks — originally warlike nomads from east-central Asia who were converted to Islam in the tenth century — succeeded in conquering much of the Middle East. They proved to be excellent administrators, who introduced significant improvements in agriculture, mining, and trade. In the mid-thirteenth century, the Ottoman Turks commenced a much greater expansion of empire, one that would spread from Algeria to the Sudan, east to Iraq, north as far as Hungary. After 1700, the Ottomans were in retreat in Europe but continued to dominate much of the Middle East. All told, they would rule for more than five hundred years.

In the nineteenth century, increasingly expansionist Europe challenged the remains of the Ottoman Empire. The French took Algeria in 1830 and Tunis fifty years later. They also gained a share of control over Egypt when the sultan failed to pay his debts to European bankers. European interest in the region was greatly intensified in 1869 with the completion of the Suez Canal, which cut 3,500 miles off the journey from England to India.

After putting down a revolt in Egypt, England would dominate that country until after World War I. Early in the twentieth century, as part of a more general colonization of Africa, France claimed Morocco and Italy took Libya.

The Making of the Modern Middle East

Many of the contemporary borders of the Middle East were created in the aftermath of World War I. The Turks, who had sided with the Germans, were soundly defeated. The European victors divided the remains of the Ottoman Empire, with only Turkey being allotted to the Turks. "Mandates," giving the right to govern, were assigned by the League of Nations: France ruled Syria and Lebanon; England ruled Iraq, Palestine, Kuwait, and Transjordon (present-day Jordan and part of Israel). Egypt and Iraq became self-governing, and two new sovereign states, Saudi Arabia and Yemen, were formed.

In the spate of independence movements after World War II, France relinquished its claims on the Sudan, Tunisia, and Morocco. However, its policy of assimilating colonies into the mother country would have devastating consequences for Algeria, where there was a sizeable number of French settlers. With France's humiliating defeat in Indochina, national pride became a significant factor. Algeria would be granted independence only after a long and vicious war.

The situation in Palestine grew exceedingly complex. Jews had spread all over Europe after their revolt against Rome was crushed in the third century A.D. In the late nineteenth century, stimulated by pogroms in Russia, a group called the Friends of Zion sought the colonization of Jews in Palestine. This would lead to a major Zionist movement. The resettlement of Jews in Palestine was greatly increased by Hitler's antisemitic policies in Germany. After World War II, a renewed flood of Jewish survivors of the holocaust sought refuge in Palestine. British attempts to control the immigration failed. Britain withdrew in 1948, establishing a small state of Israel, legitimized by a United Nations declaration. Almost immediately, the Palestinians and surrounding Arab countries attacked. In a series of wars, Israel, supported with military aid but not troops by the United States, was able to extend its land base, at one time as far south as the Suez Canal. In 1994, Palestinians in the West Bank and Gaza Strip were accorded autonomy.

The Middle East took on enormous international strategic importance because of its oil. The first major petroleum strike had occurred as early as 1908, but by 1945, only a tiny fraction of world oil was being produced in the region. The period after World War II saw a rapid increase in oil production, and it came to be recognized that the world's largest reserves lay here. Originally, multinational corporations controlled the oil, but all countries have nationalized their resources, selling concessions to large U.S. and European companies for extraction, processing, and distribution. The 1973 Arab-Israeli war stimulated an oil boycott of the West, and the Organization of Petroleum Exporting Countries took increasing control of pricing and production. In 1974 alone, oil prices increased by 400 percent. Oil made some countries in the region extremely wealthy, leaving others to look on enviously. The Middle East has been rationing its reserves; in 1983, for example, it produced only 1 percent of its estimated reserves, while the United States was producing 12 percent of its known supply. As reserves throughout the rest of the world decline, other countries may become increasingly dependent on the Middle East for their energy.

An Axis of Superpower Rivalry

Given the strategic significance of the Middle East, it was inevitable that the region be caught up in superpower rivalries. In 1956, when Egypt took control of the Suez Canal and was subsequently invaded by British, French, and Israeli troops, the Soviets hinted at intervention on Egypt's side. When the United States also condemned the invasion, the Europeans withdrew. The damage had already been done. Egyptian leader Gamal Abdel Nasser turned increasingly toward the Soviets. When the United States refused to support the construction of the immense Aswan Dam, the Soviets stepped in with the money. As a result, Egypt became an outpost of Soviet influence, with Soviet bases, troops, and arms (Egypt would reorient itself toward the West on Nasser's death). The Soviets also provided aid to the Arabs in their conflicts with Israel. Countries such as Syria and Libya took a strong pro-Soviet turn, though continuing to trade with the West. Most countries maintained an officially neutral stance, but anti-Western feelings remain high because of U.S. support for Israel and memories of colonialism.

The end of the Cold War has not cooled the region. In 1980, Iran launched what would be a long and bloody war against Iraq. Hardly had peace been established in 1988 than Iraq attacked Kuwait. The resulting Gulf War pitted the United States and several oil states, such as Saudi Arabia, against Iraq. International state-sponsored terrorism continues to be a problem and is closely allied to the rise of Islamic militancy (often referred to by the misnomer "fundamentalism"; a great many Muslims interpret the Koran literally without advocating violence). The 1979 overthrow of the shah of Iran established a base for Islamic extremists. Militants, demanding a theocracy based on Islamic law, have conducted a campaign of terror in Egypt.

The Middle East remains highly volatile, both internally and internationally. Two traditions have clashed in the Mediterranean areas: a Western rationalism and an Islamic religious culture with deep roots in Arab history and temperament. Inland and to the south — Iran, Iraq, Saudi Arabia, and much of Yemen — there has never been much Western influence. Though many of these countries have the oil wealth to promote development, it is unlikely that development here will be defined in Western terms of liberal democracy, capitalism, equality of the sexes, consumerism, and industrialization. Through thousands of years of Western conquest, colonization, and exploitation, the Middle East has maintained its own character and its own vision.

AFRICA — THE "DARK CONTINENT" IS BROUGHT INTO THE FOLD

Subsaharan Africa was the last great region to be brought into the world economy. Europeans knew of the continent for millennia, but they were kept out by forbidding terrain, hostile natives, and, above all, disease. The "White Man's Grave," as it was called during the nineteenth century, could claim the lives of six of ten settlers along the coast, and inland, the mortality rate was much higher. One African leader suggested a monument to the anopheles mosquito — the carrier of malaria — for keeping the Europeans at bay for so long. "Beware, beware the blight of Benin," warned a seaman's ditty, "For few come out, though many go in." For novelist Joseph Conrad, Central Africa was the *Heart of Darkness*, not merely a place but a "horror" of the mind and soul.

The shroud of ignorance that covered the "Dark Continent" concealed a long and vibrant past. Many paleontologists believe that the genus *Homo* — humankind — originated in Africa. One of the earliest and greatest of ancient civilizations, Egypt, began to flower in Northern Africa by 400 B.C. At that time, the Sahara was temperate and habitable. Slowly the desert spread, isolating the lands to the south behind a vast ocean of sand. Nomadic hunter-gatherers and settled fishermen lived their lives in oblivion to the rest of the world. The agricultural revolution that led to civilizations in Mesopotamia and Egypt belatedly drifted south, where people began to settle in villages, fed by yams, sweet potatoes, and other cultigens. Trade routes were established through the desert. Commercial interests and the need to protect settlers against marauding nomads gave rise to states along the edges of the Sahara — Kush, Axum, Nubia, and, much later, Ghana and Mali. Farther south, about the time of Christ, two groups, the Zande and the Bantu, spread out of West Africa, pushing east and south, bringing with them their language, their sophisticated pottery techniques, their agriculture, and their cattle raising. Islam did not significantly extend below the Sahara until three hundred years after the death of Mohammed in 632 A.D. Then it spread rapidly, following the trade routes, to include almost the entire northern third of the continent and the western coastal region.

Europe was not far behind. Portuguese ships began to trade with Western Africa and were already establishing plantation colonies on the coast by the beginning of the sixteenth century.

Three Centuries of Slavery

Africa had a long tradition of slavery, but it was not based on economics. Slaves were taken for status or domestic use and were normally assimilated into the master's social group. Europeans tapped into these existing practices but turned them to new purposes, supplying plantation labor in the Americas, where attempts to enslave the Indians had resulted in mass deaths. White traders seldom ventured far from the coast, instead inducing native tribes to do the capturing. Once in chains, a slave was lucky to reach the Americas alive; there might be weeks of hunger and disease waiting on the coast, to be followed by the two-month Atlantic crossing with captives stacked in tiers lying down so close together that they could barely turn themselves over. On arrival they could expect nothing but lives of ceaseless toil. Attempts at escape were punishable by mutilation, torture, and death.

The trade in humans started in the sixteenth century and peaked in the eighteenth, when as many as six million captives were transported. In all, perhaps ten million were captured in West Africa (plus another two million for the smaller Arab trade in the east). European ships followed a triangular route, bringing firearms, iron goods, and cloth from Europe to Africa to exchange for slaves, then taking the slaves to the Americas, and returning to Europe with tobacco, cotton, sugar, and rum. Only about 20 percent of the slaves ended up in the United States; the great majority were transported to Brazil and the islands of the Caribbean.

Large areas of Africa remained relatively unaffected by the slave trade, while others were depopulated. For three centuries, any significant social or economic development was aborted as tribe was set against tribe in warfare and communities were robbed of the labor and leadership of their young men and women.

The Scramble for African Colonies

While Africa stagnated and declined, Europe was rapidly acquiring the technology that would facilitate a more complete conquest of the continent. White penetration of the interior had been prevented to a great degree by the ferocity and prowess of native armies, but spears became virtually useless against newly developed rapid-fire guns. The breechloading rifle appeared in the 1860s, the magazine load a decade later, and the Gatling gun in the 1880s. Equally important, it was discovered that a daily dose of quinine would prevent malaria; as early as 1847, a crew of twelve sailed up the Niger River and returned without a loss.

Meanwhile, the exploration of interior Africa proceeded apace. Intrepid explorers such as Richard Burton, John Speke, and Henry Morton Stanley competed in arduous, years-long treks in search of the source of the Nile. Far to the south, the Cape of Good Hope had been settled by the Dutch as early as 1652; later, they would be pushed north into the interior by English settlers.

When colonization of the continent finally came, it proceeded with rapacious swiftness. There was no single cause. The discovery of diamonds at Kimberly on the border of the Cape Colony brought a new flood of English immigrants, while the other European powers looked on with consternation and envy. The opening of the Suez Canal in 1869 provided quick access to Eastern Africa. Britain intervened in a civil war in Egypt, leaving France — which had claims as a protectorate — furious. Finally, King Leopold of Belgium, acting as an individual, moved in to occupy the Congo Basin. The scramble was on.

In order to prevent warfare among the competing European powers, a conference was called in Berlin in 1884 with the object of peacefully dividing Africa. England, France, Germany, Portugal, Spain, Italy, and Belgium all demanded colonies, which were drawn on a large map with little regard for the on-the-ground realities of Africa. Even areas that were totally unexplored came under European jurisdiction. The original allotment left a few unclaimed regions — such as the middle of the Sahara Desert — but by 1914, just about every mile of the huge continent was in European hands.

Each colonial power established its own policies, though in common was the paternalistic notion of bringing civilization to the Africans, who were viewed as mere children needing guidance. Also, there was the common belief that colonies should not be a drain on the mother country; they had to pay for themselves. This created all sorts of taxes, rules, and punishments to force the natives to work for European interests. As would be expected, much land was turned to plantation crops for export. England, the dominant power in Africa, attempted an administrative policy of indirect rule; traditional leaders would keep their positions but with obligations to the higher white administration. As it turned out, not all traditional rulers were acceptable, and many were replaced with English-trained native elites; some of these, protected by British guns, became despots over their own people. France, the second major power in Africa, had little respect for local culture. The point of colonization was to incorporate these areas into the French empire, and this required direct rule from Paris and the creation of an interethnic elite with strong allegiance to the mother country.

Though colonialism lasted only about eighty years — a brief span in the continent's history — the effects were massive (Figure 2.3). Through the 1950s and 1960s, fifty-two countries that had never existed before would take their positions as sovereign states among the family of nations. Many of these nations would not make a lot of geographical or cultural sense. Some are huge with large populations, others are tiny. Some are landlocked. Mutually hostile ethnic groups, previously held in check by European guns, compete for power. Colonialism brought Africa fully into the world economy, but it was ill-prepared for the new role. Though most Africans are still subsistence farmers, state economies have been oriented toward external markets. Coffee, rubber, peanuts, and cocoa are exported around the world, but the wealth goes not to the people but to multinational agribusinesses, land owners, and often-corrupt governments. The case is similar with oil, copper, tin, uranium, and diamonds. Democracies introduced at the last minute by departing colonizers rapidly turned into one-man or one-party dictatorships.

FIGURE 2.3
European Possessions and Protectorates in Africa around 1914

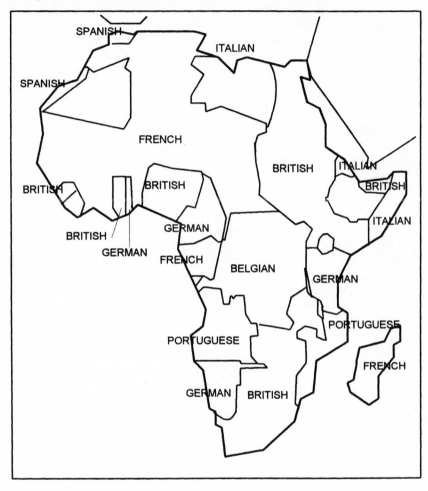

The Cold War and Beyond

Independent Africa was quickly caught up in the Cold War. The United States remained generally uninterested in the continent until it was perceived that the Soviets were gaining influence. Every internal struggle became interpreted by both sides as part of the conflict between the superpowers. Aside from its general fear that any country turning communist would have a domino effect on surrounding countries, the United States believed that the Soviets sought to control strategic naval choke points, such as the Straits of Madagascar and the Gulf of Aden. As a result, enormous amounts of arms flowed into the hands of dictators, and wars were fought over the equally alien philosophies of capitalism and communism. Cuba sent troops to protect the communist governments in Ethiopia, Angola, and South Yemen, while the Central Intelligence Agency ran major covert actions in Zaire, Nigeria, Angola, Mozambique, and Ghana. As early as the 1950s, the Chinese entered the fray, building the $500 million Great Uhuru Railway from Tanzania to Zambia and staking an ideological claim on those seeking a peasant-based communism against the Soviet model (Gavshon 1981).

With the demise of Soviet aid, the handful of communist countries quickly and unceremoniously reoriented themselves toward the West. However, for most of Africa, the end of the Cold War has had little effect, except that, lacking a security threat, the United States is less eager to provide aid. Saddled with enormous international debts, with unstable governments, with ethnic rivalries, and with population growth rates that are the highest in the world, Africa struggles to develop a definition of development that fits its unique history and character.

THE HERITAGE OF EUROPEAN EXPANSION

There remains a great deal of debate about the degree to which imperialism and colonialism was beneficial or harmful to the Third World. Walter Rodney, in *How Europe Underdeveloped Africa* (1972), argues that the effects of European penetration of Africa were uniformly negative; indigenous social systems were uprooted and destroyed, and "previous African development was blunted, halted, and turned back. In place of that interruption and blockade, nothing of compensatory value was introduced" (p. 224). Robbed for generations of their power, independence, and cultural meaning, the people were left in a permanent state of dependency, ruled by elites created to serve foreign interests. Others have argued the opposite extreme, that colonialism was a necessary precursor to development, a means of bringing backward economies into the modern world. One can point to the infrastructure — roads, railroads, factories, ports — left behind by European colonists and to the educated elites and administrators trained under colonialism. Western ideals of democracy and equality before the law were introduced.

It is easy — too easy — to dismiss these arguments by observing that the truth is somewhere in between. In reality, many areas (Peru and Zaire come immediately to mind) were much better off before any contact with Europe. Other places — and a case could be made for India — can point to a balance sheet of benefits and deficits. Almost all Third

FIGURE 2.4
The Widening Gap: Per Capita Gross National Product from 1750

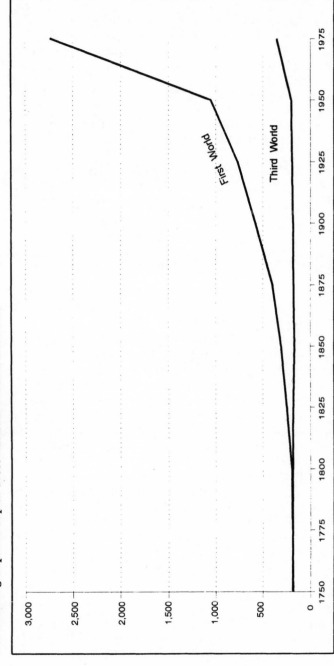

*1960 U.S. dollars and prices

Based on Bairoch, Paul, "The Main Trends in National Economic Disparities since the Industrial Revolution." *Disparities in Economic Development since the Industrial Revolution*, eds. P. Bairoch and M. Lévy Leboyer (New York: St. Martin's, 1981), p. 8.

World countries have increased their overall standards of living in terms of mortality rates, health, education, and so forth. On the other hand, it is obvious that in terms of *relative* poverty, the Third World has deteriorated greatly. It is estimated that in 1750 there was virtually no economic discrepancy between Europe and the rest of the world; by 1977, however, the developed countries were, on the average, between eight and fourteen times richer per capita than the Third World (Stavrianos 1981:38; Bairoch 1981:8) (Figure 2.4).

Whatever the blessings or curses of European expansion, it cannot be doubted that indigenous systems were hugely and permanently *changed.* Prior to European expansion, virtually all regions were "developing" in the sense that they were moving in the direction of more complex and articulated political and economic systems, larger towns or cities, and greater social differentiation. In the Americas, in Africa, in the Middle East, and in Asia, we see the rise, maturity, climax, and fall of civilization after civilization, each new one building on the accumulated knowledge of those gone before. Development, in this sense, was never something that belonged to the West.

Such development was brought to an abrupt halt by European imperialism. Natural processes of economic and political evolution were abruptly shifted in entire new and unforeseen directions, which were usually out of sync with the cultural traditions of the people. Development and progress would no longer be defined by the values of tribal and peasant peoples or by native states but would be determined by the local overlords of far-away powers. Third World countries can no more repudiate their colonial past than they can abjure their role in the present world system. What they can do, and many are trying to do, is find a place in that system that fits their own cultures and aspirations.

SUGGESTED READINGS

Beaud, Michel, *A History of Capitalism: 1500–1980* (New York: Monthly Review Press, 1983). The book clearly traces the evolution of capitalism from eleventh-century feudalism through "the great leap forward" of the 1980s. "Capitalism is neither a person nor an institution," says Beaud. "It neither wills nor chooses. It is a logic at work . . . a blind, obstinate logic of accumulation" (p. 116).

Fieldhouse, D. K., *Colonialism 1870–1945* (New York: St. Martin's Press, 1981). The author has some positive things to say about colonialism but does not have a lot of ideological axes to grind one way or another. He presents a fair assessment, with an emphasis on economics.

Open University, *Third World Atlas* (Philadelphia: Open University Press, 1983). An essential resource. The larger of its three sections is devoted to the historical development of the Third World.

Rodney, Walter, *How Europe Underdeveloped Africa* (Washington, D.C.: Howard University Press, 1982). Rodney argues that the present impoverishment of Africa is only understandable as a result of the European slave trade and colonization. The book, a classic of Marxist analysis, is highly controversial.

Stavrianos, L. S., *Global Rift: The Third World Comes of Age* (New York: William Morrow , 1981). This nearly nine-hundred–page work is, for the moment, the definitive history of the Third World. The author is a dependency theorist (see Chapter 3 in this volume) who holds that "the states of developedness and underdevelopedness are but two sides of the same coin" (p. 35).

3

Modernization and Dependency: Theories of Underdevelopment

There is no end to facts about the Third World, many in dispute but many also widely accepted. Data alone, however, tell us little about how the world works — about the way that social and economic systems are constructed. Raw statistics are quite useful, but anything beyond the simplest formulation requires some understanding of the *meaning* of those numbers. In short, understanding the Third World is very different from merely describing it, and that understanding requires theories.

A theory is a systematic attempt to define the underlying structures and the causal relations among a multitude of data. It should, therefore, allow a degree of prediction, and it should permit us to explain new facts and fit those facts within our model. A theory is usually postulated at such a high level of abstraction that it is not directly testable. In order to test the theory, we need to break it into specific hypotheses. Although evolution remains a "theory," aspects of it have been tested and found to be valid through intensive research by paleontologists and biologists. Also, evolution has undergone considerable change since the time of Darwin, as some parts of the original theory have been found to be false and new knowledge, such as genetics, has been incorporated. One of the marks of a scientific theory is that it constantly undergoes adaptation as new information becomes available. (When a theory in the social sciences becomes rigid and is considered True — with a capital *T* — and immutable, it trips over into ideology.)

A further distinction might be helpful. It is sometimes said that there are as many theories of development as there are writers on the subject. There is a certain tongue-in-cheek truth to this; it is difficult to find any serious scholar who agrees 100 percent with any other scholar. However, if we back off a bit from the dust of conflict, we can discern that most (though not all) theories of development fall into two very broad paradigms — general ways of viewing the world. Like the different geometries in mathematics, each paradigm begins with its own set of postulates or assumptions.

On the one hand, there are those who see underdevelopment as a primary condition out of which all countries must evolve if they are to attain development. There are numerous variations on this. Third World countries may be perceived as stuck in precapitalist forms of production, such as feudalism or mercantilism. Other theorists emphasize the lack of decisive characteristics that have emerged in the West, such as advanced technology, investment capital, entrepreneurial proficiency, and high levels of education. Underdevelopment, then, is intrinsic to the countries themselves, and development will come about through a diffusion of Western traits. This point of view might be termed the *modernization paradigm*. Although the history and effects of colonialism and imperialism are not denied, the emphasis is on the conditions within individual countries or within the Third World as a whole.

The *dependency paradigm* takes an opposite point of departure. From this perspective, underdevelopment was caused by Western expansion and persists because of the unequal power relationships between the First World and the Third World. The focus here is not the internal structure of the individual country but the country's place in the international system; the causes of the underdevelopment of a particular country are, thus, external. Some variations of this perspective downplay the role of states altogether, emphasizing instead economic blocs, multinational corporations, or impersonal economic forces. Countries are condemned to impoverishment not because they lack technology or capital but because of their placement within the structure of world capitalism. It is not likely, then, that development will take place through transfers from the First World; indeed, such transfers are motivated by the self-interest of the industrial countries and simply reinforce dependency and powerlessness.

CLASSICAL THEORIES

The First World/Third World distinction was not articulated until after World War II; therefore, classical economists could hardly be much concerned with it, nor with the modernization/dependency distinction. However, since the eighteenth century, theorists have devoted considerable attention to the nature of development.

Theorists of Capitalism

Adam Smith (1723–90), often considered the father of modern economics for his 1776 book *An Inquiry into the Nature and Causes of the Wealth of Nations*, wrote at a time when mercantilism was still dominant in England. Despite a burgeoning merchant class, the state remained the principal economic actor, chartering overseas companies and placing numerous restrictions on both national and international trade. The wealth of a nation was to be measured by the amount of precious metals the government could amass. Against such policies, Smith argued that the true source of national wealth was not gold and silver or bonds or land, but the labor of the people. Labor productivity would increase as specialization increased, leading to mass production, which would raise the economic level of the whole populace. The basic incentive in economic matters was self-interest, but this was not necessarily negative. The multitude of individual self-interests, if left alone by the state, would lead to the common good as though guided by "an invisible hand." Smith is credited with both defining the nature of then-incipient capitalism and, through advocating laissez-faire, helping establish the policies that would speed the growth of capitalism.

Others were not as optimistic as Smith. Thomas Malthus (1776–1834), who mainly is known for his demographic theories, believed that population growth, underconsumption, and overproduction resulted in poverty for the masses — and there was little that could be done about it. David Ricardo (1772–1823) concurred, but for different reasons. Ricardo is most famous for his theory of rents. During a country's frontier period, when there was plenty of land available, there would be no rents. As all the most fertile land was brought into production, poorer quality soil would have to be utilized. At this point, the more fertile land would begin to command rent, and the amount of rent would be determined by the degree of fertility. The higher costs of land would lead to greater intensification, that is, attempts to increase production through more labor, better irrigation, and improved seed. However, there would come a point where an increase in labor and capital would not meet with an equal increase in production. Production would decline relative to further inputs. As populations grew, this "principle of diminishing returns" would lead to stagnation and decline as well as conflict between workers and landowners. Ricardo also believed that an "iron law of wages" assured that workers would never be paid much more than enough for their barest subsistence; if their pay were increased, they would be motivated to have more children and the resulting population growth and oversupply of labor would bring wages back down. With such gloomy predictions coming from Malthus and Ricardo, it is no wonder that economics would be branded "the dismal science."

So far, most theorizing was focused on the internal causes of national wealth and poverty. Ricardo also introduced a major concept related to international trade. Underlying all commerce is the idea that different people have different things to sell. It would be ridiculous for a plumber to make his own shoes, because he has neither the ability nor the equipment to do so; he can buy them cheaper and of better quality than he can make them. The plumber sells his skills so that with the money he can purchase shoes from a specialist in shoemaking. This deceptively simple principle is the basis for the "theory of comparative advantage" among nations. A country that can produce a product at a relatively low cost will be able to profitably sell that product in the international marketplace. With money earned, that country can purchase other products cheaper than it can make them. For example, Guyana has low labor costs and an abundance of bauxite, used in making aluminum. Because it can offer a good price on its bauxite, it can gain money that can then be used to purchase automobiles or radios from the United States, which, because of its high level of assembly line technology, can produce such goods at relatively low cost.

Despite its classical origins, the theory of comparative advantage remains a virtual article of faith for modern economics. However, there are major problems with it when used as a justification for unfettered free-market economic policies. Only in statistical abstraction do *countries* sell and purchase. In reality, individual owners of land and factories do the selling and buying. As a result, most of the wealth from comparative advantage may accrue to only a minuscule elite and may not sift down to laborers.

Marx and Lenin

No single theorist has had such an enormous effect on development theory as Karl Marx (1818–83), who inspired generations of dependency theorists. Oddly enough, Marx himself had very little to say about the less developed countries, and his few ideas on the subject would fall more within the "modernization" paradigm. It was later Marxists, such as Lenin, Eric Wolf, and Immanuel Wallerstein, who would elaborate a Marxist perspective of dependency.

Marx, who emigrated from Germany to England, wrote at a time when the unregulated factory system had thoroughly established itself; men, women, and children were compelled to work agonizingly long hours under inhumane conditions for barely subsistence wages. Though best known as a revolutionary socialist, most of Marx's theorizing was a critique of nineteenth-century industrial capitalism. According to Marx's "labor theory of value," the value of a commodity is determined by the amount of socially necessary labor necessary to produce it. A worker might be able to produce enough in six hours for his own subsistence, but he is driven by low wages to work ten hours. The extra four hours' work is "surplus value," which accrues as profit to the owner of the means of production. This exploitation of the worker was protected by the state and legitimized by a "false consciousness" imbued among the masses by the schools and media. Ultimately, the exploitation would be recognized, and the proletariat (wage laborers) would rise up against the capitalists in violent revolution and establish socialism.

Underlying these ideas was a theory of the evolution of social systems. Georg Wilhelm Friedrich Hegel (1770–1831) had philosophized that the historical process grew out of conflict. In an ongoing "dialectic," there would be a struggle between the prevailing system (thesis) and its opposite (antithesis), which would result in a synthesis; this synthesis, over time, would produce a new age, and a new thesis would emerge. Marx held that this process was determined by material — that is, economic — factors, thus, creating the philosophy of "dialectical materialism." For Marx, the dialectical process came about through class struggle and was manifested in different "modes of production." Production — which includes labor, technology, property ownership, and transportation — is social in the sense that it controls the ways that people relate to each other. A particular mode of production deter-mines the very nature and structure of a society. Capitalism was the latest in a series of modes of production, superseding the feudal mode in Europe. Although pointing out the evils of capitalism, Marx believed that it was the highest form of economy yet developed and was a necessary stage before the emergence of socialism.

Implicit in this view is the idea that non-European countries are backward or undeveloped because they continue to employ precapitalist modes of production. For example, in his writings on India and China, Marx postulated an Asiatic mode of production characterized by a village economy based on agriculture, hereditary rule, and a lack of private property. Unlike the situation in the feudal mode, it was the state and not landlords that skimmed off the surplus production, in taxes. The modernizing efforts of the British colonizers in India would engender the preconditions for the change from the Asiatic to the capitalist mode.

Despite his historical and evolutionary perspective, nowhere does Marx suggest that European capitalism is the cause of underdevelopment. It was Lenin (Vladimir Ilyich Ulyanov) (1870–1924) who popularized the idea of the expansionist and destructive nature of capitalism in his pamphlet *Imperialism, the Highest Stage of Capitalism* (1916). By its very nature, the more capitalism develops, the more it requires raw materials and markets. This leads to colonialism. Meanwhile, production is increasingly concentrated in monopolies. Finance also becomes concentrated so that monopolistic banks can make huge loans for overseas investment and trade. Thus, the competitive capitalism described by Marx is transformed, and a new stage is achieved that is based on relatively noncompetitive monopolies protected by their various states. This stage, dominated by finance capital, is characterized by imperialism. War among the great powers becomes inevitable as they periodically redistribute their shares in the world market. Although Lenin does not elaborate the effects of capitalist expansion on the underdeveloped countries, it is obvious that the spread of capitalism brings about an international system of domination and subordination. This perspective, articulated by many early twentieth century writers (indeed, Lenin drew his entire theory from the works of others), would become the basis for dependency theory in the 1970s.

THE MODERNIZATION PARADIGM

Though the Third World has been evolving since the fifteenth century, it did not really come into existence in its present form until after World War II. During the long period of European and American expansionism, there was little real concept of underdevelopment. Colonies and protectorates were appendages of the mother countries, and as such, they had their particular goals of supplying raw materials, providing markets, and conferring prestige. Development was not one of those goals. It was only after the colonies had gained independence that development became a significant issue. This was not just an academic concern nor a matter of altruism. The United States and the industrial democracies of Europe needed to formulate policies toward these new countries, and they needed theories on which to rely. The Cold War lent a special urgency to the enterprise. The "losses" of China to the communists in 1949 and Cuba a decade later were seen as the wake-up calls of a worldwide threat to capitalism. Policy makers in the United States became convinced that the Soviet Union, unable to attack the West directly, was trying to take over the world through the newly independent countries. Communism, with its promise of redistribution of wealth, made its appeal to the underclasses. Development in the Third World was perceived as a matter of national security.

Theories of modernization tended to be pragmatic, that is, their aim was to provide governments with the tools to speed development, and Washington was, indeed, watching and listening. One did not have to seek far for the causes of underdevelopment; countries started out underdeveloped — that was their initial condition. The crucial questions were: How do countries become developed? and What are the major barriers to development? The way to answer the first question was to examine the progress of the First World countries. To answer the second question, it was necessary to research the internal conditions of poorer countries.

One thing was certain. Third World countries could, at least theoretically, develop much faster than had the Western nations. Though technology is not the only element of development, it is certainly a crucial one. The cotton gin, the assembly line, and the internal combustion engine were already invented and did not need to be invented again. Such technology could be transferred to the Third World. The same was true of capital; Europe and the United States had amassed huge amounts of wealth that could be invested in the Third World through multinational companies, bank loans, and foreign aid. If the "missing factor" was entrepreneurial or administrative expertise, that could also be imparted by educating Third World nationals at Western colleges.

The modernizing process inevitably created dual economies. On the one hand, there would be the modern sector, either capitalist or semi-capitalist, which would be characterized by relatively high levels of technology, openness to innovation, an entrepreneurial ethic, and an educated and progressive elite. This elite would have the money for investment in new production and, therefore, would be the engine of development. The traditional sector, on the other hand, would be feudal or semifeudal, with low levels of technology. Peasants, tied to inefficient forms of agriculture and archaic systems of land tenure, would be closed to new ideas and technique. The modern sector would be dynamic and growing, whereas the traditional sector would be stagnant. As a consequence, the gap between the two would widen.

Rostow's Stages of Growth

One of the most influential of the early works on development was W. W. Rostow's *The Stages of Economic Growth* (1960). Rostow assumed the Third World countries would have to pass through the same stages as did the First World countries. The problem, then, was to go back in Western history and sort out the developmental process. "It is possible," he wrote, "to identify all societies, in their economic dimensions, as lying within one of five categories: the traditional society, the preconditions for take-off, the take-off, the drive to maturity, and the age of high mass-consumption" (p. 4).

A *traditional society* was one based on pre-Newtonian technology and unscientific attitudes toward the physical world. Because of this, there would be a ceiling on production; lacking modern technology, there is no way to increase output beyond a very limited point. Thus, the values of the society are based on a long-run fatalism. A high proportion of resources are devoted to the primitive agricultural sector. Political power is decentralized.

As a country begins to utilize the insights of modern science, either through innovation or borrowing, it develops the *preconditions for take-off*. The idea of economic progress, both as a possibility and as something to be desired, takes root. Institutions for mobilizing capital — such as banks — appear, and investment increases, especially in transportation, communications, and the extraction of raw materials for export. The true nation-state develops as various regions and localities are united under a single government.

The "watershed stage" — *take-off* — occurs when a surge of technological improvement is combined with the emergence of an economic and political elite that makes economic progress a serious goal and has the power to enforce its aspirations as national policy. The rate of investment and savings rises to 10 percent or more of the national income, and this investment spurs the rapid expansion of new industries that yield profits that can be plowed back into further development. Agriculture becomes increasingly commercialized.

The country now moves into a sustained stage that Rostow calls the *drive to maturity*. The modern sector expands to the whole economy, overwhelming the technologically deficient traditional sector. Up to 20 percent of national income is reinvested, so that production increases above the increase in population growth. Although there is sufficient demand that goods that were formerly imported can now be produced at home, the country establishes its place in the international economy. About sixty years after take-off, the country reaches *maturity*, that is, it attains the technological and entrepreneurial skills to produce whatever it chooses.

When incomes rise sufficiently that the mass of people demand goods above the basics of food, shelter, and clothing, the country reaches the final stage, the *age of mass consumption*. Goods once thought luxuries — automobiles, televisions, suburban homes — become normative throughout the entire society.

Rostow's theories were influential in the government because of the encouraging policy implications; if U.S. allies in the Third World could be brought to the take-off stage, then their development would become self-sustaining. Take-off was largely a matter of technology and capital, which the United States had in abundance and was quite capable of transferring to the Third World. Academics were less enthusiastic. Rostow's goal of discovering universal stages of development seemed overambitious at best. It was questionable whether all Western societies had passed through such a neat set of stages and unlikely that Third World countries would or could follow the same path traveled by the United States and Western Europe. If economic "maturity" were defined as high mass consumerism, such maturity would be beyond the reach of many countries. Given the ecological implications — in terms of resource depletion and pollution — U.S.-style consumption might not even be desirable.

Vicious Circles and Internal Colonialism

Rostow and others saw the problems of underdevelopment as intrinsic to the countries themselves, but the solutions would come within the international marketplace. In accordance with Ricardo's principle of comparative advantage, by selling their raw materials, poor countries could gain currency to purchase the infrastructure and technology needed for development. The rich countries would help the process through transfers to the Third World. Logically — assuming the modernization model was correct — it should have worked, and, indeed, it seemed to be working beyond even some of the most optimistic projections. In the third quarter of the twentieth century, literally hundreds of billions of dollars were transferred from the First World to the Third through trade, multinational investment, loans, and foreign aid. As a result, per capita gross national product (GNP) grew at a rate of 3.4 percent, far faster than the rate of growth during the development of the West (Morawetz 1977).

It became evident fairly early, however, that something was wrong. Early theorists tended to equate growth with development, but by the early 1970s, it was obvious that these were two different processes and that they did not necessarily coincide. Even a substantial increase in GNP (growth) did not always, or even usually, mean that there would be a rise in the standard of living of the masses, an increase in agricultural productivity, the spread of modern technology throughout the society, or the solidifying of a strong nation-state — all things related to development. One problem with the early models was that they were additive, in the sense that they postulated that by merely adding technology and capital, the country would progress. It was now clear that problems were also, and perhaps were fundamentally, structural, that is, they had to do with the ways that societies and economies were organized.

Modernization "theory" now seems naive and simplistic if Rostow is considered its main proponent. However, if the modernization paradigm is broadly conceived — as it is here — as a focus on the *internal* processes of development in Third World countries, then there has been and continues to be some very perceptive and sophisticated analyses within this approach. These analyses tackle the second question noted above: What are the barriers to development? Many of these barriers are cultural, social, and psychological; for example, the force of tradition may be extremely strong, or there may be vested interests in maintaining the status quo (Foster 1973). However, it is the structural aspects that concern most theorists.

The Vicious Circle of Poverty

One of the cliches of capitalism is that "it takes money to make money." When applied to Third World countries, this is the principle of the vicious circle of poverty: countries remain poor because they start poor. If the people are too impoverished to save or to pay much in taxes, there will be no money for companies to borrow for investment or for the government to use to create an infrastructure to promote development. Also, if incomes are low or populations are small, there will be only slight demand for goods, so even if entrepreneurs exist, there is little stimulus to produce for the domestic market. A poor country is faced with pulling itself up by its own bootstraps.

Critics of this theory point out that not everyone in any Third World country is poor; there is always an elite that does have money to save and invest. Furthermore, personal savings are only one source of finance capital; corporations, governments, insurance, and pension funds also provide savings. It is also noted that low-income countries normally spend 3 percent of their GNPs on the military and somehow manage to finance periodic wars.

Though these criticisms are apt, the vicious circle of poverty should not be too cavalierly dismissed. High inflation rates tend to discourage savings even by the wealthy; often, the rational approach is to get one's money out of the country (though this may be illegal) and into a stable currency such as the U.S. dollar or the Swiss franc or to invest in a safe overseas business. Also, the lack of a domestic market does, indeed, discourage production for the masses. One of the arguments for foreign aid is that it is needed to break the vicious circle by an infusion of investment capital from outside.

Internal Colonialism

In contrast to unilineal theories of economic evolution, it is evident that different countries develop in very different ways. Even within a single country, not all elements modernize at the same rate; industry may leave agriculture behind, or vice versa. Some countries have attained high levels of industrial production but retain low levels of literacy. Very poor countries have achieved pluralistic democracies, while relatively wealthy ones have been mired in archaic dictatorships. Truly balanced development — in which all sectors move together — may be an unrealistic goal, but the extremes of imbalance are sometimes phenomenal.

One very common example of this is where one city or region within a country achieves a high degree of modernization, while the rest of the country is stagnant or actually deteriorates. This city — be it Bangkok, Thailand, or Lima, Peru — is the nerve center of the country. National politics, and, thus, all power, is centered there as well as most industry and, if the city is a port, most international trade. National wealth flows into this one city, which will also become a magnet to attract migrants in search of jobs. The government may hold agricultural prices at artificially low rates in order to feed the city's millions inexpensively, which means that farmers are forced to subsidize the city. The powerless hinterland remains traditional not because peasants are conservative and fatalistic, as is so often claimed, but because their profits and savings are being siphoned off and little investment is made outside the city. This situation, sometimes called "internal colonialism," is based on a relationship of exploitation between a country's urban center and its underdeveloped periphery. One of the problems of measuring development by GNP statistics is that the core city, representing perhaps a tenth of the population, may be responsible for virtually all the rise in GNP.

Social Differentiation and Social Mobilization

Early modernization theorists believed that as a country developed, its traditional institutions would fade away; people would come to identify with the nation-state rather than with their tribal or ethnic groups. S. N. Eisenstadt (1973a, 1973b, 1990) has observed that just the opposite is often the case. Disruption of traditional institutions is more likely to lead to turmoil and discord than to modernization. Tribes, lineages, ethnic groups, and secret societies may change goals and functions but often actually increase their cultural cohesiveness. In Liberia, for example, the ancient male secret society, the *Poro*, has become a strong force for the maintenance of tribal autonomy and the status of the elders in the face of government infringement on local power.

This said, Eisenstadt observes that the core of modernization is social differentiation and mobilization. If a society is to be sufficiently adaptive to embrace new technology and new structural forms, the political sphere must be sufficiently differentiated from the religious sphere. In Islamic countries, such as Saudi Arabia, modernization has been retarded by the close association of religion and political power despite the availability of high levels of finance capital.

Social mobilization refers to the process by which traditional social and psychological loyalties are broken down and reoriented so that new social and economic arrangements become possible. Traditional structures do not cease to exist, nor is cultural collapse a necessary part of the process. Rather, traditional groups restructure themselves and reorient themselves toward new goals consistent with modernization.

THE DEPENDENCY PARADIGM

Modernization theorists had a hard time accounting for the growing inequalities within Third World countries and for increasing international inequality. Theoretically, infusions of capital and technology from the First World to the Third World should have been closing the gap between the two, but in reality, the gap was growing at a frightening rate. Few countries were achieving anything resembling Rostow's "take-off," and even for those few, growth was often unbalanced and erratic. Some scholars began to look beyond the countries themselves to the structure of the international system. Whereas the cause of underdevelopment had not been a problem for modernization theorists — all countries started underdeveloped — it became a central problem for the new generation of scholars.

The Economic Commission for Latin America Model

Dependency theory is often seen as a 1970s reaction to moderniza-tion theory, but it actually had its origins in the 1940s, when a group of economists from the United Nations' Economic Commission for Latin America (ECLA) began to focus on international capitalism as the source of underdevelopment. The world was divided between an under-developed *periphery* and a developed *center*. According to classical economics, both groups should benefit from comparative advantage, that is, each would sell what they could produce most economically and with the money earned purchase needed goods. The problem, according to the ECLA model, is that this exchange is fundamentally unequal. The periphery exports mainly raw agricultural and mineral products, importing manufactured goods from the center. In the industrialized countries, the power of labor unions and other pressures push up wages, and manufacturers raise prices to compensate. There are no similar pressures driving wages in the periphery; unions are weak, if they exist at all, and the large supply of labor keeps wages low. As a result, exports from the periphery remain comparatively cheap, while imports from the center become increasingly expensive.

Also, as individuals and countries become richer, they spend a smaller proportion of their incomes on raw materials and a larger proportion on manufactured goods. To the extent that prices follow demand, relative demand decreases for foodstuffs and other raw materials and increases for factory-produced goods. People can drink only so much coffee, so the demand for the product will be relatively stable even if people have a raise in income; however, the demand for cars and radios expands as people get wealthier, so such manufactured goods increase in price.

The problem of unequal terms of trade — the widening gap between prices for raw materials and manufactured goods — was seen as critical. If it continued unchecked, the periphery would fall farther and farther behind. Fidel Castro (1983:62), in his report to a summit of nonaligned countries, complained that in 1959, the sale of twenty-four tons of sugar provided income to purchase one sixty-horsepower tractor; by 1982, the same tractor required the sale of 115 tons of sugar. In such circumstances, he argued, increases in productivity are not matched by increases in wages, so the level of the masses stagnates despite arduous attempts by countries to produce more.

The problem was not perceived by the ECLA economists as capital-ism, per se, but rather as a conflict between domestic capitalism and international capitalism. Countries are prevented from developing local manufacturing capabilities by foreign competition and by the inequali-ties in the terms of trade, but they desperately need foreign capital. Throughout Latin America, the state stepped in to implement ECLA-recommended "import substitution" policies; prohibitively high tariffs were placed on formerly imported goods that could be produced internally. Although antithetical to classical market-driven economics, the policy was accepted by the United States, at least for a while. Multinationals saw an opportunity to profitably invest as state-protected monopolies in domestic production, especially in countries with large populations. Brazil, after 1964, became the bellwether of ECLA policy. The government assumed a strong guiding role in the economy, combining import substitution policies with an openness to foreign investors. The military dictatorship held down wages by force of law and restrained expenditures on social programs. This, plus a national stability enforced by severe repression, created an attractive investment climate, and multinational money and industrial technology flowed in. Unfortunately, after a period of rapid growth in GNP, Brazil found itself with a large marginalized population (most benefits accrued to the top 20 percent) and the highest debt in the Third World. Such experiences led to disenchantment with the ECLA model. It appeared that the "terms of trade" theory of underdevelopment, although perhaps accurate, was simplistic. There would be no magic formula for rapid development.

The "Development of Underdevelopment"

The ECLA put equal emphasis on internal and external factors; both traditional landowners and international terms of trade were impediments to development. If land reform and import substitution policies were enacted, then investment from the center would be a positive force for progress. Other theorists, such as Andre Gunder Frank (1969), went much further; he argued that world capitalism was itself the cause of underdevelopment.

Frank draws a useful distinction between *un*development and *under*development. Undevelopment is an early stage of economic and social evolution, similar to Rostow's traditional society; underdevelopment, on the other hand, involves the systematic exploitation of the poorer countries by the richer ones. In other words, underdevelopment was not intrinsic but was *created* (in Frank's own terminology, by the exploitation of "satellites" by a "metropolis"). Because the wealthy countries were never underdeveloped, stage theories drawn from an analysis of Western history are irrelevant.

From this perspective, many of those activities that modernization theorists propose as solutions — such as multinational investment or the Western education and training of Third World elites — are actually causes of underdevelopment. Only by delinking from world capitalism can a poor country hope to develop.

Johan Galtung (1971) views imperialism as a sophisticated type of dominance in which the center establishes a "bridgehead" in a periphery nation. This is similar to the idea of comprador elites — native people who represent First World interests in Third World countries — but Galtung is not thinking of individuals so much as structural relationships. A harmony of interest between this small sector and the elites of the center assures that the peripheral nation will serve as a mere appendage of the center. Inequalities of living standards will increase both within the peripheral country and between the periphery and the center.

Imperialist exploitation takes place in three stages. First is a simple looting of raw materials with nothing given in return, as we see in the conquest of Latin America. Second, something is offered in return, but the price is ridiculously low. Incipient political and economic development has brought the peripheral country's power level from zero to some low positive value, but there is still a marked inequality between the trading partners.

At the third level of exploitation, there may be some balance in the flow of goods between the periphery and the center, but there will be enormous differences in the *effects* of trade. Such differences result from the different levels of processing of the goods involved in the exchange, and the "spin-off effects" of such processing. For example, a peripheral country may exchange oil with the United States for tractors. Oil is a natural product that can be put on a ship for export with little or no processing. The extraction of oil provides relatively few jobs, requires little research, and needs no domestic auxiliary companies to support it. The spin-off effects of production are, thus, minimal. Producing tractors, on the other hand, involves great amounts of labor, high levels of education for researchers and scientists, considerable job specialization, numerous auxiliary producers and suppliers, and a strong infrastructure of roads and railroads — that is, numerous spin-off effects. The production of raw materials may make good profits but is relatively self-contained, with little dissemination of benefits to other parts of the society or economy, and, thus, leads to stagnation. High-tech production, however, has a great ripple effect throughout society, leading to increased development.

After this third stage of imperialism is reached, there is no need to use force to maintain it; rather, the structure of the system assures domination and inequality (though Galtung notes that "professional imperialism" has not been perfected, and, therefore, direct violence may sometimes be required to keep the structure intact).

The People without History

Cultural anthropology has been characterized by small-scale field studies of particular peoples. In his influential book *Europe and the People Without History* (1982), Eric Wolf broadened the scope of anthropological investigation, arguing that even tribal and peasant cultures can be understood only in terms of the international system. Wolf shows how European expansion and domination affected every aspect of life even in some of the most remote regions of the globe.

Basic to Wolf's analysis is Marx's concept of "mode of production." In the year 1400, which Wolf uses as a convenient baseline, the dominant mode of production in what we now call the Third World was "kin-ordered." Kinship within a lineage or a clan determined the division of labor. There was a clear distinction between those who belonged to the kin group and those who did not. Tasks were determined by gender, age, rank, and relations of marriage. There was little concept of private property; land or hunting territory would belong to the group. Society was not stratified into classes, and, thus, there was no domination of one economic group over another. Symbolism held the system together; for example, kinship, and, thus, membership within the group, might be determined by reference to mythological ancestors.

The spread of European mercantilism introduced the "tributary mode of production" throughout the world (here Wolf combines two of Marx's modes of production, the "feudal" and the "Asiatic"). In contrast to the kin-ordered mode, tributary relations are based on domination and subordination. Society is organized into two classes, a ruling elite of surplus takers and an underclass of surplus producers. Unlike capitalism, people do not produce for wages but, rather, because they are coerced by military might or because the elite controls an essential part of the production process, such as the land or irrigation. This mode encompasses a wide range of variations, from the tight control of monarchs and colonial viceroys to the loose domination of local strongmen. In some cases, the kin-ordered mode could subsist, in modified form, with the tributary mode; a new layer of power would be added, and much formerly subsistence production would be turned to export, but the original tribes, bands, and chiefdoms would persist. In most cases, however, the tributary mode supplanted the kin-mode, transforming many aspects of society. Among the Plains Indians of North America, the fur trade and the introduction of the horse from Europe changed a formerly sedentary people with a subsistence economy into widely ranging buffalo hunters heavily involved in commerce.

In the tributary mode, the underclasses may still control their own land and resources, whereas under the "capitalist mode," it is the elite that owns the means of production. Also, takers of tribute simply demand a surplus, whereas under capitalism, workers must sell their labor for wages; otherwise, lacking access to the means of production, they cannot survive. In addition, capitalist competition requires that in order to stay in business, the owner of production must constantly increase output and cut costs. This puts the worker in the precarious position of being threatened with losing his job to new technology (and having no fallback for survival) or having his pay cut. Unlike the kin-ordered mode, both the tributary and capitalist modes of production require an apparatus of coercion; this is the state, which provides the laws, the courts, the police, and the armies to maintain the system.

For Wolf, the capitalist mode of production emerged only in the eighteenth century with the mechanization of the textile industries in England. Because of its efficiency and technological superiority, this mode spread rapidly throughout the world, virtually replacing the tributary mode and radically transforming the cultures it encompassed. The kin-ordered mode, to the extent that it had survived mercantilism, was obliterated. Everywhere capitalism created a system in which labor was bought and sold as a commodity. Rigid class stratification emerged where none had existed before, and in many places, the results were cultural collapse, detribalization, and mass immigration in search of jobs. The Mundurucú, a horticultural tribe in Brazil, was brought into the capitalist economy by the development of rubber tapping in the region. Highland villages disappeared as workers moved to the river-bank groves of rubber trees. The rubber trader replaced the chief, and men became caught up in a web of debt bondage to village stores that they could not escape in their lifetimes.

Though a Marxist, Wolf turns Karl Marx's original theorizing about peripheral countries on its head. As we have seen, Marx believed that capitalism was the highest level attained in his time (to be succeeded by socialism) and that underdevelopment outside Europe and North America resulted from the continuation of precapitalist modes of production. For Wolf, underdevelopment results from the encroachment of capitalism on other modes of production and on capitalism's destruction of these other modes.

In one sense, the capitalist economy imposes a unified system on the world. Yet, each individual culture had a different starting point, and each was transformed in its own way and at its own rate. Thus, we should not expect a single proletariat culture but a multitude of cultures, all subsumed under capitalist domination.

The Capitalist World System

For Immanuel Wallerstein (1974), the primary focus of analysis is not individual nations or even the relationship between nations, but the workings of a single global capitalist economy. Though there have been major changes over time in the ebb and flow of power, the basic characteristics of the world system emerged five hundred years ago and have remained relatively constant. Unlike Wolf, Wallerstein does not see wage labor as a defining quality of capitalism; rather, capitalism is simply a system in which the owners of the means of production — individuals, private companies, or states — compete with each other in order to maximize profit.

Ancient empires such as Rome and China also developed "world systems" — that is, integrated and interdependent economies that covered extensive regions. What distinguishes the modern capitalist world system is that it is not confined within the boundaries of an empire; it is truly global. It began in the fifteenth century in Europe. Government-centered mercantilist policies gradually gave way to capitalism as states shifted to increasing reliance on the merchant class, which had developed more resources than the monarchies. The influence of the aristocracy diminished with the growing power of the merchants. The major functions of the state became the support of the capitalists through controlling laborers' demands, protecting property rights, safeguarding foreign markets and trade routes, and opening new geographical areas to exploitation.

The system works through the market and not through states. Although there is only one world economy, there are numerous political units. It is the competition among sovereign nation-states that maintains the economic system. If there were a single political center, competition would disappear and the capitalist system would collapse.

The structure of the system, which developed through complex cycles of expansion and contraction, is based on an international division of labor between the *core*, the *periphery*, and the *semiperiphery* (Figure 3.1).

The core first formed as a small group of Western European nations intensively involved in foreign trade. After the industrial revolution, the core came to include all fully industrialized countries. These countries are characterized by wealth, capital-intensive production (increasingly focused on high-tech manufactures, services, and communications), and a relatively small proportion of workers in agriculture. In the mid-twentieth century, there was a core shift from Europe to the United States, which for two decades held core "hegemony" (dominance by a single state). Today, the United States increasingly shares its economic power with Japan and the European Union.

Historically the role of the periphery has been to supply unprocessed mining and agricultural goods to the core, and this exploitation has shaped its societies, politics, and economics. Because profits from periphery production accrue to the core, these countries cannot accumulate sufficient capital for modernization. Money and resources needed for investment flow into the hands of the core capitalists. What investment exists — for example, in mining or manufacture for export — is for the benefit of the core. One of the few defenses that the periphery has against such exploitation is the erection of protectionist barriers against core products and investment.

The semiperiphery includes characteristics of core and periphery, for example, both high levels of industrialization and large marginalized populations. Countries such as South Africa, Argentina, and Taiwan have more independence than periphery states and may act as regional powers. However, because they are still heavily dependent on

FIGURE 3.1
The Capitalist World System

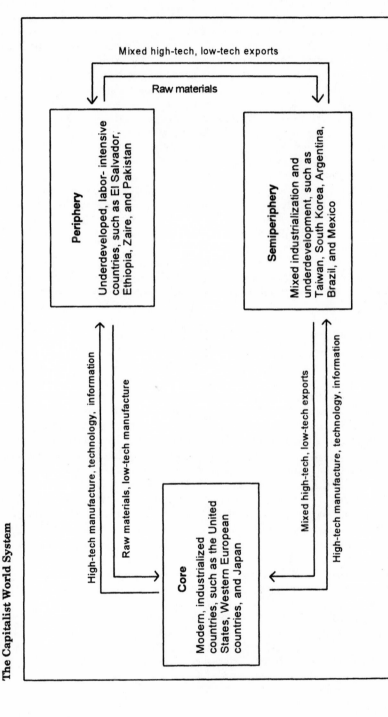

trade, they are forced into a delicate balancing act, asserting their own sovereignty while placating the core. Politically they tend to be closely allied with the core and might depend on it for military protection.

The system as a whole is relatively stable, but there is some movement within it. Once-major powers such as Spain, Portugal, and the Netherlands have become minor players in the core. The British Empire maintained hegemony for a hundred years but lost it in the twentieth century. Japan moved from the core to the periphery after its defeat in World War II, then rapidly returned to the core. Semiperiphery states such as Taiwan, South Korea, and Singapore are rapidly claiming their place in the core. The position of the Soviet bloc was always ambiguous, but with the collapse of socialism, some countries seem to be moving into the core, others into the periphery, and others into semiperiphery status (Table 3.1) (Hopkins and Wallerstein 1982; Shannon 1989).

TOWARD A SYNTHETIC THEORY

An odd incongruity has emerged over the last decades in U.S. academia. By the 1970s, most social scientists adopted at least some aspects of the dependency approach, while economists have tended to reject or ignore dependency arguments. Ricardo's principle of comparative advantage remains a foundation doctrine of economists, although it is largely repudiated by dependency theorists. There is probably enough truth — and enough that is questionable — in each perspective to keep the opponents arguing for some time.

The dependency paradigm has a number of strengths. For one thing, it recognized that the dynamics of the Third World are very different from those in the First World; simplistic prescriptions based on development in Europe and the United States are not applicable to poor countries. Early modernization theorists tended to see poverty and wealth in terms of production; those countries that produced more would develop faster (thus, development was measured by increases in GNP). The dependency theorists added an important dimension by viewing the issue not as a matter of production but of the structural relations of capitalist exchange. Also, the dependency idea of a world economic system based on a division of labor between center and periphery is a valuable one. Finally, such theorists as Wolf and Wallerstein placed a strong, and badly needed, emphasis on the history of the Third World and the effects of that history over hundreds of years.

Critics have pointed out that much theorizing — especially that of the world system approach — tends to be at such a high level of abstraction that it is difficult to apply in specific cases or to meaningfully test empirically. Dependency theory tends to focus almost exclusively on economic factors (an inheritance from Marx) to the exclusion

TABLE 3.1
The Modernization and Dependency Paradigms

	Modernization Paradigm		Dependency Paradigm	
	Early Theorists	Later Theorists	Dependency Theory	World System Theory
Focus of analysis	The internal systems of individual nations.		The international system as historically developed.	
Causes of underdevelopment	Nations start out underdeveloped. Lack of modern technology, capital, entrepreneurial spirit, modernizing elites.	Vicious circle of poverty. Internal colonialism. Lack of social differentiation and social mobilization.	Capitalist exploitation. Unequal terms of trade. Comprador elites. Lack of spin-off effects of primary export production.	Historical emergence of capitalist world system since sixteenth century creates international division of labor, within which each country has its function.
Structure of the system	Internationally: developed and underdeveloped countries. Internally: traditional and modern sectors.	Internationally: developed and underdeveloped countries. Internally: dual traditional and modern economies. "Colonial" dominance by a major city or region.	Developed center and underdeveloped periphery.	Developed core, underdeveloped periphery, partially developed semi-periphery.
Path to development	Underdeveloped countries must follow the paths traversed by developed countries. The latter can help by transferring technology, expertise, capital, etc.	Foreign aid and foreign investment to overcome vicious circle of poverty. Open trade. Export production — at first of primary resources, then of manufactured goods.	Import substitution to develop the domestic economy. Acceptance of foreign investment but with strong controls to break dependency.	May be necessary to "delink" from the capitalist world system for a time. Countries can move from periphery to semi-periphery to core.
Key theorist(s)	W. W. Rostow	S. N. Eisenstadt	Andre Gunder Frank Johan Galtung	Immanuel Wallerstein

of political, military, social, and cultural factors. Critics also charge that dependency theorists ignore factors internal to the various countries, overemphasizing the international domain.

Though often argued in categorical terms, modernization and dependency perspectives may not be as mutually hostile as they first appear. The previous chapter — on the history of the Third World — assumed a clearly dependency perspective, arguing that the characteristics that define the Third World are not intrinsic but were developed through interaction with the West. However, implicit in the dependency paradigm is the added assumption that underdevelopment persists today because of *ongoing* structures of inequality. One might argue that though such structures certainly exist and are formidable, there are *also* powerful forces internal to various countries. The fact that such forces were developed historically from Western expansion does not make them any less real or less internal now. An example would be the continuity of elites in Latin America. These elites, who date back hundreds of years to the conquest and colonial periods, are more interested in the maintenance of their own power and position than in supporting or benefiting the core states (though they may use core investment and military support to their own advantage). Another example is the emergence in many Third World countries of huge informal economies — shantytowns, gypsy transportation, and illegal markets — that are relatively divorced from the dictates of international capitalism.

Some recent theorists have sought to reclaim the state, rather than the economy, as the focus of analysis. These scholars see the Third World state not as a mere servant of international capitalism but as an autonomous entity in its own right, with the power to direct (or misdirect) development through policy decisions and through acting as a primary investor in indigenous production.

One thing is certain: there will be no agreement among theorists about the causes of national poverty or the best road toward development. However, each skirmish in the intellectual battle leads to new and valuable insights into this single most critical issue of our times.

SUGGESTED READINGS

Brewer, Anthony, *Marxist Theories of Imperialism: A Critical Survey* (London: Routledge and Kegan Paul, 1980). After giving a detailed overview of Marx's views of capitalism, the book critically describes the ideas of individual authors, such as Paul Baran, Andre Gunder Frank, and Immanuel Wallerstein. Final chapters discuss current debates within the Marxist tradition.

Castro, Fidel, *The World Economic and Social Crisis: Report to the Seventh Summit Conference of Non-Aligned Countries* (Havana: Office of Publications, Cuban Council of State, 1983). Obviously written by a committee of professional Cuban economists, this report offers a clear synthesis of Marxist dependency theory. The theory is supported by numerous graphs and charts taken from World Bank and United Nations statistics.

Chilcote, Ronald H., *Theories of Development and Underdevelopment* (Boulder, Colo.: Westview, 1984). This short overview describes the theories of the major writers on development, such as Marx, Lenin, Prebisch, Cardoso, Baran, Wallerstein, and Amin. A final chapter is devoted to new perspectives.

Rostow, W. W., *The Stages of Economic Growth* (London: Cambridge University Press, 1960). Though considered outmoded, this classic statement of early modernization theory has had a great impact on U.S. policy toward the Third World.

Shannon, Richard Thomas, *An Introduction to World Systems Theory* (Boulder, Colo.: Westview Press, 1989). This is a clear and objective overview of the influential theories of Immanuel Wallerstein and his followers. Maps illustrate the growth of the world capitalist system. The final chapter offers some cogent criticism of the theory.

Wolf, Eric R., *Europe and the People Without History* (Berkeley: University of California Press, 1982). The author, an anthropologist, takes a Marxian perspective, showing how the tributary and capitalist modes of production introduced by Europeans altered (for the worse) the social and economic structures of Third World peoples.

4

Import Substitution, Basic Needs, and the Physical Quality of Life Index: The Domestic Economy

In Lima, Peru, a private research group attempted to set up a small clothing factory in order to determine what sorts of obstacles an entrepreneur would face. The anticipated hurdles were not, as one might expect, lack of capital, appropriate technology, or skilled labor; rather, they were an intricate maze of regulations established by a government that poured out an average of 27,000 laws and administrative decisions annually. Just getting the company legally registered required several lawyers and almost three hundred days of full-time work. The direct cost was $1,230, the 1983 equivalent of thirty-two minimum monthly wages. The research group, determined to remain legal, tried to avoid paying bribes. It was solicited for bribes ten times and ultimately was forced to pay two of them. Another study revealed that it took over two years to get a commercial minibus route approved. Once a business was established, legal expenses could eat up over 70 percent of profits, while another 22 percent went to taxes.

Little wonder that the large majority of entrepreneurs chose to work in the informal or illegal sector! Over 80 percent of the markets in Lima were black markets, often employing their own self-defense organizations in lieu of reliance on the police. Virtually all public transportation was unlicensed and, therefore, illegal; more than a billion dollars had been invested in trucks, busses, and gypsy cabs. The situation was similar in private housing. Almost half of all families lived in squatter settlements, on land that they did not own — partially because it took up to seven years just to complete the legal processing requirements for a house. These were not necessarily cardboard and scrap wood hovels; the average resale value of these houses was $22,000. Indeed, squatters were spending four times as much as the government was investing in low-income housing (De Soto 1989).

Although the Peruvian case may be extreme, it is not that atypical. In many countries, a flourishing informal sector has challenged the formal sector, which might be weak, corrupt, and inefficient.

Throughout the Third World, countries have had trouble achieving strong, self-generating domestic economies.

NATIONAL VERSUS INTERNATIONAL ECONOMIES

Few subjects relating to the Third World are so hotly debated as the economics of development. Is poverty the result of conditions internal to the various countries, or has exploitation by the industrial powers distorted and retarded indigenous capacities for growth? Is the road to development through exports, or is a country better off concentrating on domestic industries and establishing high tariffs to protect them? Does the investment of multinational corporations help or hinder development? Should countries be forced to reorient their economies toward paying their huge foreign debts, or should the debts be written off or reduced? Should a country make a priority of reducing income inequalities, or should it focus on growth of gross national product (GNP)? Finally, what does "development" mean anyway?

Where one stands on these questions depends a great deal on whether or not one assumes a modernization or dependency perspective. The former position — that the causes of underdevelopment are internal and that a free market approach to development is best — would be supported by most economists. Whether this is because of their more thorough understanding of the data, because of their reliance on ahistorical mathematical models, or a matter of the political culture of the economics profession is a moot question. Many social scientists outside economics (as well as some inside) would tend more toward a dependency perspective, viewing the structure of the international system as at least a significant part of the problem.

What do the data reveal? Nothing conclusive. Statistics can support either side in many arguments, and there is so much variation in the experiences of individual Third World countries that specific examples can be found to buttress or refute just about any general claim. It is at the ideological extremes — whether a rigid laissez-faire approach or a dogmatic Marxism — that the arguments seem weakest. The fact is that almost everything has been tried, from complete immersion in international capitalism to delinking from the capitalist system, and no universally effective model has emerged.

One of the most important realities of Third World countries is their reliance on international capital. Unlike the industrialized nations, which raise the bulk of their revenues domestically through taxes, most developing countries have to depend on external sources: trade, multinational corporate investment, loans, and foreign aid. It is somewhat artificial to separate the internal from the international, so closely are the two fused. However, for purposes of simplification, we will do so, examining the domestic economy in this chapter and surveying outward-directed commerce in the next.

CHARACTERISTICS OF THIRD WORLD ECONOMIES

As we have seen, despite the wide variation among Third World economies, most hold a number of characteristics in common. Internally, there is a large proportion of the labor force and a high percentage of national output in agriculture, accompanied by a relatively small manufacturing sector. Labor is mostly unskilled and cannot move easily from one sector to another. Though the concept of "dual economies" has been challenged — it has been shown that virtually all people participate in some way in the world economy — there is often a marked discrepancy in living standards between modern urban enclaves and traditional rural areas. Technology may be inadequate or inappropriate (as when high-tech assembly lines contribute little to employment).

In the First World, saving is crucial to domestic development, because it provides the primary source of investment. Banks, savings and loans, stock markets, pensions, and insurance all provide money for business. In the Third World, however, high inflation rates, often combined with interest rates maintained at artificially low levels by government edict, discourage savings. For example, if a legal interest ceiling of 8 percent were combined with 10 percent inflation, savers would lose 2 percent of their money each year. The result is that people either spend their money on luxuries, rather than save it, or get it out of the country, investing in more solid currencies or foreign enterprises. Often, because of personalistic banking practices or corruption, what little savings exist will be selectively loaned to family, friends, or political patrons rather than the most promising entrepreneurs. Farmers and small businesses may be completely cut off from loans. Because of a religious prohibition against "usury," some Islamic countries officially discourage lending at interest rates sufficient to make a profit, with the result that there are few lenders. The lack of savings means that domestic sources for investment are extremely limited (Wight 1994).

Despite such problems, the overall growth rate of the Third World was impressive during the 1960s and 1970s, averaging 3.7 percent, higher than the rates of growth in Europe and North America during their developmental periods. However, there was considerable variation. Predictably, the highest income countries had the greatest growth (4.2 percent), while the poorest countries fared the worst. With the major exceptions of India and China, which performed reasonably well, per capita incomes in the poorest countries increased less than 1 percent during the two decades after 1960; considering their extremely low starting points, that 1 percent is negligible in real-money terms. Economic growth in Africa was a mere 0.2 percent. In the 1980s, a world recession brought even these small gains to a halt; per capita gross domestic product (GDP) in Africa *declined* over 2 percent per year.

Though a few of the higher income countries of Southeast Asia and Latin America continue to grow, many countries entered the last decade of the twentieth century either stagnating or declining (Figure 4.1) while burdened with enormous international debts (Gordon 1992:75; Weiner 1987b:49).

Absolute Poverty

Poverty is a relative concept. In terms of income, a family earning below the official poverty line in the United States would be considered wealthy in Bangladesh. Poverty in Uruguay does not mean the same thing as poverty in Chad. Because of this, there have been attempts to define the concept of "absolute poverty." Former World Bank President Robert MacNamara once characterized it as "a condition of life so degraded by disease, illiteracy, malnutrition, and squalor as to deny its victims basic human necessities" (quoted in Chenery et al. 1974:12). A more or less accepted definition considers access to minimal levels of nutrition by South Asian standards, namely, income levels sufficient for a diet of 2,150 calories per day. This definition may be *sub*minimal insofar as it fails to consider the quality of those calories (How much is protein? Are all necessary vitamins included?). Based on this concept, it was estimated that in 1975 as much as 40 percent of people in the Third World lived in absolute poverty. There were wide disparities from country to country and region to region: in Asia the figure was over 56 percent, in Africa nearly 50 percent, and in Latin America over 17 percent. The United Nations Economic Commission for Latin America adopted poverty lines specific to that continent and estimated almost 40 percent lived in poverty (Chenery et al. 1974:12; Ahluwalia and Carter 1979).

The real characteristics of absolute poverty extend well beyond caloric intake. As much as four-fifths of income may be spent for food, and that food would be a monotonous regimen of only a few cheap staples, such as rice, yams, or cassava. As a result, many are under-nourished, often severely so, with the inevitable listlessness and susceptibility to disease and parasites. Two out of ten babies die within their first year, and another dies before the age of five. Fewer than 10 percent of children at this level of poverty are vaccinated against diseases that have virtually disappeared from First World countries, such as diphtheria, whooping cough, and polio. The average life expectancy at birth is forty years, compared with about seventy-five in developed countries. Only one-third are literate, and less than half complete more than three years of often poor-quality primary school (Nafziger 1984:82–83).

In all regions of the Third World, from 70 percent to 80 percent of these poor are located in rural areas. Despite this, by far the largest share of government expenditures have been focused on the cities.

FIGURE 4.1
Comparison of Per Capita Gross National Products

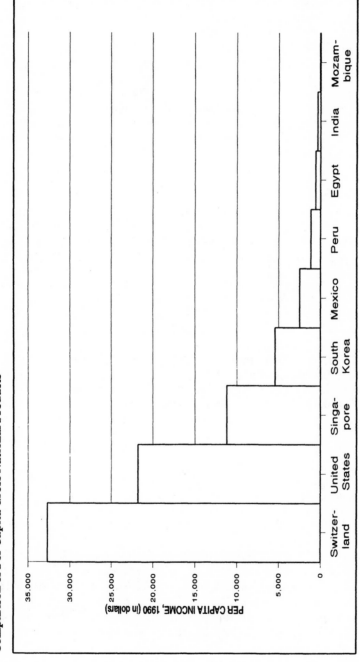

Source: World Bank. *World Development Report 1992* (New York: Oxford University Press, 1992), pp. 218–219.

In both cities and rural areas, poverty disproportionately affects women, who normally have less status than men, are less educated, and have fewer employment opportunities. Women perform a dual economic role. At home, they are responsible for housework, food preparation, child care, gathering food and water, caring for animals, and often weeding, sowing, and harvesting crops. Outside the home, they are relegated to working in the agricultural sector and in informal small businesses with long hours, hard labor, and low wages. The problems are exacerbated because poorer women tend to have more children and because males are increasingly absent from the home. In some areas of the Caribbean and Africa, as many as 40 percent of households are headed by women.

The Physical Quality of Life Index

The primary means of measuring economic development remains per capita GNP (or the very similar GDP). The World Bank bases its classification of countries on such statistics, which also furnish measures of improvement over time. However, it is the "gross" in GNP that should be emphasized; this is, at best, a very crude instrument. For example, the ratio of per capita GNP between the United States and India is fifty to one; however, if purchasing power is considered, the ratio drops to fourteen to one. Although GNP might be an adequate measure of economic growth, it tells us little about the standard of living of the masses.

To circumvent the problems of GNP, the Physical Quality of Life Index (PQLI) was designed primarily as a measure of the world's poor countries in meeting the most basic needs of the people (Table 4.1). The relatively simple measure combines the rates for infant mortality, life expectancy at age one, and literacy. A top score of one hundred would signify a very high level of basic needs provision (most First World countries score above ninety-five). When first calculated for the early 1970s, Mali scored lowest, with only fifteen.

Life expectancy and infant mortality ostensibly demonstrate the effects of nutrition, public health, income, and the general environment. Although it would appear that both rates measure the same thing, in reality, there is not always a strong correlation between infant mortality and longevity.

Unlike GNP, the PQLI avoids the assumption that there is only one pattern of development or that Western economic values are supreme, nor is it concerned with the manner in which basic needs are attained; the socialist countries of Eastern Europe scored very close to their Western counterparts, although there were large differences in income. Another advantage of the PQLI is that its data are easy to come by and relatively accurate.

TABLE 4.1
Physical Quality of Life Index Compared with
Per Capita Gross National Product

	Per capita GNP $	PQLI		Per capita GNP $	PQLI
Mozambique	80	32	Peru	1,160	73
Somalia	120	31	Cuba	1,494	96
Chad	190	33	Jamaica	1,500	93
Rwanda	310	41	Costa Rica	1,900	94
India	350	54	Chile	1,940	91
China	370	81	Algeria	2,060	66
Haiti	370	49	Mexico	2,490	84
Sri Lanka	470	88	Brazil	2,680	79
Bolivia	630	64	South Korea	5,400	92
Philippines	730	80	Saudi Arabia	7,050	67
Guatemala	900	64	Israel	10,920	96
El Salvador	1,110	72			
United States (for reference)				21,790	98

Note: GNP per capita is of limited use in measuring development, because it may mainly reflect the wealth of the upper 40 percent of the population. The PQLI is an attempt to measure a country's provision of basic needs, such as health and nutrition. It is based on a scale from 0 to 100. If life expectancy at age 1 is 38 years, the country would score 0; if 77 years, it would score 100. Infant mortality ranges from 229 per thousand (score of 0) to 7 (score of 100). Raw literacy scores are also included.

As might be expected, there is a rough correlation between per capita GNP and PQLI, but there are a number of exceptions, such as Sri Lanka and Cuba and, at the other extreme, Saudi Arabia.

Sources: Formulas from Morris 1979; statistics from World Bank 1992.

How does PQLI compare with GNP cross-nationally? There is a correlation, to be sure, but it is not nearly as strong as we might guess. One would expect that the higher the per capita income, the higher the standard of living. To some extent, this is true, but there are numerous exceptions. Sri Lanka with a per capita GNP of only $470 has a relatively high PQLI of eighty-eight; Saudi Arabia with a GNP fifteen times higher than Sri Lanka has a PQLI of only sixty-seven. India and China have almost identical per capita GNPs, but China, which assumed a basic needs model of development, scores twenty-seven points higher on the PQLI. Before the loss of support from the Soviet Union and the collapse of the economy, Cuba with a per capita GNP of less than $1,500 attained a PQLI of ninety-six. Though Brazil has a per capita GNP of $2,680, its PQLI is nearly the same as the Philippines, which has a per capita GNP of $730. The lower-middle income countries of Jamaica and Costa Rica score almost as high as First World nations.

The PQLI is itself a crude measure. There is no clear proof that it actually measures all the things it claims. Its critics point out that the equal weighing of its three indicators unreasonably places literacy on a par with infant death. However, PQLI discrepancies with GNP do point out a crucial fact: a high GNP does not necessarily mean that people have a high standard of living. Conversely, a low GNP does not mean that people are necessarily hungry, lacking access to health care, or uneducated. If a country is truly devoted to supplying basic human needs, it would appear that it has options beyond merely increasing its GNP.

Defining Development

The term "development" is used so commonly — including in its many manifestations such as "less developed" and "underdeveloped" — that one would think the term had a universally accepted definition. Hardly. Its meaning is closely tied up with various competing ideologies, paradigms, and theories.

The traditional meaning was exclusively economic and closely associated with GNP, or perhaps with GNP per capita. A country that could sustain a GNP growth of, say, from 5 percent to 7 percent per year was considered developing. A by-product of this was that the share of agriculture in the GNP would decline and that of manufacturing and services would increase. As one group of researchers put it, "A national economy is considered developed if it has high levels of internal differentiation, integration, and energy consumption, employs scientific technology in production, and has a high level of labor productivity" (Bornschier et al. 1978:654). There is no hint that the standard of living of the masses has anything to do with development or that development encompasses aspects of society other than the economic.

The "dethronement of GNP" as the basis for definitions of development occurred in the 1970s as it became evident that not everyone was sharing in the fruits of growth. Studies of income distribution revealed that quite often the poorest 40 percent or more of the population was being left behind and that economic growth often had little relation to the physical quality of life of most people. Development began to be perceived as much more complex. There were social and political aspects that were not incorporated in purely economic definitions.

The 1984 Kissinger Commission for Central America adopted a definition that was almost identical to that of the Alliance for Progress two decades before. It included the elimination of a climate of violence and civil strife, the emergence of democratic institutions and processes, the evolution of strong and free economies with diversified production for both external and domestic markets, sharp improvement in social conditions of the poorest sectors, and better distribution of income and wealth (Huntington 1987:9). Both the Alliance for Progress and the

Kissinger Commission were motivated first and foremost by U.S. national security interests and the perceived threat of communism; therefore, this is a political rather than an economic or even social definition of development. It is notable, however, that there is no mention of industrialization or "high rates of energy consumption" or "scientific technology" (none of which would have had much application to Central America).

Many economists continue to support traditional economic measures of development on the grounds that a rise in GNP will inevitably lead to more equalization of income and to a rise in the standard of living of all sectors (as we will see, this is not true). However, the need to reorient developmental policies away from a strict reliance on GNP toward broader social objectives became widely accepted. Development is best viewed as a multidimensional process and one that might not be the same for all countries. A country just beginning development may focus on such fundamentals as nation building, establishing a strong state, and creating an infrastructure of roads and communications. In parts of Africa, for example, progress may be measured in personal terms: electric lights for the village, a health clinic within walking distance, and low prices for rice and flour.

For countries that have already realized such basics, development might include the following: first, economic growth that entails a reduction of inequality and rising standards of living, preferably for all population groups but at least for the lowest 40 percent; second, a sufficiently strong and self-sustaining *domestic* economy so that people have employment and, thus, the earning power to create demand for domestic and imported goods; third, a diversified economy with at least some manufacture and a balance between export and domestic production; fourth, effective citizen participation in government (though not necessarily Western-style democracy); fifth, education available to all sectors and both sexes; sixth, governmental and social stability; and, finally, a respect for human rights.

As general as these criteria are, few Third World countries would qualify as anywhere near developed, though some are seriously moving in the right direction.

Growth and Equality

For most Third World countries, GNP mainly measures the rate of growth of the upper 40 percent, or even much fewer. For example, between 1954 and 1963 India had a GNP increase that averaged just over 4 percent per year. In reality, the wealthiest fifth of the population grew by 5.3 percent, while the poorest fifth grew by only 2 percent. In absolute terms, the gain of the poorest was minuscule; even if their individual incomes were as high as $100, their increase would have been only two dollars per year (Todaro 1985:161).

The fact that economic growth left much of the population in the dust was recognized as early as the 1950s. Simon Kuznets' (1955) study of development in the West revealed that early growth had been accompanied by increased inequality. However, after a certain level of per capita income had been achieved, the income gap narrowed. This process was assumed to apply equally to the Third World. As the modern sector took off, the traditional sector would be left behind, so that inequality would, at first, increase. Then, as modernization gradually encompassed the entire country, the standard of living of the poor would increase and inequality would diminish. Kuznets' principle became — and continues to be — a rationale for development policies based on modernization theory and on growth of GNP. Essentially the idea is: Don't worry about inequality because it will automatically self-correct as growth continues.

Is this true? One way to find out is to compare Lorenz curves for various countries (Figure 4.2). The simplest and most common method of expressing inequality is to divide the country's population into fifths according to income share. For example, in Ghana, which boasts a relatively low level of inequality, 7 percent of income goes to the lowest fifth while about 29 percent goes to the highest fifth. Comparisons between the First World and the Third World are often distorted by demographics; a much larger proportion of the population in developing countries tends to be in the younger age groups, which would not be expected to have established themselves economically yet. However, comparisons within the Third World, where age distributions are roughly similar, are more valid. Another problem with comparing distributions is that such information is hard to come by. The World Bank lists such statistics for only nineteen of over a hundred Third World countries.

Based on the best data available in the 1970s, there did appear to be a rough correlation between income distribution and per capita GNP (Ahluwalia and Carter 1979:465), thus, supporting Kuznets' hypothesis. However, more recent statistics show no strong or obvious relationship (Todaro 1985:156–158; World Bank 1992:276–277). Bangladesh and Pakistan, both low-income countries, fare much better than high-income countries like Brazil and Uruguay. Income distribution may have more to do with the history of a region and with such characteristics as land tenure and the depth to which elites are entrenched than with GNP. If there is a relationship between equality and GNP, it is subtle and not particularly significant. This suggests two conclusions. First, a developmental emphasis on growth of GNP cannot be justified on the grounds that inequalities will diminish after a certain level of income is reached; the gap between rich and poor is just as likely to continue to widen. Second, policies that focus on redistribution of income early in the developmental process should not be discounted;

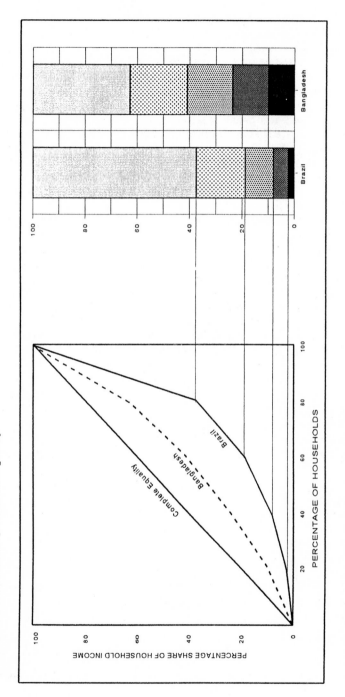

FIGURE 4.2
The Lorenz Curve, Showing Income Inequality

The greater the curve, the greater the degree of inequality.

Sources: Open University, *Third World Atlas* (Philadelphia: Open University Press, 1983), p. 16; World Bank, *World Development Report 1992* (New York: Oxford University Press).

there is apparently no necessary trade-off between equality and growth (Nasar 1994).

As with GNP, there are some real problems with using income distribution as a measure of development. For one thing, the poor may be improving their standard of living in absolute terms even if they are declining relative to the wealthy (of course, it is also often the case that the poor suffer a real decline in income). Subsistence agriculture may be undercounted; if a peasant family is forced off its land by the spread of plantation agriculture, the family's money income will increase as it enters the wage labor market, but its security and ability to feed itself may diminish immeasurably. On the other hand, barter and services in the informal economy may be severely undercounted as income.

A much more important measure of inequality is *wealth* distribution. Whereas income represents only the earnings per year of an individual from all sources (wages, rents, royalties, interest), wealth includes all privately held money and property, not only stocks, bonds, and savings but also houses, plantations, and factories. Income may feed a person through a day, but it is wealth that provides long-range security, especially in countries without insurance, pensions, or welfare. It is wealth, not income, that translates into political power, as well as the economic power of ownership of productive facilities. Wealth is vastly more maldistributed than income. In the United States the upper fifth is eleven times richer in income than the poorest fifth but 380 times richer in wealth; in fact, the top 1 percent has more wealth than the bottom 90 percent. We would expect even greater maldistribution of wealth in many Third World countries. It would be most enlightening to look at what happens to wealth distribution as countries experience economic growth. The problem: wealth distribution is too politically explosive. Such statistics are seldom calculated in the First World and never in the Third World (Lewellen 1984).

Redistribution as a means of generating more equality within a country conjures images of an autocratic Robin Hood government stealing from the rich and giving to the poor. Such a policy would bring about deterioration, because the transferred funds would not lead to increased production. More realistic strategies include land reform, progressive (but reasonable) income and wealth taxes, minimum wage laws, low-interest loans to farms and small businesses, and investments in education, health, and nutrition. Such reforms can greatly raise the level of productivity of the people at the bottom of the economic pyramid and, by putting more money in the hands of the poor, can increase demand for domestically produced goods.

INNER-DIRECTED MODELS OF DEVELOPMENT

Every Third World country must choose a path to development, if only by default. This is not to say that every government deliberately and systematically follows a rational, well-thought-out strategy. The reality is that a government may be so corrupt or chaotic or faced by internal crises such as revolution or famine that development is a low priority. However, many countries do formulate detailed short- and long-range plans based on particular theories or ideologies. In any case, all countries must make choices. Whether to rely on exports or focus on the domestic economy, whether to deliberately try to raise the level of the poorest or to emphasize the productive role of the elites, whether to use scarce funds to stimulate the agricultural sector or manufacturing — such hard decisions cannot be avoided. The appropriateness of a given model depends on a number of factors, such as the size and population of the country, its natural resources, its historical evolution, the distribution of wealth, and the degree of dependence on external powers. Brazil, China, and India have sufficiently large populations to support extensive manufacturing for domestic use, whereas a smaller country like Botswana would be more likely to import even its low-tech manufactured goods. By taking advantage of international demand for critical raw materials, a country with plenty of oil or copper might be able to delay industrialization. A country with large Islamic or Hindu population might choose a course in keeping with its religious traditions.

In popular conception, there are only two dominant models of development, the capitalist and the socialist. This is extremely simplistic. Neither "capitalism" nor "socialism" means quite the same thing in the Third World as in the West. Capitalism can be inward directed, with an emphasis on competition among domestic producers, or it can be outward directed toward the international market. Even the most capitalist of Third World countries have nationalized their primary resources, and many support a wide range of state-owned enterprises. Socialism can run the gamut from a moderate democratic populism to Cuban-style communism. In a sense, each country invents its own model of development.

This said, "ideal types" can be delineated. It is the nature of such categories that they are seldom reflected exactly in reality, and most countries would blend elements from two or more patterns. However, four models cover most of the available options actually employed in the world today: the basic needs approach, the import substitution strategy, neoliberal capitalism, and the Southeast Asian model. In this chapter, we will look at the first two, which are inward-focused; in the next chapter, the export-oriented models will be examined.

The Basic Needs Model

All countries ostensibly wish to raise the living standards of their poorest citizens, but this is seldom the primary goal of development. For one thing, the political and economic elites are usually those who control the developmental process, and they are seldom amenable to the drastic redistribution that such a strategy implies. Also, the prevailing ideology may be that the poor are best served by a general growth in GNP, even if increased initial inequality is the result.

Some countries, however, have chosen to concentrate immediately on supplying all of their citizens with the most basic needs of adequate food, sanitary water, housing, health services, and education. This option has been chosen almost exclusively where there are a large number of extremely poor people ruled over by a small wealthy elite. The strategy, then, requires a radical restructuring of society. The elite, and possibly the middle class dependent on the elite, must be either eliminated or divested of power. The government will then derive its authority and legitimacy from support of the lower classes. This is a process most effectively attained through violent revolution (though modified versions have emerged through democratic or at least peaceful means, as in Chile under Allende and Indonesia under Sukarno). The successful versions of this strategy — that is, those that have lasted for any length of time — are all Marxist.

For Marxists, the causes of underdevelopment are perceived to lie in the structure of the capitalist system. This requires at least a degree of delinking from that system, though in the past, dependency on the capitalist West was sometimes traded for an equally strong dependency on the Soviet bloc. A strong central government, formed around a socialist ideology, controls almost every aspect of the economy. The priority of providing basic needs to all sectors of the society funnels capital into education, domestic agriculture, housing, and medicine, with the result that industrialization may be put off. Ideally, medical treatment and education are free, and food and housing are subsidized to make them accessible to even the poorest. At the outset, standards may be extremely low; for example, a few years of grade school for everyone is seen as preferable to high levels of illiteracy accompanied by a few college graduates. It is more important that even the most remote rural family have access to a clinic than that expensive modern hospitals be built in the cities. Manufacturing is devoted to supplying necessary commodities; luxury goods are neither produced domestically nor imported.

China, North Korea, and Cuba have all been relatively successful in their initial basic needs aims; though their per capita GNPs have remained low or moderate relative to other countries in their regions, they have attained high scores on the PQLI. These countries have been effective in providing a low but adequate standard of living for the larger part of their peoples, but they have found it difficult to evolve beyond the basic needs approach. In that sense, there may be a sort of built-in self-destruct mechanism within socialist economies. If the state is successful in providing basic needs to all or most of its citizens, the second or third generation after the revolution will no longer see this as a priority; having grown up with their basic needs supplied, their dreams will tend toward more consumer goods, expressive freedom, and political participation. China, which by 1994 had attained the fastest growing large economy in the world, was experimenting with limited capitalism and greatly expanded consumerism but seemed unable to provide similar social and political reforms.

Several other countries that have chosen the Marxist model have failed miserably even at their basic needs goals, including Cambodia, Ethiopia, Tanzania, South Yemen, Angola, Mozambique, Chile, Nicaragua, and Vietnam. Failures of socialism are usually ascribed to structural weaknesses of the model itself, such as the lack of incentives to produce, the emphasis on redistribution over production, overly rigid centralized planning, and the necessity for high levels of repression to maintain the system. However, it would be difficult to find a Marxist government in the Third World that was not relentlessly attacked by the West, either covertly through Central Intelligence Agency destabilization or overtly through embargoes and open warfare, so, it is difficult to say how a socialist country might have fared if it were left in peace and allowed to trade freely in the international marketplace.

Import Substitution Industrialization

We have already seen how import substitution developed out of early Latin American theories of dependency. The logic of import substitution was so persuasive that, sooner or later, virtually every Third World country adopted it to some extent. That logic is not necessarily anticapitalist; rather, the underlying assumption is that indigenous capitalism needs protection from international capitalism. If cheap imports can undercut any attempt by entrepreneurs to build even modest industries, it will be impossible to develop a domestic capitalist class, and foreign capitalists will control the economy to their own advantage. To be sure, most countries were able to export primary products — ores and agricultural goods that might be locally owned and controlled — but such exports would not lead to the emergence of a manufacturing sector.

A government can stimulate investment in domestic manufacturing through quotas and high tariffs on competing foreign goods. The emergence of a domestic manufacturing sector provides jobs that, in turn, train a factory labor force. Ideally, one factory acts as a catalyst to the creation of supporting enterprises. When domestic demand is saturated, factories can, it is hoped, export their manufactures. Though industry is the focus of import substitution, domestic food crops also often are protected.

Some problems were obvious even before the policies were put into effect. At least initially, the quality of indigenously produced goods would be less than that of imports, and prices would be higher.

Smuggling, and the corruption that goes with it, would be inevitable if a country with high tariff protection bordered on a country without import substitution. Countries with small populations have very limited demand for manufactured goods, and, thus, it might not be worth it to even attempt such production. So much government control of the economy would lead to an unhealthy concentration of political power. Officials would be tempted to unrealistically overvalue their exchange rates; such a policy would, indeed, protect local industries but would have the negative effect of making the country's exports too expensive for foreign buyers. First World countries, which form the biggest market, can retaliate against import substitution by closing their own markets.

Nevertheless, the advantages were seen to outweigh the drawbacks, and as it turned out, the early stages of import substitution industrialization were relatively easy. In the early phases, there is little need for a well-trained managerial force or skilled laborers, because industries grow out of existing artisan workshops. Most manufacturing at this stage is small-scale, perhaps a family operation making shirts, so even less-populous countries can take advantage of limited demand. As more and more people become employed in these enterprises, often moving out of subsistence agriculture and into wage labor, the market grows. Profits at this early stage are virtually assured. Government subsidies and loans for start-up costs help new entrepreneurs.

Early import substitution was often, though by no means always, successful in its limited goals of creating indigenous factories, a domestic capitalist class, experienced managers, and skilled factory workers. Before being derailed by the rising price of oil, Brazil's "economic miracle" took place in an environment of one of the most severe import substitution programs anywhere. (In this case, however, many of the protected companies — often partially financed from abroad — belonged to the state rather than to private entrepreneurs. Protected state monopolies became increasingly inefficient and corrupt.)

Domestic production of basic commodities often evolved into more sophisticated manufactures, so that in the second phase — reached as early as the 1950s in Latin America — even radios and automobiles fell under tariff protection. In these cases, large multinational corporations such as Sony or General Motors set up factories to assemble imported components into finished products. It might be thought that multinational corporations would have been the strongest opponents of import substitution, but many of them were quite happy to invest as monopolies in protected markets and reaped handsome profits.

In large countries, such as Brazil, domestic markets may be big enough that protected industries can prosper indefinitely. More often, however, import substitution will reach a point of crisis when markets become saturated. Indigenous capitalism is as expansionistic as its international counterpart. When there are no new customers for products that were formerly imported, companies will find themselves with stagnant markets. Ideally, they then would be able to expand their markets through export. However, a company that grew up in an environment protected from international competition may not have a product that can compete in the international marketplace. Although import substitution has its value in the initial phases of industrialization, the limits of internal demand may bring an economy to a dead halt.

Import substitution is now routinely criticized for its antiexport bias, overvalued exchange rates, market inefficiencies, and concentration of political power. Early successes are forgotten. It may not be the model itself that is deficient but the failure of countries to make other changes — such as land reform, educational improvements, and political reform — at the same time. Also, because vested interests benefit from protectionism, import substitution is often continued as the major economic model long after it has reached the limits of its developmental potential.

THE THREE SECTORS

Most Third World countries are characterized by relatively weak domestic economies. Populations may not be large enough or people may be too poor to create sufficient demand to justify production for the internal market. Without such production, there are not enough jobs available and wages are so low that a vicious circle is created: simplistically speaking, no money means no demand, no demand means no factories, no factories mean no jobs, and no jobs mean no money. Such an economy may have to rely on exports and imports to a much greater degree than is the case in the First World, and such dependence may further weaken the domestic economy. In addition, for many Third World countries, whether capitalist or socialist, the primary goal of economic policy is not growth or development but the consolidation and maintenance of the state. Resources are taken from those lacking political power and reallocated to those with such power.

A country's economy can be divided into three distinct but overlapping sectors. The *primary sector* is that of the exploitation of unprocessed resources — agriculture, fishing, mining, and oil extraction. Manufacturing comprises the *secondary sector*. The *tertiary sector* encompasses commerce, government, the military, and services, such as medicine or teaching.

The Primary Sector

Though manufacturing is of increasing importance to the Third World, primary commodities remain dominant, accounting for 80 percent of all exports (by contrast, in the industrialized countries, only a quarter of exports are primary) (Todaro 1985:41). In some countries, oil or minerals are the main source of foreign exchange, but these enterprises employ relatively few workers. In almost all Third World countries, it is agriculture that engages the bulk of the population, and it is this population that is the poorest, least nourished, and least educated.

In the United States, less than 3 percent of workers are employed in agriculture; in the Third World, an average of 60 percent work on the land, with the rate rising above 80 percent in some countries of Africa. Despite so many more people involved in agriculture in the Third World, per capita productivity is less than 4 percent of that in the developed countries (Todaro 1985:293). Land is very unevenly distributed. It has been estimated that in the world as a whole, the 2.5 percent of landowners with over 250 acres own nearly three-quarters of all the land, with the top 0.23 percent controlling over half (George 1977:35). This is not necessarily an issue in industrialized countries, where the larger part of the labor force works in manufacturing or services, but it can be a severe problem in the agrarian economies of the Third World.

Rural areas are often considered relatively homogenous; in reality, they are highly differentiated, with complex structures consisting of wealthy landowners, sharecroppers, tenants, peasants, plantation workers, artisans, and traders. There are numerous ways that people own and rent land, ranging from large-scale modern farms to small subsistence plots. Patterns of land tenure strongly affect productivity. Though it is often assumed that larger farms produce more because they can efficiently use such machinery as tractors, the fact is that small family farms boast greater output per acre. Studies in India showed that labor-intensive small farms also invested more capital per acre. The general rule seems to be that if the person who tends the land profits directly from increased production, the land will be used more efficiently.

Malnutrition amid Abundance

In a process sometimes called "the rationalization of agriculture," traditional feudal-style landholdings, such as the haciendas of Latin America, have become plantations, producing commercial crops through the use of machines and wage labor. Serf-like peasants and sharecroppers have been expelled, taking their places among the army of landless farmworkers. Throughout the twentieth century, and especially since about 1950, there has been a tendency for large-scale landholdings to expand at the expense of small holdings. In Latin America, for example, 8 percent of landowners hold 80 percent of the agricultural land, and that would include almost all of the most fertile soil. Even those peasants who are able to maintain plots cannot feed themselves; by 1980, three in five rural households — 132 million families — had holdings too small for their own subsistence (Harrison

1992:126–127). Large farms employ only one-quarter the number of workers per acre as small farms.

Though many displaced peasants migrate to the cities, rural populations continue to increase in absolute numbers because of natural population growth. Most must make do laboring at barest wages only a few months of the year, during planting and harvest, sometimes travelling long distances to find work. Subsistence farmers eke out a meager existence using traditional techniques on marginal lands, while the more fertile lands produce export crops. Small-scale farmers who grow for the commercial market must sell their products through a chain of middlemen, each of whom takes a cut, so that the actual producer may receive only token payment for his crops.

This extremely common phenomenon in which widespread and severe malnutrition exists side by side with agricultural abundance has often been blamed on cash cropping. However, cash crops of themselves are neither good nor bad; indeed, it is hard to see how cities would be fed if all production was for subsistence only. The basic questions are: What is produced? For whom? If the poor do not have sufficient money to create demand for food, food for domestic use will not be produced. Huge amounts of land will be taken out of domestic food production and put into crops such as coffee, cotton, peanuts, coca (to make cocaine), or sugar cane for export. India, which has the largest absolute number of malnourished people in the world, including a child malnutrition rate of nearly 50 percent (World Bank 1993:234), exports enormous amounts of agricultural products each year. Although some workers benefit from export crops through minimal wages, most profits accrue to a small group of wealthy landowners.

It was once believed that the Green Revolution would solve the problem of hunger in the Third World. The Green Revolution is based on high-yield varieties of seeds that require extensive inputs of fertilizers and pesticides. A number of countries have been able to greatly increase their agricultural output using Green Revolution crops. This has often lowered prices, making food more available to the poor. However, the results have not always been beneficial. Green Revolution technology tends to favor bigness and has added to the concentration of landholding when tenants and sharecroppers, unable to afford the expensive inputs, are thrown off the lands they have worked for generations. Often, Green Revolution crops are exported, rather than sold cheaply in the domestic market. In addition, there are ecological consequences; land has been overused, leading to erosion, and chemical pesticides and fertilizers have contaminated water sources.

Although agriculture is the largest sector in virtually all Third World countries, it is also the least likely to receive adequate governmental support. Power lies in the cities, not in the agricultural areas, and most governments have chosen to devote their resources to the industrial sector; only about 20 percent of an average Third World nation's investment goes to agriculture (Nafziger 1984:128). More schools, hospitals, roads, and electrical systems are built in urban centers than in the countryside. Wealth may be drained off from the rural areas through taxes on agricultural sales to provide investment in manufacturing. In addition, many governments have established low ceilings on the prices of agricultural goods in order to make food accessible to the impoverished masses who have flooded the cities. Often, state-owned agencies act as buyers and distributors of agricultural goods, allowing them to determine prices at artificially low levels. The already-impoverished farmer ends up subsidizing urban enclaves. The effect of such policies has been so devastating in Africa that per capita food production declined an estimated 1.5 percent per year throughout the 1970s and 1980s (Weiner 1987b:56). The signs are hopeful, however; increasingly, governments are realizing that agriculture must receive its due in the overall process of development.

Land Reform

Because so much land is concentrated in so few hands, land reform is often seen as a partial solution to rural poverty. However, if the landed oligarchy remains powerful, anything but cosmetic change is difficult; attempts at land reform in the Philippines and Brazil have been repeatedly thwarted in the legislatures. Land reform can range from rent reductions and the enactment of laws protecting tenants to land-to-the-tiller redistributions. These latter, which were successfully enacted in Taiwan and Peru, involved taking land away from the large-scale landowners and giving it to the tenants who have actually worked it for generations.

One of the most successful of land reforms was that enacted in the 1940s and 1950s by South Korea. Agricultural land was redistributed in a land-to-the-tiller program that raised the percentage of landowners from 15 percent to 70 percent. Individual holdings were limited to about seven acres, with the average postreform holding only about two and a half acres. The reform resulted in a 20 percent to 30 percent increase in income for the bottom four-fifths of the population and laid the foundation for mass rural marketing, which, in turn, provided the money for a manufacturing base. The reform was strongly supported by the government, which enacted laws enforcing the seven-acre limit, provided subsidies for fertilizer, and oversaw the marketing of produce.

In cases where feudal estates have been worked by collective labor, jointly owned cooperatives, in which all members get a share of profits, may be preferable to independent family farms. If the original landowners are compensated at all — and in revolutionary situations, they may not be — it will be through long-term payments or perhaps through government bonds that must be reinvested in the industrial sector.

The motives for land reform often are more political than economic. A government may want to appease rural unrest, to keep it from turning into revolution, or a revolutionary government may want to consolidate its rural base by buying the loyalty of the peasants. A basic argument has been that private ownership will encourage peasants to make improvements and work harder. The results, however, are ambiguous. If efficient, modern farms are redistributed, as has occurred in Mexico, Kenya, and Malaysia, there may be a significant decline in production, because peasants do not have the knowledge or capital to continue advanced farming practices, and the smaller units may not be able to take advantage of tractor plowing. The greatest successes tend to be where lands formerly kept out of production on large estates are redistributed and where inefficient farms owned by absentee landlords are given over to tenant ownership. In any case, land reform must be a serious long-term commitment by the government, which must be able to provide low-interest loans, fertilizer, and distribution networks to the new owners. Even if there is a short-term decline in overall production, land reform may be successful in providing security for thousands of peasants formerly dependent on minimal wages earned during only a fraction of the year.

The Secondary Sector

The secondary sector — manufacturing — consists in fabricating products through the use of machines. "Industrialization" would be the process by which manufacturing evolves into a major part of the economy. Almost all countries have recognized industrialization as a positive goal (exceptions may be some oil-rich Islamic countries and some very traditional agrarian societies). There are many advantages to establishing an industrial base. Manufacturing can provide costly goods to the domestic market that would otherwise have to be imported, thus, reducing a country's dependency and increasing its power within the international system. Manufacturing supplies jobs while it trains a skilled labor force and proficient managers for further development. Ideally, manufactured goods can be exported, bringing in higher and more stable profits than primary goods. There is also something self-generating about industrialization. Jobs in industry pay more than in agriculture; as people have more money, they tend to spend a smaller percentage of their incomes for food and more for manufactured products. Thus, it is the secondary sector that has the greatest growth potential.

Developing a Manufacturing Base

Initially, there are numerous difficulties in establishing industries. First, manufacturing requires mass output for profitability; therefore, there must be an economy of scale, that is, sufficient population with sufficient money to provide a market for the goods produced. Countries with under a million citizens or that are extremely poor may have a hard time getting beyond modest artisan enterprises. Second, factories are capital intensive; a country may have to seek outside funds, or the government itself may have to provide the investment. Third, the techniques of manufacturing are highly complex; the factory must be constructed, an assembly line organized, workers trained, and distribution systems established. Such skills may not be locally available. Fourth, competent management must be created.

Finally, factories do not stand alone. They need other factories to supply them. This can be both a curse and a blessing. A factory may have to import machinery and components at high cost. On the other hand, a single factory may have a ripple effect through the economic system, as other entrepreneurs hasten to support it or to use its products. *Backward linkage* is the process by which the manufacture of a product generates other supporting factories, as when a bicycle factory need tires and chains. *Forward linkage* occurs when new factories are built to take advantage of readily available products, as might be the case if a sewing machine company were established to use locally made small electrical engines. In planning development, many governments seek industries that promise both forward and backward linkages.

State-Owned Enterprises

Often in the Third World there is a confusion between the secondary and tertiary sectors, as governments get involved in creating, owning, and running industries. State-owned enterprises (SOEs) or "parastatals" are more common in Third World capitalist countries than in the First World. The government may not claim outright ownership of a company but retains controlling stock. It is not unusual for a country to invite a multinational to invest in 49 percent of a corporation while the state holds 51 percent. What distinguishes a parastatal from a public agency — such as an electrical utility — is that the company is engaged in the production of goods (or services) for sale with profit as the goal. Many parastatals are autonomous legal entities, which are formally free from government involvement and act as independent corporations.

Governments have many reasons for owning businesses. They may be the only entrepreneurs within a country that can afford the initial investment for an expensive factory. The government might view the direct control of industry as an essential part of its overall development strategy; for example, in South Korea, state control of the fertilizer industry was deemed essential to the success of the land reform. Parastatals also allow governments to reap all the profits and can be used as a means of consolidating state power. The government might take over a failing business in order to preserve jobs, or it might create a business with a primary objective of providing jobs. Often, ideology and public sentiment play a strong role; foreign corporations, especially those controlling natural resources such as oil or copper, have been nationalized because of public antipathy to outsider domination of the economy. Such nationalizations are usually negotiated with the affected company, which may retain a primary, and highly profitable, role as processor and distributor.

Early SOEs tended to be small-scale monopoly producers of liquor, beer, tobacco, salt, matches, and other commodities, often protected by import substitution. Today, however, there are no limits on size, and, sometimes, they are the largest corporations in a country. In 1980, there were over five hundred such companies in Mexico and four hundred in Tanzania. These figures may represent the extreme, but SOEs are very common and seem to be independent of ideology; they are found in both capitalist and socialist states. Such companies contribute half of all annual investment outside agriculture in India and Turkey and, at one time, nearly a third in Brazil.

Though there are many examples of efficient and profitable SOEs, as a whole, they have not performed well. Even though government-controlled natural resources could be expected to make a profit, many persistently run deficits that must be financed from state revenues, and some losses have been so large that they virtually crippled the country's economy. Pertamina, the state-owned petroleum industry in Indonesia, at one time rang up a $10 billion debt. Because many SOEs are protected monopolies, there is little pressure on managers to minimize costs or to adopt new production techniques. Often, governments use such industries to increase employment beyond the real needs of the company, and officials may be reluctant to let their pet projects die (Gillis et al. 1987).

The Tertiary Sector

Population growth, the mechanization of farming, and the expansion of plantations push more and more people out of agriculture every year. Manufacturing has not been able to keep up with the demand for employment — in fact, proportional to population, there are fewer jobs in industry than there were in the early 1900s. As a result, people must make their livings in the tertiary sector, which covers a wide range of occupations from street vendor to soldier to government employee. In most First World countries, the tertiary sector is about the same size as the secondary sector, but in Third World countries, it may be three times as large. The tertiary sector plays an absolutely crucial role in the economy; commerce, education, and banking, for example, are essential to any country's development. However, unlike agriculture, mining, and manufacturing, the tertiary sector contributes no tangible goods to the GNP while using up much domestic and imported production. This is not a severe problem in the First World, because capital-intensive industry is so efficient that per capita production remains quite high; in more labor-intensive Third World countries, the inflated tertiary sector may mean low national levels of production.

Many in the tertiary sector might be considered "marginal" in the sense that, as individuals, they add little and take little from the economy. True unemployment may be relatively low; lacking access to welfare assistance or unemployment benefits, everyone has to do something to live. However, *underemployment* and job redundancy is rampant. There are too many small-time tradesmen, too many waiters, too many store clerks. Anyone who has a business of any kind may be obligated to hire relatives. Whereas in industrialized countries, the tertiary sector is predominantly middle class — consisting of teachers, lawyers, salesmen, and so forth — in the Third World, the largest proportion is very poor.

The Inflated Bureaucracy

The government itself may act as a huge employment bureau, adding layer upon layer of bureaucratic jobs virtually as a disguised form of welfare. In Africa and Asia, the political branch grew rapidly during the first decades of independence. By 1970, over 60 percent of African wage earners were state employees, and by 1980, half of all government expenditures went to pay salaries (Gordon 1992:73). As a result, a simple task, such as getting a license to open a small business, can become a complex ordeal as paperwork wends its way through a bureaucratic labyrinth and each employee legitimizes his meager job by blocking the process for a few days or weeks. Underpaid workers are often tempted to charge bribes for their services. It may be necessary to find a high-level patron who can grease the wheels to get anything done.

The military may also be much larger than necessary (though it should be noted that in some countries, voluntary or conscripted service may fulfill an important function of providing literacy, job skills, and health benefits not otherwise available to the poorest sectors). In the common situation where militaries are autonomous, and, thus, a power unto themselves, they can often claim an excessive amount of the national treasury. In 1984, Third World countries imported over $30 billion worth of arms. On the average, military costs exceeded the combined expenditures of both education and health, although few countries are truly threatened by external enemies (Sivard 1987:10, 23). Higher-level members of the officers corps may live elitist life styles.

The Informal Economy

In most countries, there is contained within the tertiary sector — and overlapping the secondary sector — an *informal* economy, such as that of Peru described at the beginning of this chapter. The formal sector is characterized by numerous obstacles to entry, large-scale and capital-intensive enterprises, imported technology, legal contractual arrangements, skills acquired through formal schooling or training, and markets protected by tariffs and licensing. The informal economy is almost the opposite; entry into it is easy, and it is distinguished by small-scale and labor intensive enterprises — often family owned and operated — indigenous technology, informal deals, skills learned outside the school system, and unregulated and highly competitive markets (Drakakis-Smith 1987:65). This subsector consists of squatter housing, unlicensed businesses, gypsy cab drivers, shoeshine boys, repairmen, and so forth, as well as some small-scale manufacturing. It also encompasses an underground of petty criminals, prostitutes, drug dealers, and smugglers.

Though often considered to be a refuge for the truly marginalized, in reality, the informal economy may be quite dynamic. Freed of virtually all legal restrictions, it is the last bastion of true free-market capitalism (though, in many cases, there are monopolies and mafia-like bosses who control various occupations). In Latin America as a whole, the informal sector accounts for between 30 percent and 40 percent of the GDP and has grown more than three times as fast as the formal sector. A manufacturing job in the informal sector of Columbia can be created with an investment of just $1,000, whereas it takes $10,000 to create a job in the formal sector (IDB 1989:8).

As vibrant as the informal sector might be, there are real problems: because clandestine and unlicensed businesses pay no taxes, they do not contribute to the national economy. Contracts have no legal validity, so businesses exist in a state of uncertainty and are limited in how far they can grow. A company or an individual vendor can be rousted by the police at any time, as can people living in squatter housing. A large informal sector denotes the failure of the state to establish the economic conditions that can legally incorporate some of the most energetic entrepreneurs in the country.

TOWARD THE TWENTY-FIRST CENTURY

The latest solution to Third World economic problems to be proclaimed by the First World is outward-directed capitalism, which, if unaccompanied by internal structural change, might make for stronger international economies but weaker domestic economies. Foreign trade can enrich elite owners of production and strengthen the state in the international arena but may have little trickle-down effect, especially if it fails to provide jobs for rapidly growing populations. Domestic savings are increasing in some countries but are always threatened by high inflation rates and unrealistic government ceilings on interest. In the agricultural sector, the deteriorating quality of the land through erosion and leeching is reaching the crisis stage in many regions, as is the reduction of the availability of water in northern Africa and the Middle East. Manufacturing has not been able to offer jobs to displaced peasants or rapidly increasing populations, with the result that the bloated tertiary sector continues to grow. With the exception of the few newly industrializing countries of Southeast Asia, the prospects for domestic development do not look good.

SUGGESTED READINGS

Chenery, Hollis, Montek Ahluwalia, C.L.G. Bell, John H. Duloy, and Richard Jolly. *Redistribution with Growth* (New York: Oxford University Press, 1974). Starting with statistical analyses of income inequalities in Third World countries, this now-classic anthology goes on to examine the political framework and to suggest strategies for greater equity.

De Soto, Hernando. *The Other Path: The Invisible Revolution in the Third World* (New York: Harper & Row, 1989). The author was head of a research group that probed the huge informal economy of Peru. They found that a maze of "mercantilist" government regulations has so stifled the legal sector of the economy that the only real capitalism is in the informal sector.

Dietz, James L., and James H. Street, eds. *Latin America's Economic Development: Institutional and Structuralist Perspectives* (Boulder, Colo.: Lynne Rienner, 1987). The various theories of development that have been implemented in Latin America are analyzed, followed by discussions of the import substitution strategy, multinational corporations, and foreign debt.

Loewenson, Rene. *Modern Plantation Agriculture: Corporate Wealth and Labour Squalor* (London: Zed, 1992). The author argues that the plantation system in the Third World, though viewed as necessary to national development, has resulted in the ill health, malnutrition, and social poverty of millions. An in-depth study of Zimbabwe shows how the system works.

Morris, Morris David. *Measuring the Condition of the World's Poor: The Physical Quality of Life Index* (New York: Pergamon Press, 1979). This book, which introduced the PQLI, compares material living standards — as opposed to per capita GNP — among Third World countries. The book contains numerous charts and tables that are now dated, but there are formulas with which the reader can calculate current PQLIs using easily available World Bank statistics (the formula for calculating life expectancy at age one is on page 126).

Seligson, Mitchell A., ed. *The Gap Between the Rich and the Poor* (Boulder, Colo.: Westview, 1984). There are two significant gaps: within countries and between countries (especially between the Third World and the First World). This anthology seeks the causes of these gaps and the effects of various development strategies on them.

5

Between Debt and the Deep Blue Sea: The Third World in the International Economy

Poet John Donne once observed that "No man is an island, entire of itself." He might have added that no country is an island. Despite revolutionary proposals to "delink" and despite cases of relative isolation (such as North Korea and, until recently, China), all countries are inevitably and inextricably enmeshed in a web of economic and political connections with other countries. The *world* economy is a reality, not just a theory (though the nature of that reality is debatable). Even if a nation opts for a basic-needs approach or chooses an import substitution strategy, development is still, to a great degree, an international issue. All countries need to trade for essential goods that they cannot produce themselves. The market within which trade takes place is, for good or ill, a capitalist market, and that is not likely to change within the foreseeable future.

By definition, capitalism is not centrally controlled, and, although it might be regulated to an extent, it works by its own inner logic. Part of that logic is that those with the money also have the power. Most Third World nations have scant control over either supply or demand within the world economy, which is dominated by the First World, and, thus, they have little effect on prices for their imports and exports. Their freedom of action is limited, and they must sometimes adjust their internal and external policies to fit the demands of richer nations in order to get loans, foreign aid, multinational investment, and military protection.

The poorer countries' relative impotence within the global economy is clear from the widening hiatus between the Third World and the First (see Figure 2.4), which more than doubled between 1913 and 1977; by the latter date, citizens of the developed countries were eight times better off than those in the underdeveloped countries as a whole (Bairoch 1981:8). The hope that many countries will soon follow the examples of Taiwan and South Korea in closing in on First World status is unrealistic. It is the most impoverished countries that are falling behind the fastest; the gap between the world's richest fifth and poorest fifth is widening at an alarming pace (Figure 5.1).

To be sure, there are continuing efforts to empower the Third World. Developing countries themselves have formed such international policy groups as the Non-Aligned Movement and the Group of 77, and there are numerous regional associations and alliances. Aside from the well-known Organization of Petroleum Exporting Countries (OPEC), there are cartels in bananas, rubber, copper, bauxite, and coffee. Most of the 184 member states of the United Nations (UN) belong to the Third World, and the UN has been a promoter of development objectives through major conferences on food, agrarian reform, energy, and so forth. The primary mission of the World Bank, originally established to assist European postwar recovery, has evolved to helping Third World countries with both loans and technical assistance. The Third World has participated in UN Conferences on the Law of the Sea. Third World countries participated in negotiating the General Agreement on Tariffs and Trade, which was endorsed by the United States in 1994. Over a hundred signatory countries agreed to lower tariffs and end import quotas toward the goal of more open world trade. Significantly, the governing body of the General Agreement on Tariffs and Trade, the World Trade Organization, gave equal votes to all participating countries.

Such empowerment is countered, however, by the structure of the system itself, which puts the bulk of decision making in the hands of those with the largest militaries and the greatest wealth. Of the five permanent members of the UN Security Council — each with veto power — only one (China) is a Third World country. All primary-resource cartels, including OPEC, are weak, lacking both political cohesiveness and sufficient control of their product, and they are opposed by stronger manufacturers' cartels or oligopolies that can control prices. Extremely influential nongovernmental policy organizations such as the Council on Foreign Affairs and the Trilateral Commission — each of which includes many of the world's most powerful industrialists, bankers, and politicians — exclude Third World membership altogether.

Developing countries have to function within this international environment the best they can. Because their domestic economies are weak, they depend for most governmental resources on import and export duties, royalties and taxes from multinational corporations, direct aid from First World treasuries, loans from international banks and lending agencies, and income remitted from expatriates working in foreign countries. Liberia and Sierra Leone derive up to 80 percent of their income from such sources (Clapham 1985:94).

More and more countries are turning outward toward export-led growth, encouraged by the industrial powers. Some studies have suggested that export-oriented developmental strategies have fared

FIGURE 5.1
Distribution of Global Income between the Richest Fifth and the Poorest Fifth

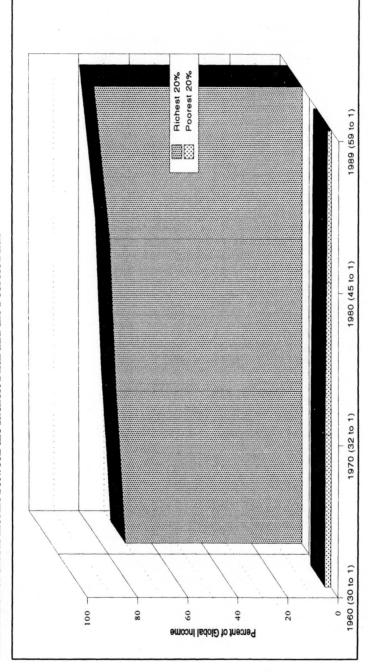

Source: Sandra Postel, "Carrying Capacity: Earth's Bottom Line," in *State of the World, 1994*, ed. L. Brown (New York: Norton, 1994), p. 5.

better, at least in terms of growth of gross national product (GNP), than inward-looking models, though such statistics may be skewed by a handful of countries that have moved from primary exports to the export of manufactured goods. Yet, despite an enormous increase in trade by the Third World, First World trade has been expanding even faster; the world share of developing countries has been declining, from about 30 percent in 1950 to a mere 20 percent in 1980.

TRADE IN AN UNEQUAL MARKETPLACE

Unlike socialism or other ideological "isms," capitalism was not invented by theorists. It was already well formed when it was described by Adam Smith and David Ricardo. There is something intrinsically organic about it; given certain initial conditions, capitalism is perhaps inevitable (on this point, Marx seems to be in agreement with many classical economists). According to its most ardent proponents, it works best (that is, most efficiently) when left alone, or at least when government's role is limited to the protection of private property and the enforcement of contracts. The theory of comparative advantage — that countries specialize in exporting those things they can produce at lowest relative cost — is, thus, half descriptive and half prescriptive. The descriptive part is simply that this is the way the system works; this is very much what countries actually do and *have to do* in order to play in the game. There do not seem to be many other alternatives. The prescriptive part, which is more debatable, is that this is morally good, because it leads to the benefit of all.

Comparative Advantage . . . and Disadvantage

Early theories of comparative advantage were based almost exclusively on the availability and costs of labor. It is now recognized that the decision as to what goods will be produced for export is dependent on numerous factors, such as natural resources, technology, capital, and education levels of the populace. Each product requires a unique set of factors of production. Individual countries will possess these factors, or be able to attain them, in different degrees. Because coffee is a labor-intensive crop, a tropical country with much fertile mountainous land and a large, cheap labor force can produce it more economically than can a country that is similarly endowed in terms of physical resources but has a highly skilled labor force. The latter country might choose to assemble radios. The coffee-growing country would require an adequate road system and vehicles to transport workers and crops. These might be irrelevant to the radio-producing country, which would do almost all its work in the city but which would need a good educational system to train workers and managers and sufficient domestic wealth for the start-up investment. In a sense, both countries *could* grow coffee and produce radios, but in the international economy, it is to each one's advantage to focus its efforts on those products for which it is best adapted. Countries gain comparative advantage by using their most abundant factors of production most intensively while importing goods that would require scarcer factors of production.

Theoretically, everybody benefits. By selling what they can produce most efficiently, countries can get the foreign exchange to purchase that which they cannot make at all or that which they cannot make as cheaply as they can purchase. Poor countries need tractors and costly fertilizers to improve their agriculture; they need trucks, roads, rail-roads, and ports for transportation; they need communication networks; they need machinery and technical advice for starting local factories. All these must come, initially, at least, from outside the country. Even if loans from the World Bank are used, the loans themselves must be paid off through trade. Export industries also create jobs that did not exist before.

There are, however, serious problems. Trade often is associated with growth but not necessarily with development. First, benefits are not distributed equally. The owners of the means of production may get rich while peasants and workers remain poor. It is true that coffee provides jobs, but only during part of the year and at extremely low wages. Agriculture that employs tractors will inevitably displace workers. For beef exports, formerly subsistence agricultural land that supplied food for thousands might be turned over to ranges that require very few workers. Second, local producers may be harmed. If soy beans are traded for cloth, a few large landowners will greatly benefit, but local textile workers will be put out of business. Third, there are few spin-off effects of primary exports; that is, agricultural goods and raw ores have few backward or forward linkages that promote other industries and services in the society. Fourth, declining terms of trade mean that countries get less and less for their raw materials relative to what they must pay for imported manufactured goods. Finally, many markets are highly unstable. Synthetics have significantly reduced the demand for rubber, sisal, wool, cotton, and many other products. Also, there is always the chance that a country with a lower-paid workforce will undercut another country's export price, leaving the latter with expensive equipment or mines and no place to sell the product.

Primary versus Manufactured Exports

Primary specialization — that is, the export of natural resources — may not be a development strategy so much as a necessity for some countries. This is basically a policy of deferred industrialization. "Fiscal linkage" occurs when raw or minimally processed agricultural products, fish, ores, or fuels are used as a means of obtaining foreign exchange for investment in factories. This can be a trap, however. For very small countries, with little domestic demand, it may be difficult or impossible to expand beyond the primary-export stage. With some significant exceptions, the smaller the country, the more likely it will be a "monoculture," that is, it will depend on only one or two exports, such as coffee in Colombia or bauxite in Jamaica. The result may be extreme concentrations of wealth in very limited enclaves, with relatively little of the types of spin-off effects that lead to development. Demand for primary goods tends to be much more sluggish than demand for manufactured goods, which is one reason why terms of trade have continuously declined at an average rate of about 1 percent per year (Gillis et al. 1987:421). Countries trapped at this stage may be quite poor and have inefficient and corrupt governments that fritter away foreign earnings rather than investing them in development. Ghana, for example, was the richest country in Subsaharan Africa at independence in 1957, with a per capita income of $500 per year. However, its reliance on cocoa as its single dominant crop, comprising 60 percent of its export earnings, and its failure to diversify were major factors in the country's economic decline. By 1983, per capita income had dropped almost 40 percent.

By no means are all poor countries monocultures. Bolivia exports tin, gas, silver, and zinc; Thailand specializes in rice, rubber, corn, tapioca, and sugar. Although diversification is certainly preferable and gives the country more flexibility in riding out the inevitable fluctuations in export earnings, it may be no better at supporting the development of a manufacturing base. At the other extreme from these impoverished primary-good exporters are those oil-producing countries that fail to industrialize because they do not have to; their wealth is sufficient without it.

Balanced development would include both primary and manufactured exports. The Third World is, indeed, increasing its sales of industrial goods, but only a small group of countries — Hong Kong, Singapore, Taiwan, South Korea, Brazil, Mexico, and a few others — account for almost all such exports. Most countries are still stuck at the primary-export level. The process of developing a manufacturing base is a long and difficult one, requiring such painful procedures as periodic devaluations, caps on wages even during periods of inflation, and borrowing that can lead to severe indebtedness.

EXPORT-ORIENTED MODELS OF DEVELOPMENT

In the last chapter, we examined two inward-oriented strategies of development, the basic needs model and the import substitution model. There have been some short-term successes of these approaches, as well as many failures. Today, the pressure from the West and from international lending institutions is increasingly toward outward-directed policies. Although many countries follow no particular philosophy, simply exporting what they can and importing what they have to, two competing, but somewhat overlapping, ideal models have emerged (Table 5.1).

The Neoliberal Model

Ever since Adam Smith proclaimed the "invisible hand" of the unfettered market and David Ricardo extolled the virtues of comparative advantage, laissez-faire capitalism has been virtually a religion for many Western economists. Briefly displaced by a Keynesian model (which postulated the necessity for government intervention) arising out of the Great Depression, classical economics reemerged in the 1970s and has been dominant since then. This neoliberal model — so-called in reference to nineteenth-century free-market liberalism — follows a modernization approach and pays scant attention to theories of dependency. Third World underdevelopment is not seen as the result of the evolution of world capitalism; indeed, macroeconomic mathematical models do not deal with history at all. Problems are seen as the result of state intervention in the economy (such as import substitution) and the inevitable price distortions that result. The free operation of unrestricted markets is the ideal. The role of government is to assure that trade is unobstructed and that prices accurately reflect the laws of supply and demand.

Herein lies a fundamental problem. Supply and demand are basic to the definition of capitalism; production will automatically increase to meet demand, and once the market is satiated, production will be reduced. The result is a degree of efficiency that is impossible if demand is controlled through price subsidies or if supply is determined by government edict. The argument is persuasive. A difficulty lies in the nature of demand. Demand is determined by purchasing power — money — and has very little to do with *need*. For example, in the United States, there is substantial need for low-cost housing, but very few entrepreneurs are investing in such construction. The people who need housing the most do not have the money to pay for it. Therefore, almost all new housing is devoted to middle- and upper-middle-class buyers. In the Third World, where 40 percent or 60 percent of the population may be extremely poor, this dilemma is greatly amplified. In El Salvador, the malnutrition rate approaches 70 percent. People desperately need food. However, poor people do not have money to create effective demand, so virtually all the most fertile agricultural land is turned over to crops such as cotton and coffee for export. The *need* is in El Salvador, but the *demand* is in the United States. There is no assurance within an economy based upon the logic of supply and demand that production will be oriented to supplying the needs of the large majority of the people. Scarce resources may be turned over to producing or importing automobiles for the wealthiest 5 percent of the population. Unlike the

TABLE 5.1
Four Models of Development

	Internal-Focus Models		International-Focus Models	
	Basic Needs	Import Substitution	Neoliberal	Southeast Asian
Perceived causes of underdevelopment	Capitalist exploitation. Elite dominance. Inequality of wealth.	Terms of trade favor developed countries. Imports prevent development of domestic economy.	Government intervention in the economy. Socialist policies. Import substitution.	Reliance on primary exports. Lack of investment capital. Lack of domestic demand.
Goals of development	Adequate food, housing, clothing, medical care, education for all.	A strong domestic economy, with an indigenous entrepreneurial class. Less dependency.	Increase in GNP. Pay off foreign debt.	Increase in GNP while raising the standard of living of all sectors of the society.
Guiding ideology	Marxism, socialism.	Dependency theory, especially Economic Commission for Latin America.	Laissez-faire capitalist theory; Adam Smith and David Ricardo.	Capitalist, but no rigid theory; pragmatic.
Policies	Centralized planning of economy. Redistribution of wealth through land reform, government subsidies.	Prohibitively high tariffs on imports that compete with domestic production. May invite multinational investment. Government-owned industries.	Low tariffs, export-oriented production. Little government regulation of the economy. Open to investment by multinational corporations	Early import substitution and continued protection of domestic industry. Manufacturing exports. Extensive government involvement in economy.
Examples	China, Cuba, Chile under Allende	Brazil until about 1990, Peru	Chile after 1974, Hong Kong	Taiwan, South Korea, Singapore

United States, most Third World countries lack much in the way of a social safety net for those whose needs are not met within the capitalist economy; there may be no welfare, unemployment insurance, or social security. The burdens of growth tend to fall most heavily on the people at the bottom.

The response of neoliberal theorists is that as countries develop through free-market policies, new jobs will be created so that the income level of the poor will increase. As the masses get money, their power in the market will grow so that more and more will be produced for them. It is important that money be spent on new production that will create new jobs, rather than on social benefits that produce nothing. Short-term austerity is necessary for long-term prosperity.

The neoliberal model might be called the "American model," because it is here that it has been most promoted. This is somewhat ironic; the U.S. government adopted strong antimonopoly laws in the late nineteenth century, pays farmers to take large amounts of acreage out of production in order to keep prices high, enforces numerous tariff barriers and import quotas, and contributes over $100 billion a year in direct subsidies and tax breaks to corporations (Donahue 1994). In other words, the United States is preaching to the Third World a policy it has never practiced itself.

The model was clearly explicated at the 1982 international economic meeting in Cancún, Mexico, is represented in the Caribbean Basin Initiative, and is embodied in policy reforms insisted on by the United States in rescheduling debts. Among the requirements of this model are a reduction in public expenditures and the selling of state enterprises to private investors. Education and health are seen as proper objects of government spending, because this is investment in human capital, but food and housing subsidies and other welfare projects should be curtailed. There is little pressure to reduce the size or expenses of the military (perhaps because arms sales are such a huge part of U.S. exports and because many of these countries need large armies to keep the poor from rebelling). Expenditures for infrastructure are also considered beneficial. Interest rates and exchange rates should be determined by market forces. Trade should be outward oriented and as free as possible, with moderate tariffs of 10 percent to 20 percent acceptable. The country should be open to private investment from foreign businesses and should offer low taxes and minimal state regulation of prices or of profits removed from the country (Williamson 1987).

Advocates of this approach often point to Singapore, South Korea, and Taiwan as shining examples of its success. However, as we will see, the Southeast Asian model of development is very different from, and in many ways diametrically opposed to, the U.S. model. The only two successes of the neoliberal model are Hong Kong and Chile. Hong Kong, an island city-state that was established as a financial outpost of the

British Empire, is an exceptional case, with few lessons for any other country, but a brief look at Chile is instructive.

In September 1973, Chile's socialist President Salvador Allende was overthrown in a violent coup by the armed forces under General Augusto Pinochet. At that time, the country was suffering from hyperinflation, rampant strikes, and shortages of food. The new military government established dictatorial power by means of state terror; opponents of the regime were eliminated or neutralized by a campaign of political murder, disappearances, imprisonment, and torture.

In a complete reversal of the socialism of the Allende period, the government adopted the developmental theories of U.S. economist Milton Freidman and his Chicago school of economics. The two most important aspects of these reforms were, first, privatization of government-owned firms and, second, export-oriented trade. Under Allende, over five hundred commercial firms and banks were controlled by the state; by 1980, this number was down to a mere twenty-five (Chile's biggest industry, copper, remained nationalized). The high tariffs of import substitution were reduced to an exceptionally low flat rate of 10 percent, and other trade barriers such as quotas and deposits for imports were eliminated. Foreign capital — mainly in the form of purchases or investments in newly privatized companies — was invited and made attractive with low taxes and few regulations. Stability was achieved through the strong arm of the military government. All opposition political parties were outlawed. Labor unions were banned, so there was no collective bargaining. Real wages dropped precipitously, and firings were made legally easier. The state eliminated price controls, so that prices rose as wages fell. Spending priorities shifted; health and education expenditures declined slightly while defense spending rose from 10 percent to 16 percent of total state expenditures.

An "economic miracle" resulted from these policies, similar to that of Brazil a decade earlier. After 1981, while other countries were caught in a world recession, the gross domestic product increased about 6 percent per year. Inflation dropped. Chilean exports increased phenomenally, from $1 billion to almost $10 billion (U.S. dollars) between 1970 and 1992. Privatized companies turned out to be more efficient, in terms of profits, than their state-owned counterparts. Contrary to dire predictions by labor leaders, employment was not significantly reduced because of privatization. Among eleven privatized firms, employment dropped less than 2 percent, and most of these firms actually added workers. When Chile returned peaceably to democracy between 1988 and 1990, the elected government chose to continue the economic policies of the Pinochet era and has done so with considerable success (Meller 1990, 1993). By the mid-1990s, other countries of the Third World were enviously looking to the Chilean model for guidelines.

The Chile experiment has its critics. The government is accused of playing "Santa Claus" to the elites and to foreign investors in selling off state-owned corporations at half of their actual value. Electricity, the national airline, and communications were divested, even though they were efficiently run and were remitting their profits to the government. The recession of 1981 turned out to be the worst economic crisis in fifty years in Chile and, according to detractors, resulted from the dogmatic assumption that laissez-faire policies would self-adjust without government intervention.

The biggest controversy has to do with the effects on Chile's poor. Statistics suggest that the truly indigent, that is, families with income insufficient to purchase even their basic food needs, almost doubled between 1969 and 1989, while the number of moderately poor increased by 8 percent. In total, the number of poor grew from about 30 percent to over 40 percent. Though privatization did not significantly increase unemployment, other policies did; unemployment rose from under 6 percent to over 27 percent between 1970 and 1984, and real wages dropped 10 percent. In other words, there was not only a widening gap between rich and poor, but the poor also lost out in absolute terms. At the same time, however, there was a significant betterment in nutrition, health, and infant mortality and an increase in consumer possessions, such as radios and television sets, at all levels. This contradiction is explained by the Pinochet policy of increasing health and nutrition services for the very poor — a policy in direct opposition to neoliberal theory — and price reductions on some manufactured consumer goods because of the lowering of tariffs and increased imports (Graham 1991; Meller 1991).

It is unclear how far the Chilean experience can be generalized. Long before embarking on its neoliberal economic path, Chile was already one of the most developed countries in the Third World, with a good infrastructure of ports, roads, and communication networks. In addition, the country boasted relatively high incomes, high levels of literacy, a competent managerial force, and experienced factory labor. Very few Third World countries even remotely resemble Chile in this respect. The neoliberal model may be best suited to countries that have already attained a relatively high level of development.

The Southeast Asian Model

What makes Taiwan and South Korea truly unique among Third World nations is not their rapid industrialization (a few other countries have experienced similar spurts) but that their development seems to have reached a point where it is self-sustaining. More importantly, all sectors of the population have benefited from economic growth. The two countries have acheived greater levels of income equality than the United States and most other Western nations.

Taiwan (formerly the island of Formosa) was part of China for ten centuries before it was invaded and occupied successively by the

Portuguese, the Dutch, and, finally, the Japanese, who invested heavily in building an infrastructure of ports and roads. After World War II, the island reverted briefly to China. In 1949, when the communists were successful in taking over the mainland, the remnants of Chiang Kai-shek's Koumintang party escaped to the island to set up what became virtually a separate country. The newcomers were an educated elite that made their escape with an army in tow and many financial resources. They quickly displaced the landed oligarchy, bought their legitimacy among the natives with an extensive land reform, and established a one-party dictatorship with absolute power (a person could be sentenced to death for publicly opposing the regime). The United States viewed Taiwan as a bastion against Chinese communism and even seems, for a while, to have deluded itself that the Koumintang could retake the mainland. As a result, foreign aid — both military and developmental — poured in. Other countries have received such preferential aid with little to show for it, but the government of Taiwan set out on a deliberate and systematic process of economic development. The results have been little short of amazing. Per capita income in 1950 was a mere $224; by 1992, it was $8,486. An average growth rate of almost 10 percent was sustained for twenty years. After 1970, Taiwan's exports grew at an average of 22 percent per year.

South Korea has a similar history of Japanese occupation, land reform, massive U.S. aid, and planned economic development, with much the same results. Both countries (which, along with the relatively affluent city-states of Hong Kong and Singapore, are referred to as the "Gang of Four") will soon enter the First World. Other countries of Southeast Asia, such as Indonesia and Malaysia, seem to be following a similar pattern of growth, though starting much later.

Superficially, these countries would appear to vindicate the methods of neoliberal capitalism. In reality, their policies are quite different in many ways.

First, the laissez-faire approach opposes government intervention in the economy; in Taiwan and South Korea, the state was so deeply involved in every aspect of development that one writer refers to their policies as "state capitalism" or even "mercantilism" (Harris 1986). Initially, the government owned many of the crucial industries. Private enterprises were subsidized by the state and worked closely with the state in developing export and import policies. As in Chile under Pinochet, wages did not reflect market demand but were held artificially low. Trade unions were kept weak, strikes banned, and welfare legislation avoided. Economic growth was planned by the state at every level and enforced through strong government intervention.

Second, both countries employed almost two decades of import substitution in order to build up their own businesses and their domestic labor forces. Import protections were dropped only as domestic markets were sated and indigenous companies could turn to export. Some local industries remained protected into the 1990s.

Third, right from the beginning, both countries gave priority to domestic demand. In South Korea, between 1965 and 1975, only 15 percent of total manufactures were exported. Even as the role of exports increased, it went hand in hand with the rapid growth of the domestic economy (Donnelly 1985a:36–37). By contrast, the neoliberal model gives priority to the international marketplace, with the assumption that the domestic market will follow.

Fourth, in opposition to the neoliberal emphasis on the sanctity of private property, both countries enacted extensive land reforms, forcibly dividing the lands of large-scale owners among the peasants. In these then-agrarian societies, perhaps no other action was so significant in redistributing wealth and bringing all of the people into the national economy. (The United States has an ambiguous record in relation to land reform: it overthrew the Arbenz government in Guatemala in 1954 partly because a modest land reform threatened some property of the U.S.-based United Fruit Company; in the 1980s, the United States promoted land reform in El Salvador at the same time it was violently opposing similar reforms in neighboring Nicaragua.)

Fifth, redistribution of wealth and equalization of income took place *before* export-led industrialization. The neoliberal model assumes that free-market policies will work at any level of development. This has yet to be proved. The Chilean and Brazilian examples suggest that if income equalization measures are not enacted early in the developmental process, rapid export-led industrialization will exacerbate inequities.

Sixth, in both South Korea and Taiwan, the indigenous elites were displaced or destroyed, permitting modernizing elites to take their place. In both countries, the power of the entrenched traditional elites were at least partially broken by Japanese occupation; in Taiwan, the landed elite that had survived Japanese occupation was simply replaced by the Koumintang. In contrast, the neoliberal "trickle down" model works through existing elites, strengthening them. In Latin America, with its tremendous concentrations of wealth and power, this is a severe problem.

Finally, the U.S. model encourages immediate democratization. It is unclear whether democracy really promotes development; there are arguments on both sides of the question. What is clear is that in South Korea and Taiwan, specifically, the periods of most rapid development took place under strong and brutal one-party dictatorships. As Nigel Harris (1986:53) aptly puts it, "The invisible hand was more of an armed fist."

The Southeast Asian model is not one policy but a sequence of government-controlled programs, each building upon the previous ones. The industrial export phase is only the last of a series of carefully planned stages, from land reform to primary import substitution to secondary import substitution to the export of small-scale manufactures to high-tech export. There is no point in the process at which one can say "This is it. This is the correct policy." The U.S. model, on the other hand, is a static set of principles that is supposedly applicable to any country at any level of development. Taiwanese and South Korean policy has been dynamic and evolutionary.

The strategy may be chiefly applicable to Southeast Asia. It might be very difficult to transfer the final export-led phase to countries in Africa, Latin America, and elsewhere in Asia that have not already experienced extensive land reforms, massive infusions of U.S. aid, and the displacement of traditional elites and that are not ruled by dictatorships that can enforce low wages and floating prices. Redistribution of income before industrialization, a crucial element of the Southeast Asian model, is hardly an option in countries that have already industrialized, such as Brazil, Mexico, and India. Although an outward-oriented strategy may be advantageous, neither of the two models that are now dominant may be particularly applicable to the rest of the Third World.

MULTINATIONAL CORPORATIONS

According to a 1977 policy paper by the influential Trilateral Commission, "The public and leaders of most countries continue to live in a mental universe which no longer exists — a world of separate nations" (quoted in Sklar 1980:3). In the new universe, multinational corporations (MNCs) are the basic units of power.

Funeral arrangements for nations may be premature — indeed, scholars are increasingly "rediscovering" the importance of the state — but the point is a good one. MNCs have assumed an enormous economic power in the world today. When both countries and corporations are ranked together according to GNP or annual sales, one-third of the top sixty are MNCs. Exxon is larger than all but eighteen nations, and even the twentieth biggest MNC is larger than the majority of Third World countries. The three top oil companies alone have a combined annual product greater than the GNP of Canada (Todaro 1985:435). When a Third World country negotiates with an MNC, it is not necessarily bargaining from a position of power.

In the international sphere, MNCs operate as oligopolies, that is, only a handful of companies control world production of a specific product. In almost every commodity, from wheat and sugar to rubber and automobiles, fifteen or fewer MNCs command 90 percent of the global market, and, in many commodities, only three or four companies dominate. There is some question if competition really determines prices in situations of oligopoly or if prices are inflated by a tacit agreement among producers. Although oligopoly is the rule in the international marketplace, monopoly is the norm within individual Third World countries. Usually only one company, protected by the government, will control a single export or import sector, or a subsidiary of an MNC will exclusively produce a certain commodity for the domestic market.

MNCs have their roots in the joint stock companies of the early period of expansionist capitalism. In the sixteenth and seventeenth centuries, not only was buying and provisioning large ships an expensive proposition, but an investor had to possess sufficient resources to wait out months or years before the payoff or to survive the not-rare cases of shipwreck or piracy. Only princes or prosperous businessmen owning shares in large enterprises could assume such risks. The English became especially adept at running such companies, which had not only their own fleets but also their own police and armies. Stock companies flourished as monopolies, with the active support of governments. Laws restricted trade, assuring a flow of goods back and forth between colonies and the mother country.

It was only after 1895 that true MNCs, in the modern sense, developed, that is, corporations that are relatively independent of their home governments and with the ability to trade anywhere. A threatened monopoly on petroleum in the United States was countered by antitrust laws that broke up Rockefeller's Standard Oil into thirty-eight smaller companies. Monopoly quickly gave way to oligopoly as five of these Standard progeny joined two overseas companies — British Petroleum and Royal Dutch Shell — to become the Seven Sisters that controlled most of the world's oil supply. This era also gave rise to huge multinational agribusinesses, such as the United Fruit Company, which owned large tracts of land throughout Central America and the Caribbean and manipulated governments at will.

The true age of multinational expansion and power did not come until after World War II. The war left the United States with a considerable amount of investment capital, which was used to move into the global economy. By 1960, of the top two hundred MNCs, 127 were based in the United States and accounted for over 70 percent of revenues. The collapse of the colonial system opened up new opportunities for MNC penetration in Africa and Asia. The proportion of the United States' participation has declined as new MNCs from Europe and Japan have joined the competition (as well as some from Third World countries, such as South Korea's Hyundai).

The traditional MNC, which handled a single product or economic sector — whether bananas or automobiles — has given way to the conglomerate. These much larger corporations have many subsidiaries that may be engaged in unrelated activities. Encouraged to diversify by unstable international conditions and by tax laws that reward such policies, conglomerates are continually on the lookout for companies to purchase. Often, an independent enterprise can be assimilated through a "hostile" takeover, in which a large corporation buys controlling stock of a company that does not want to be purchased. Many conglomerates are simultaneously involved in agriculture, industry, and services. R. J. Reynolds, once exclusively a tobacco company, owns Del Monte fruit, Heublein beverages, Seal and Service shipping, Kentucky Fried Chicken, and Aminoil petroleum, among many other subsidiaries.

The ownership of multiple companies allows MNCs to supply themselves. An industrial subsidiary may purchase raw materials from a mining subsidiary and give the final product to a marketing subsidiary. Such control of an entire range of production allows a company great leeway in determining prices and maximizing profits. Corporations seldom really need the countries in which they operate. If labor costs or taxes become uncomfortable, the company can move its operations elsewhere. If the demand for a product drops, a conglomerate can cut back production and shift emphasis to another commodity.

Third World countries, especially if they are monocultures, are often highly susceptible to such decisions but have little power to affect them. Also, in order to attract and keep investment, Third World countries must compete among themselves to provide the best "investment climate." This would include such attributes as a stable economy and government, low wages (and perhaps weak, government-controlled, or nonexistent labor unions), an adequate infrastructure, low taxes, liberal laws allowing profits to be removed, and sufficient domestic savings that much or most of the initial investment can be borrowed within the country.

Almost all major MNCs operate in Third World countries. Historically, they focused on mining and agriculture, but now, manufacturing accounts for over a third of such investment. Because of revolutionary and nationalistic sentiments, the outright ownership of foreign property is rare today. In agriculture, for example, an "associate producer" system is widely employed in which locals own the land but large agribusinesses determine what is grown, supply the seed and the harvesting machinery, and perform the processing and distribution. Many states have nationalized their resources but contract MNCs for the extraction and shipping.

Do MNCs help countries to develop?

On the positive side, it is argued that MNCs supply badly needed investment. There is always a gap between a country's development aspirations and what it can afford from available savings and export earnings. Foreign investment can provide the needed money. Equally important, countries do not start with a technological base; it must be imported. MNCs have been a primary mechanism for the transfer of technology — whether tractors or assembly lines — to the Third World. Foreign corporations also supply experienced management from abroad and management training for locals. By investing in new factories, mining operations, and plantations, MNCs create jobs that would not have existed without them, and these jobs commonly pay more than jobs in locally owned industries. Such jobs provide training in skills badly needed by developing countries.

On the other hand, several empirical studies have drawn a much darker picture. Volker Bornschier and colleagues (1978) analyzed a score of statistical studies on foreign investment in the Third World and concluded that such investment increased economic inequality and, over the long run, *decreased* the rate of growth (short-term effects were positive). These negative effects were found in both richer and poorer developing countries, although they were stronger in the better-off nations (perhaps because these were more attractive to investors). These effects were also found in all geographical regions of the Third World. Later statistical studies have concluded that dependency on MNC investment has a negative effect on the provision of basic needs and on income distribution (London and Williams 1988; Wimberly 1991).

Part of the explanation might lie with the type of regime that offers a good investment climate to MNCs. Repressive dictatorial regimes often have been preferred to unruly and unpredictable democracies, with their demanding unions and their populist calls for nationalization of foreign property. In Bolivia, Brazil, Chile, Greece, and Indonesia, multinational investment increased enormously when military dictators took over from democracies and ruled through state terror. None of these regimes was much concerned with equalizing incomes or providing basic needs to those at the bottom of the economic pyramid.

It is not true that MNC investment transfers a great deal of wealth to Third World societies. For a number of reasons, corporations try to borrow as much of their investment as possible from banks within the target country. A study of U.S. MNCs from 1966 to 1976 found that 49 percent of all new investment funds were reinvested earnings, half were acquired locally, and only 1 percent were funds transferred from the United States (Szymanski 1983:692). Another study of MNCs in Latin America revealed local financing of 83 percent of investment. Because of their credit worthiness, MNCs are priority customers for host-country banks, and this tends to dry up funds available to domestic entrepreneurs. Once established, MNCs traded mostly with themselves; fully three-quarters of exports and imports tended to be with other subsidiaries of the parent company so that prices could be artificially controlled. It was estimated that exports were underpriced 40 percent below similar exports on the open market. This meant that, often, profits were hidden and tax revenues were minimal (Barnet and Müller 1974:17, 153–158). Local managers and owners of subsidiaries tend to be comprador elites, whose interest is more in benefiting the mother company than in developing the home country.

Although it is true that MNCs transfer technology, it is technology designed for profit maximization, not for the needs of poor countries. A single tractor may displace ten or more rural laborers. Global corporations use only about half the number of employees per $10,000 in sales as local firms do. The International Labor Organization estimates that of the sixty-five million people employed by MNCs worldwide, only seven million are in the Third World, accounting for less than 1 percent of the economically active population (Zlotnik 1993:47). Capital-intensive factories may put many domestic artisans out of work and drive out local businesses. The goods produced may also be inappropriate. For-profit production inevitably will be oriented toward demand, which, as we have seen, may have little relation to the actual needs of most of the people. In a country with a high rate of malnutrition, soft drinks and nonnutritive processed foods are sold through expensive advertising campaigns designed to associate such consumption with upwardly mobile life styles.

In order to attract foreign investment, countries must spend domestic funds to build up a supportive infrastructure, resulting in barely disguised public subsidies. Governments try to require that some or most profits be reinvested locally, but competition with other countries often necessitates liberal policies on money leaving the country. It is difficult to determine what real profits are because of conglomerate trading with its own subsidiaries. Overall, much more wealth leaves the country than is invested (otherwise, why invest?), with relatively few jobs to show for it.

Several scholars have contested Bornschier's negative findings (Szymanski 1983; Firebaugh 1992). The debate remains a lively one. Arguments may rest not only on statistical analysis and interpretations of data but also on different ideological perspectives. Those who see growth of GNP as the primary measure of development and who extol free-market capitalism generally hold a positive view of MNCs, whereas those who see development in terms of basic needs and income equalization take a more jaundiced view.

Third World countries themselves may feel that the argument is academic, because they have little choice. In desperate need of foreign exchange, they may see no option but to turn to MNCs. In any case, MNCs are, like capitalism, a "given" of the international scene. They are not going to go away. The problem may be for both Third World countries and the MNCs themselves to be aware of and to realistically deal with negative impacts in order to assure that foreign investment truly works toward long-term development goals.

FOREIGN AID

Although many different ideological perspectives on the Third World compete, there is general agreement that development is a positive goal. From a moral position, teeming hordes of hungry people are intolerable. From a purely pragmatic standpoint, improvements in Third World standards of living mean expanded markets for goods produced in the industrialized countries and greater political stability. Foreign aid — along with multinational investment and export earnings — is considered an essential part of the mix that helps countries in their developmental aspirations.

A basic definition of foreign aid is the transfer of resources on terms that are more generous or "softer" than loans at market rates. This definition may seem odd, because the popular conception of aid is that it consists of goods or services that are provided gratis to Third World countries; the reality is that most aid is in the form of loans, though loans made for longer periods and at better interest rates than are available through private or multilateral banks. Most developmental aid is for specific projects and also involves professional planning and technical assistance. Such projects take a multiplicity of forms, from building a huge hydroelectric dam to setting up a cooperative for marketing locally produced textiles. Usually, the term "foreign aid" is used exclusively to apply to undertakings by official agencies, rather than to the many types of aid offered by nongovernmental organizations.

Aid may be purely or largely humanitarian, as when it is sent to relieve crisis situations such as earthquake or famine. Much aid, however, is provided with the self-interest of the donor in mind. It may be used to strengthen the donor's political and ideological allies, to buy votes in international bodies such as the UN or the Organization of American States, to propagate capitalism against the threat of socialism, or to open markets. For example, the Alliance for Progress — a multibillion dollar aid program for Latin America inaugurated by President Kennedy — was motivated by national security concerns growing out of the emergence of communism in Cuba. Some of the "development" funds were spent on top-secret police and military training. The program fizzled out when the predicted security threat did not materialize and other crises, such as the Viet Nam war, assumed priority. The recipients' motives in seeking or accepting aid may not be entirely humanitarian or developmental either. Aid must be funneled through governments and cannot help but become a source of political control for those in power.

Virtually all First World countries provide aid. Norway contributes 1.5 percent of its GNP, the most of any country. During the Cold War the United States gave the most aid in absolute terms, though even then it ranked seventeenth out of eighteen First World donors in relation to GNP (only Ireland was lower), giving about 0.25 percent (World Bank 1992). Between 1985 and 1993, total U.S. aid dropped $4 billion, making Japan the world's primary aid giver. France and Germany are the next largest donors after the United States. The

Soviet bloc was a major aid competitor with the West, providing mainly military and major infrastructural assistance, but with the collapse of communism, these countries have become recipients rather than donors. The OPEC countries of the Middle East provided over $6 billion in 1990, mainly to other Islamic countries of the region.

Aid is either bilateral, between two countries, or multilateral, funneled through international agencies. Most aid is multilateral. Both types are commonly "procurement-tied": as a condition for receiving the aid, the recipient must purchase all needed goods and services from the donor country. For example, a large agricultural project may require the purchase of tractors, seed, fertilizer, and technical assistance from the donor. Food aid is often used as a means of getting rid of agricultural surpluses in the donor country. Obviously, business lobbies play a significant role in the planning and approval of projects that can be worth billions of dollars for domestic companies. More than 40 percent of all foreign aid is "tied," rising to 63 percent for U.S. bilateral aid (Cassen 1986:286).

A main channel for multilateral aid is the International Development Bank, sometimes referred to as the World Bank's "soft-loan window." Loans provided are identical to regular World Bank loans except for the lower interest rates and easier terms of payment. Aid is also funneled through regional banks, such as the African Development Bank, and a number of specialized UN agencies such as the Food and Agriculture Organization and the World Health Organization. Recipient countries usually prefer multilateral loans over bilateral aid, because they are less political, support a broader range of activities, and are somewhat less likely to be procurement tied.

U.S. aid has been most effective in agricultural development. In Guinea-Bissau, for example, a U.S. project helped hundreds of small farmers increase rice yields by 400 percent to 900 percent in merely two years. Almost all of the rice was consumed locally, raising the nutritional standards of the populace. The United States is also notable — except during the Reagan administration — for assisting countries in reducing their rates of population growth. In general, however, U.S. aid over the last decades has often been less concerned with development than with national security. Between 1981 and 1986, over 40 percent of bilateral aid consisted of loans to countries to purchase military equipment and receive training. Another 30 percent were Economic Support Funds, aid specifically designed to prop up about ten mainly middle-income countries that the United States believed were of national security importance (especially Israel and Egypt). Only 12 percent of bilateral aid went to food assistance and 18 percent to development. The end of the Cold War has reduced the political importance of aid and, thus, the amounts given. During the peak aid period of the rebuilding of Europe after World War II, the United States donated 60 percent of the world's foreign aid; by 1993 it gave only 16 percent. Much aid has been shifted to Russia and Eastern Europe, so that the decline in aid to some Third World countries has been enormous. Aid to the Philippines, for example, was cut 85 percent (Holmes 1993).

World Bank studies suggest that about 80 percent of its aid projects met their objectives. It is difficult, however, to determine the overall effects of aid by evaluating specific undertakings. A project may meet its goals, but have a broader detrimental effect. Aid projects often emphasize the modern sector, which tends to exacerbate inequalities within the country and perhaps downgrade the role of agriculture. During the 1970s, the West poured over $22 billion in developmental aid into Subsaharan Africa, but per capita food production decreased at a steady rate. Merely a quarter of expenditures were devoted to agriculture, and only half of that actually reached the rural areas. Even then, most went to large landowners, not the small holders who are Africa's most numerous and most efficient producers (Shepherd 1986). It often has been noted that food aid can undercut local food prices, driving farmers out of business. Aid in Latin America, closely tied to U.S. national security concerns, has been used to prop up dictators. Because aid is mainly loans, not gifts, it adds to the already heavy debts of Third World countries. Studies that have attempted to consider the Third World as a whole show little relation between foreign aid and development, except for the lowest income countries, where aid may be a substantial percentage of all revenues.

Both bilateral and multilateral aid agencies have learned much from experience. There is an increasing tendency to try to bypass elites and reach aid down to the level of grass-roots development, with greater success rates in alleviating poverty. Whether aid actually benefits the poor will continue to depend on the nature of the project itself and the degree to which the project is motivated by humanitarian and developmental concerns, rather than the self-interest of the donor.

THE DEBT CRISIS

If the United States were to pay 8 percent of its GNP to service its external debt, its annual expenditures would be almost $450 billion, considerably more than the government now spends for defense and education combined. Savings would evaporate, making expansion of the economy through new investment very difficult. Wages would have to be cut, and living standards would fall. Social unrest would be inevitable.

This is the real situation in many Third World countries today, where entire economies are being reoriented toward servicing their debts, which includes paying interest and expenses but little, if anything, on the principle. In 1980, Peru was billed 8 percent of its GNP in debt service. Mozambique's total debt in the 1990s is almost four times its annual GNP, and Jordan's debt is almost twice its GNP. Bolivia,

Colombia, and Côte d'Ivoire must pay almost 40 percent of their annual export earnings in debt service, and Algeria must pay almost 60 percent. Between 1977 and 1983, Brazil's total debt grew from $35 to $92 billion; 85 percent of all new borrowing during this period went just to pay interest (by 1990 Brazil's debt, the largest in the Third World, stood at $116 billion). Many Third World countries owe so much that all new loans must be devoted entirely to servicing old loans. On the whole, the interest on the debts is being paid (forget about the principle) to the tune of more than $65 billion a year. Banks have reaped enormous profits, but the effects on the Third World are devastating.

How did the Third World get into this predicament? Many observers believe that the causes were not corruption or irrationality but, rather, a series of unforseen circumstances. Lenders and borrowers may have been acting rationally at the time. During the 1960s and early 1970s, most Third World countries were growing at a healthy pace. Bankers were not concerned with income inequalities or broad definitions of development; growth of GNP alone meant good credit risks, especially when a whole country would be the collateral. Developing countries were willing to pay more in interest than domestic borrowers, which gave higher profit margins. After oil prices quadrupled in the mid-1970s, suddenly rich OPEC oil producers flooded banks with recycled "petrodollars," which then could be lent out. Not only huge international banks such as the Bank of America, Citicorp, and Chase Manhattan got into the act, but so did hundreds of smaller banks. Multilateral institutions, such as the World Bank, were also intensely involved.

From the Third World perspective, the availability of money and the willingness of banks to lend it seemed a godsend for their development ambitions. During the 1970s, the dollar was depreciating on international markets almost daily, which made loans a bargain. Also, although interest rates were high, inflation was sometimes even higher. There were cases when interest rates were effectively zero or even negative. For example, if the interest rate was 10 percent but inflation was 12 percent, real interest rates would be –2 percent. With money so amply available and so cheap, borrowing seemed the logical thing to do.

The Collapse

It turned out that the structure was built on sand. Most countries borrowed at "variable" rather than "fixed" interest rates, which meant that interest rates could change over time. In the 1980s, inflation fell faster than interest rates, leaving countries obligated for great amounts. Few people realized at the time the extent that development had been predicated on the availability of cheap energy. The very factor that made petrodollars available in the first place — oil price rises — forced countries to borrow more and more just to stay even. Oil price increases alone accounted for a quarter of all Third World debt. In addition, terms of trade for primary goods — the main exports of Third World countries — fell 40 percent just between 1980 and 1982. Finally, the 1980s ushered in a worldwide recession that shriveled markets and depleted export earnings.

Though much of the money was well spent on development projects, many countries emerged from their borrowing binges with little tangible benefit. It is estimated that 20 percent of Third World debt is directly attributable to arms purchases. Some money disappeared through corruption, and some was devoted to prestige projects that added nothing to development. West Germany loaned Togo money for an expensive new steel complex. When it was completed, the government realized that there was little available iron or scrap metal for start-up. With the credibility of the country's leaders at stake, German technicians dismantled a fully functional iron pier in order to feed the steel mill. When the pier was used up, the mill had to close down (George 1988).

Such episodes, although not rare, account for only a small proportion of debt. Third World leaders have complained that the crisis was not caused mainly by domestic folly but by external factors — recession, rising oil prices, and so forth — yet, they are given sole responsibility for resolving it. In desperation, Peru once proposed limiting debt payments to 10 percent of export earnings. Periodically, default — simply repudiating the debts — is suggested. The penalties for default or unilateral reduction of debt servicing would be unbearable for most countries. Foreign assets would be attached throughout the world, exports would be seized at the docks, national airlines would not be permitted to land in foreign countries, foreign aid would be cut off, access to spare parts would be curtailed, and no new loans would be forthcoming.

The International Monetary Fund to the Rescue

The International Monetary Fund, or IMF, has emerged as the superagency in charge of global debt. The IMF grew out of the Bretton Woods Conference in New Hampshire in 1944, which also established the World Bank. Its main function was to promote free trade, but it would also make loans to correct trade imbalances. By the 1980s, there were 146 member countries, each paying a "quota" to belong. The United States alone provides a fifth of IMF funds and, therefore, is the dominant influence on the organization. In contrast to the World Bank, IMF loans tend to be relatively short term and directed toward stabilizing economies rather than for developmental projects.

A crucial component of loans is "conditionality." This means that in order to borrow, a country must agree to make often-major "structural adjustments" in its economy. In collaboration with IMF loan officers, a country submits a letter of intent specifying the steps it will take to correct the situation leading to the deficits. It then accepts a "stand-by agreement" by which the money will be dispersed over months or years as the conditions are met. At any given time, the IMF may be overseeing stand-by agreements in forty countries of the Third World.

Though IMF officials insist that they are quite flexible and that a great number of different arrangements have been made according to the needs of different countries, in reality, most agreements follow a very similar pattern based on the export-oriented neoliberal model of development. Among the most frequently imposed reforms is the devaluation of currency, often highly overvalued, in order to discourage imports and encourage exports. Foreign investment should be actively sought and a good investment climate created. Government expenditures must be reduced. Food and fuel subsidies are discouraged. Wage increases should be tightly restricted and price controls abolished. Government-owned enterprises should be sold to the private sector.

There can be no doubt that such requirements often have the beneficial effect of reducing bloated bureaucracies, increasing efficiency, and getting governments to divest inefficient parastatals. Many countries do need the discipline imposed by IMF conditionality. However, IMF policies are growth oriented, not development oriented. Countries' economies are turned to a focus on GNP with the main purpose of paying debt service. The burden falls on the lowest classes, who had no say in incurring the debt, with the result that poverty and inequality may increase. According to the *Washington Post*, five months after fourteen African nations were forced to radically devalue their joint currency under pressure from the IMF, "the clearest result so far is that millions of people in some of the world's poorest nations have been forced deeper into poverty" (Singletary 1994). As wages are held down and prices allowed to rise, internal demand may diminish, weakening the domestic economy even though the export sector improves. However, exports do not necessarily improve. Because the IMF has the same export-led strategy for all countries, pressing two producers of the same product to increase output could well cause a glut that drops the price, so that neither country gains. The IMF also urges countries to diversify their exports, but this can be quite expensive in the best of circumstances and may be impossible when so much money is being spent in debt servicing. As we have seen, the successful Southeast Asian model was an ongoing process, not a standard set of procedures. That process included periods of import substitution, state ownership, and intensive government involvement in the economy, all of which are discouraged by IMF conditionality.

Despite the IMF's ideological committment to its prescriptions for the Third World, it is not at all evident that those prescriptions promote either growth or development. A 1985 IMF study observed that "little empirical evidence exists on the long-run effects of Fund programs, and none at all on the effects of various combinations of stabilization policies on economic development" (Khan and Knight 1985:7). Three years later, the World Bank published a comprehensive review of the structural adjustment program, comparing performances in thirty "adjustment lending" countries with forty-eight countries that had not made such adjustments. The differences were not statistically significant. As one critic noted, "Indeed, what the study actually shows is that only high middle-income, manufacture exporting countries were able to turn these policies to their advantage" (Bienefeld 1994:36).

In essence, the debt crisis has given the United States — through the IMF — the power to impose its particular philosophy of growth on much of the Third World. It is true that many countries do benefit from the belt-tightening requirements. However, both the problems and the solutions may be simplistically diagnosed and simplistically resolved. The focus of conditionality is on the economic policies of individual countries, with little recognition of the need for structural adjustments at the international level.

"When governments must devote every last centavo to servicing debt," writes Susan George (1988:44), "they cut expenditures at home, drive down salaries, sack public workers, stop paying for health, education and welfare and generally neglect their own populations." As a result of such policies, there has been rioting in Peru, the Dominican Republic, Brazil, Venezuela, and Bolivia. If countries were actually escaping their debts, IMF conditionality might be more bearable, but, even while adhering to IMF mandates, many countries continue to fall ever deeper into debt, with little real alleviation in sight.

THE NEW INTERNATIONAL ECONOMIC ORDER

Poverty looks very different from the periphery than it does from the core. In its governmental policies and business arrangements, the First World takes a modernization approach, viewing problems as internal to the various underdeveloped countries. The Third World itself is more acutely aware of the international structures from which it cannot escape. Exporters of primary products have little control over global terms of trade, nor can they penetrate the high tariffs of protected markets in the First World. They receive only a small percentage of the final price of their exports; the lion's share goes to processors and distributors. They have little or no decision-making power over the policies of the richer countries and are even in a subordinate position dealing with wealthier MNCs.

It is mainly in the UN that Third World countries can make their voices collectively heard. At the Sixth Special Session of the UN in 1974, the General Assembly committed itself: "to work urgently for the establishment of a new international economic order based on equity, sovereign equality, common interest and cooperation among all states . . . which shall make it possible to eliminate the widening gap between the developed and developing countries and ensure steadily accelerating economic and social development and peace and justice for present and future generations" (quoted in Todaro 1985:560).

From this initial declaration emerged the New International Economic Order, or NIEO. A primary concern is debt; such solutions were proposed as cancellation of debt, moratoriums, rescheduling, and the provision of subsidies to help pay interest. The IMF should be reformed so that Third World countries themselves will have a say on terms of conditionality. The NIEO presses for a redefinition of terms of trade so that the prices of primary commodities are tied to those of manufactured goods. It calls for a common fund to stabilize price fluctuations on raw materials. Third World countries insist that their needs to protect domestic industries be recognized and that there be a nonreciprocal lowering of tariffs on the part of the industrialized countries to give greater access to these markets. Because so much wealth flows from the Third World to the First World, an official foreign aid target of 0.7 percent of GNP should be imposed on the developed nations and aid should not be politically motivated or procurement tied.

This "wish list" of international reform shows little potential for becoming a reality. Only the Nordic countries and France meet the foreign aid goals. The United States has a policy of *not* cancelling debt (though there have been many cases of rescheduling), and there remains little Third World input on the IMF. In contrast to the demand for nonreciprocal lowering of tariffs, the United States, the World Bank, and the IMF follow a policy of requiring Third World countries to abandon import protection. In reality, implementation of the NIEO would require a major shift in the power balance between the two worlds, and there is no evidence that this is happening.

What the NIEO does accomplish is to provide a Third World viewpoint. For much of the Third World, the economic future seems quite bleak. Quick fixes, such as IMF loans to pay interest on other loans, do not go far in solving problems that the Third World perceives as basically international and structural. Although it is undoubtedly true that many economic difficulties are internal to Third World countries, the international dimension cannot be discounted. Unfortunately, it is much easier to require impoverished nations to alter their policies than it is to change immensely powerful international structures.

SUGGESTED READINGS

Barnet, Richard, and Ronald E. Müller, *Global Reach: The Power of Multinational Corporations* (New York: Simon and Schuster, 1974). The authors examine the global structure and worldwide impact of MNCs, arguing that they have retarded development in the Third World and distorted the economy of the United States.

Dell, Sidney, *International Development Policies: Perspectives for Industrial Countries* (Durham, N.C.: Duke University Press, 1991). The author recognizes the crucial importance of the international political and economic system to Third World development and advises the industrial countries what they must do.

George, Susan, *A Fate Worse than Debt: The World Financial Crisis and the Poor* (New York: Grove Weidenfeld, 1988). The kindest thing that George has to say about the IMF is that it "is the messenger, watchdog, international alibi and *gendarme* for those who [really] hold financial power," namely, private banks. Using specific examples in Africa and Latin America, she shows the devastation caused by debt.

Harris, Nigel, *The End of the Third World: Newly Industrializing Countries and the Decline of an Ideology* (London: Penguin, 1986). The ideology that is in decline, according to the author, is laissez-faire capitalism. In analyzing the development of Southeast Asia's Gang of Four, he shows that only Hong Kong used the neoliberal model, while Singapore, South Korea, and Taiwan developed through extensive government involvement in every aspect of the economies.

Lappé, Francis Moore, Rachel Schurman, and Kevin Danaher, *Betraying the National Interest* (New York: Grove, 1987). A scathing (and well justified) indictment of U.S. foreign aid during the Reagan administration, when almost 70 percent of bilateral aid was devoted to military programs or national-security related Economic Support Funds.

Todaro, Michael P., *Economic Development in the Third World*, 2nd ed. (New York: Longman, 1985). Of the numerous textbooks available on Third World economics, this one offers a balanced, nonideological, and easily accessible approach to what can be a dense and difficult subject.

World Bank, *Trends in Developing Countries* (Washington, D.C.: World Bank, annual). An outstanding yearly sourcebook that provides brief economic analyses of the World Bank's 120 or so Third World members (notably missing are Taiwan and Cuba, which are not members). Two pages of charts and tables follow each brief country description.

6

Dictatorship and Democracy: Politics in the Third World

June 30, 1960, was a day of great promise for Africa. On that day, Belgium granted independence to the Congo, ending 75 years of one of the most oppressive colonial rules the continent had experienced.

The misnamed Congo Free State was created in 1885 as the personal property of Belgian King Leopold II (it did not become officially a colony of Belgium until 1908). It quickly acquired the nickname *Bula Matari*, literally "he who breaks rocks." The appellation was fitting, because the Belgians ruled through a brutal and crushing repression. Full responsibility for financing the colony — including the military, administration, transportation, and other expenses — fell on the Congo itself. Onerous taxes were imposed, and natives were pressed into arduous forced-labor crews to gather ivory, tap rubber, and, later, mine gold, tin, and copper. The whole system of state terror was legitimized under an ideology of the "civilizing mission" of the colonizers.

In 1955, bowing to liberal postwar pressures, Belgium permitted the first establishment of political parties, unleashing the creation of innumerable tribal-based movements. The only organization that promised to unite rather than rend the country was that of Patrice Lumumba, whose National Congolese Movement called for independence while opposing the demands for tribal or regional secession. Independence was achieved only after many a bloody confrontation. Lumumba became prime minister via an election that was about as fair as it could be in a country with no history of democracy and virtually universal illiteracy.

Within days, the copper-rich province of Katanga announced its secession. When Belgium landed parachutists to salvage some of its lost wealth, Lumumba made the terminal mistake of requesting Soviet aid to expel them. The prime minister quickly retracted his invitation, but the damage was already done; he was written off as a communist by the Eisenhower administration. In a confused series of violent events, the United Nations under U.S. influence intervened with a "peace-keeping" invasion, the Central Intelligence Agency (CIA) sent three separate hit men to kill Lumumba, and the president staged a coup against the hapless prime minister. Lumumba was captured and assassinated before the Americans could get to him (Weissman 1979; Garwood 1985:59–60).

Years of political discord followed, with sputtering attempts at democracy alternating with violent coups and considerable manipulations by the increasingly activist CIA. The man to emerge as the only one strong enough to bring order out of chaos was General Joseph Desiré Mobutu, who took over in a coup in 1965. The country assumed a degree of stability but at a high price. After renaming the nation Zaire and renaming himself Mobutu Sese Seko, the new "president" banned all political parties except his own, restricted and then abolished parliament, assumed central control over virtually all institutions — unions, student organizations, even churches — and instituted the personalist rule of Mobutism. Political opponents could face imprisonment in concentration camps, torture, and death. Despite a brief falling out with Washington over the nationalization of Zaire's copper, Mobutu became a key instrument of U.S. policy in the region, especially in opening the country to U.S. business and in sheltering CIA-supported forces fighting the communist government in Angola.

Mobutu was successful in extending state control over myriad tribal groups and for a while was able to sustain economic growth and the appearance of strength. After 1974, however, the top-heavy system began to disintegrate, as overreliance on exported copper and undervaluation of domestic literacy and health drove the dictatorship from crisis to crisis. Governmental corruption became rampant and institutionalized. Self-sufficient in food during and immediately after the colonial period, by the 1980s, the country was importing 40 percent of its food. Despite its mineral and agricultural wealth, purchasing power for the already impoverished people continued to decline; up to 40 percent of workers were unemployed, and inflation averaged 35 percent a year. The great promise of independence had brought only dictatorship, corruption, and impoverishment (Young and Turner 1985; Gibbs 1991; Kwitny 1984:49–103).

The experience of Zaire exemplifies the political processes that took place in many decolonized countries. An initial flush of nationalist optimism and the promise of democracy was frustrated by disintegration into tribal or ethnic conflict, followed by increasingly personalist and corrupt one-person, one-party dictatorship. Virtually all countries were dragged, willingly or not, into the Cold War conflict between the United States and the Soviet Union. Economies, even those once showing promise, collapsed under the weight of bureaucratic corruption, international dependence, massive debt, and internal conflict.

To be sure, the pattern was not universal. A handful of democracies, such as India, survived the stresses of decolonization. A few others, such as Vietnam and North Korea, became communist and initiated their own forms of despotism. The countries of Latin America, with over a hundred years of independence and somewhat better-off economies, assumed patterns of government different from those of Africa and Asia, but even here, the greatest extremes of repression erupted.

Although U.S. and European models of multiparty democracy remain integral to the ideal of modernization and development promoted by the West, almost nowhere in the Third World was that aspiration achieved. Just as modernization theorists were to learn belatedly that economics in the periphery was substantially different from that of the industrialized countries, so, it became increasingly obvious that the underlying dynamics of politics were very different from those of the Western democracies.

BUILDING A NATION-STATE — THE PROBLEM OF UNITY

In the vast span of the human sojourn on earth, the state is a relatively recent political structure, dating back to Mesopotamia in the third millennium B.C. Anthropologists have classified a number of simpler stages in political evolution. Societies based on hunting and gathering have tended to live in nomadic, egalitarian *bands*, groups of twenty-five to fifty people with no formal leadership. *Tribes*, too, lack formal leaders, but the groups are larger, are dependent on small-scale agriculture and herding, and are organized into lineages (people tracing their descent, exclusively through either the male or female lines, to a common ancestor) and clans (related lineages). Tribes also may be united by secret societies and other associations that crosscut lineage divisions. The *chiefdom* level of political organization is characterized by some form of centralized political authority and by pervasive inequality. True class stratification is absent, but both individuals and lineages are ranked; those closer to the chief's lineage receive the deference of those below (Service 1962; Lewellen 1992:21–45).

Although the state has invariably encompassed these less complex political arrangements, it does not always supersede them. In many Third World countries, these lower-level structures continue to exist, requiring loyalties that are in conflict with the demands of the state. In Yemen, for example, hereditary sheiks control almost all rural regions despite the attempts of a federal government to unite the country.

It is this problem of unity that makes it so difficult to build a true nation-state. Though the term "nation" has no universally accepted definition, it is often considered to be a group that shares a culture, religion, traditions, and language. A nation may or may not be territorially based; even migratory peoples or peoples pushing into a new territory, such as the Zulu in the nineteenth century, may qualify. The nation-state — a collection of perhaps diverse peoples who share common loyalties, culture, and heritage — is a relatively recent development, dating back only a few hundred years. Within such a political entity, individuals are "citizens," who claim the country as their legal home. A uniform system of law overrides local custom and regulation. Despite its enormous diversity, even in language, the United States qualifies as a nation, partially because it has a common "referent culture" to which immigrants tend to aspire and because there is a general acceptance of the political authority of the Constitution (Spindler and Spindler 1990). This would be more or less true of all First World countries. Although all Third World countries have established some form of centralized government (though these may periodically collapse under stress, as in Lebanon and Somalia), few have been able to unite their multiple ethnic, tribal, and religious groups into true country-wide nations. One obvious reason is that it is difficult to claim a common history or culture of much depth when your country is only thirty years old. Tribal loyalties continue to take precedence over loyalties to the state; local chiefs and strongmen exercise power over their localities.

Theorists of the 1950s and 1960s predicted that ethnicity would dissolve into a single common national culture as a country developed. Exactly the opposite has been the case. Ethnic groups that had virtually disappeared under colonialism or had become increasingly dispersed were solidified by the processes of modernization. In Nigeria, the pressures of party politics and of state antipathy to tribalism severely weakened the Hausa, a group of traders who had developed a widespread reputation as shrewd businessmen, traders in cattle and kola nuts. Detribalization threatened not only their self-identity but also, and more importantly, their livelihood. To maintain control of their lucrative personalized trading networks required an in-group mentality that had nearly been lost. The answer was to reemphasize the tribal unit around a Moslem religious brotherhood, the Tijaniyia. Their strongly fundamentalist religion not only set them off as morally superior to outsiders but also furnished a religious hierarchy that provided the leadership that had been lost with the decline of the old tribal chiefs. Through retribalization, ethnicity was politicized and used as a crucial weapon in the control of their trading networks (Cohen 1969).

The failure to integrate tribal or ethnic groups is not always just a matter of in-group traditions or economic protectionism. Ethnic groups, especially those composed of peasants or horticulturalists, are often at the bottom of the class pyramid and are deliberately and systematically excluded from political power by the reigning elites. In many countries, those elites may themselves be an ethnic group, such as the Sinhalese in Sri Lanka, the Javanese in Indonesia, or the Arabs in Mauritania. In India, the relatively weak federal government is multiethnic, but individual states are run by dominant linguistic groups, such as the Assamese in Assam (Weiner 1987a).

The Power of Elites

Competitors for power are not restricted to such traditional groups. The end of colonialism and the processes of development have created multiple elites as well as populist movements that often retain their power no matter who runs the state.

Perhaps the strongest of these is the officer's corps of the military, which may be autonomous of government control. The common experience of officer's school, the force of tradition, and the esprit de corps of warfare gives the military a continuity and ideological unity denied the government. Even where the military does not constitute a hidden but de facto government, it may, through the ever-present threat of a coup, hold a tacit veto power over state decisions.

In Latin America and parts of Asia, traditional large-scale feudal landowners will have their own organizations and their own agendas. Composed of historically prestigious families, they demand to be left alone, allotting the state only the power to repress peasant organizations. Commercial farmers may have a completely different agenda, demanding easy credit, low tariffs, high price supports, and the infrastructure to get their products to market, such as roads and ports. If the country derives much of its national wealth from export agriculture, this may put enormous political power in the hands of wealthy farmers. In Brazil and the Philippines, even under democratic rule, a minuscule group of large-scale farmers has been able to thwart long-overdue land reform.

Business elites — the owners of large industries and financial institutions — form another power bloc. They are interested in many of the same things as commercial farmers, such as export infrastructure and low taxes, but, in addition, they demand tight controls on militant labor unions, if not their actual repression. Bureaucrats, high-ranking civil servants who may have the power to implement or impede government initiatives, form another power bloc with which the government must reckon.

Competitors for power are not restricted to domestic elites; multinational corporations and foreign governments may exercise considerable — at times even dominant — power within a Third World country (Table 6.1). The days when the United Fruit Company could help destabilize Guatemala or International Telephone and Telegraph would work closely with the CIA to bring about the downfall of the government of Chile may not be over, but such instances are rarer than in the past. Multinationals have found that directly tampering in domestic politics, beyond the necessary bribe or two, can be both embarrassing and financially detrimental. However, so-called *comprador elites*, local investors and managers of multinational subsidiaries, may be among the wealthiest people in the country and may exercise enormous power. Because their interests are those of the multinationals — low minimum

TABLE 6.1
Competing Players in Third World Politics

	Composition	Political Objectives	Political Resources
Traditional large-scale landowners	Owners of large estates more interested in traditional social and economic roles than maximizing production.	Want to be left alone by the federal government, assisted by local police and courts. Minimum taxes and regulations. Repression of peasants.	Economic dependence of rural labor, often reinforced through patron-client relationships. Wealth. Social prestige. Control of local law enforcement
Commercial farmers	Landowners devoted to maximum production for profit, using modern technology. Often export oriented and tied to multinational agribusinesses.	Stable government. Low taxes and low tariffs, high support prices, easy credit, and adequate infrastructure (roads, ports, etc.). Control of rural labor organizations.	Production of essential domestic and export crops. Personal and economic ties with commerce and industry. Ties with agribusinesses.
Business elites	Owners of large domestic industries and financial institutions, including subsidiaries of multinationals.	Stable government, low taxes, high tariffs, easy credit, free market pricing, government protection without regulation. Control of militant labor unions.	Control over critical economic activities. Wealth. Economic and technical expertise.
Military	Officers corps of the army, navy, and air force.	Strong government that maintains order and promotes national development. Financial and political support for military institutions.	Force of arms. Hierarchical organization, continuity, ideological coherence, managerial skills.
Organized ethnic or religious groups	Powerful ethnic and religious groups that are sufficiently organized and effectively led. May include all strata of the society, from top to bottom.	May demand either control of the government or autonomy from the government. At minimum, want freedom for their culture and religion.	Mass protest — riots, demonstrations, rebellion. Control of an economic sector or a geographical region.

Bureaucrats	High-ranking civil servants and technocrats who staff government agencies.	Personal wealth and social status. Political power. Influence over policy decisions.	Bureaucratic authority. Ability to implement or block policy decisions. Expertise. Control of goods and services both nationally and locally.
Multinationals and comprador elites	Foreign-owned companies: manufacturing, mining, banking, utilities.	Political, economic stability. Access to raw materials and labor. Minimal regulation. Infrastructure paid for by state. Subordination of labor unions.	Investment capital. Technology. Access to foreign markets. Job creation.
Foreign governments	Agencies of powerful First World governments, such as the United States and Japan.	Investment opportunities and markets. Political and economic stability. Cooperation in mutual security efforts. Support in international organizations.	Military and economic power. Foreign aid. Influence (including destabilization) through covert action.

Source: Based on Wynin, Gary, *The Politics of Latin American Development* (Cambridge: Cambridge University Press, 1978), pp. 46–47.

wages and subordination of labor unions, access to raw materials, and
the development of export infrastructure such as ports — the economy
may be turned outward rather than inward. Comprador elites aside,
multinationals exercise political power through their ability to invest or
withdraw investment. During the Cold War, the U.S. and Soviet
governments were notorious for their interventions in Third World
politics, but the decline of east-west hostility has by no means brought
an end to foreign-power influence. Foreign aid, international loans, the
opening or closing of markets, support in interstate or civil wars, and
even the threat of invasion or destabilization put great political power
in the hands of First World nations, especially the United States
(Wynia 1978).

Political Parties

In Western democracies, political parties are the most important
actors in electoral politics. This may or may not be true in Third World
countries, where parties may be inordinately strong or very weak. In
either case, political parties in the Third World tend to be different in
many ways from those in the First World.

The nature of parties varies depending on whether they exist in
single-party or competitive-party systems. In the former, such as Iraq
under Ba'athist rule and Cuba under the communists, the party may be
virtually identical with the state. Other parties are legally banned or so
persecuted that they cannot exist. Such parties are not necessarily
monolithic, however. Factions struggle for dominance within the party,
and, if elections are allowed, individuals may be identified with these
factions, thus, providing a system that is crudely competitive.

In many countries, one finds a mixture of single-party and competitive-party systems. This occurs when multiple parties are legally
permitted, but one dominant party holds virtually all power for long
periods of time, either through election fixing or by control of political
machines reaching down to the local level. In recent times, such have
been found in Mexico, India, Senegal, and Malaysia.

It is also necessary to distinguish between mass and elite parties. In
the nineteenth and early twentieth centuries in much of Latin America,
parties tended to be oriented around factions of the elite. The
traditional feudal *latifundistas* were represented in the conservative
parties, while the budding industrialists and export-oriented landowners favored the laissez-faire capitalism of the liberal parties.
Excluded by literacy restrictions on voting, the masses were not
represented at all. Over time, however, where universal enfranchise-
ment has been introduced, elitist parties have been forced to become
more and more mass oriented, often overriding divisions of ethnicity or
class (Randall 1988; Cammack, Pool, and Tordoff 1988:81–114).

One of the most longstanding parties of Latin America is Peru's APRA — the *Alianza Popular Revolucionaria Americana* — which was founded by Victor Raúl Haya de la Torre in 1924. At a time when most Peruvian parties were temporary organizations formed around individual strongmen, APRA offered a true ideology. Originally an attempt at a pan–Latin American party, it promoted antiimperialism, the economic and political unity of Latin America, nationalization of land and industry, and "the solidarity of all the oppressed people and classes of the world" (Haya de la Torre 1961:15). Though never repudiated, in practice, the grand vision was considerably narrowed to appeal specifically to the demands of the coastal agricultural workers who formed the backbone of the organization. Continually persecuted and driven underground by a series of dictatorships, APRA survived more because of its organization and ability to serve the needs of its members than because of its ideology (which, over the years, changed from radical to liberal to conservative). Local APRA headquarters were social and recreational centers, complete with cut-rate lunchrooms. APRA-affiliated support institutions included labor unions, a popular university, a feminist organization, and a youth arm. Rallies consisted of torchlight parades, bonfires, an anthem, the chanting of the official slogan "Only APRA will save Peru!" and huge pictures of Haya, who was virtually worshipped. When literacy restrictions on voting were revoked in 1980, the party extended its appeal to peasants and shanty-town dwellers, losing much of the tight coherence of the original party. Haya died in 1980, never having attained national office (he was once elected president but was kept out by a coup). However, in 1985, APRA leader Alan García attained the presidency of Peru. The economic collapse that occurred during García's tenure destroyed much of APRA's support, and the party lost its place in government after only four years (Lewellen 1989).

THE POWER — AND WEAKNESS — OF THE STATE

A controversy exists among political scientists over the nature and role of the state. Is the state invariably the primary political actor in a country, to which all competitors to power aspire? Or is it one power bloc among many? The answer may depend on the particular country, but there has been a tendency to put more and more emphasis on the state and its internal workings (Evans, Rueschemeyer, and Skocpol 1985; Clapham 1985).

Max Weber (1964:156) defined the state as an organization composed of numerous bureaucratic agencies coordinated by an executive authority that makes the binding rules for all people in the country, using force, if necessary, to implement those rules. (This emphasis on a legitimate monopoly over the use of force has also been central to many anthropological definitions.) In addition, most states have at least three distinct levels of organization: a central executive that establishes policy, federal agencies that have the power of appointment and patronage, and state agencies or officials at regional and local levels that implement policy. Such an ideal-type definition would be subject to numerous exceptions (for example, there are states where the use of force may, in reality, rest with local chiefs or warlords). Whatever definition one chooses, the state is different from the nation, the country, or any particular elite. Indeed, state actions and policies may, and often do, conflict with nationalist sentiment or elite interests. Increasingly, the state is viewed as a separate and distinct actor within the political arena.

Early theorists of modernization believed that the primary function of the state was national unification and economic development. This turned out to be highly optimistic; in many — if not most — cases, the primary function of the state is its own survival and the aggrandizement of power and wealth by its leaders.

The Third World state maintains itself and expands its power by extracting resources, in the form of taxes or control over agriculture, mining, and industries as well as international trade. Often, the domestic tax base is small; in countries with large informal economies, only a fraction of the populace is taxed, and those who are — the wealthy elites — are exactly those in the position to best avoid paying their legal share. The temptation, often perceived as a necessity, is to obtain income from government ownership of major corporations — so called parastatals — and from tariffs. This occurs, as we have seen, under both socialist and capitalist regimes. Theoretically, this makes a great deal of sense, because profits accrue to the whole people, rather than only to elite owners of production. However, the state is not the people; often, the state in no way even represents the people. State ownership and control of profits may reinforce the power of the official leadership with no more trickle-down effect than if these corporations were privately owned. "Where the state is by far the strongest source of political power," observes Christopher Clapham (1985:41), "government of the state, by the state and for the state becomes extremely likely." This may be true of both dictatorships and democracies. Such a view of the state confounds ideologies of development based on the intrinsic logic of either socialism or capitalism; many of the underlying principles of power are the same no matter what development strategy is adopted.

Strong State, Weak State

States operate in two broad overlapping spheres of power: first, they function as international entities, interacting with multinational corporations, global and regional organizations, and other states; second, they seek to rule within their own countries. States may be strong or weak in either of these areas, depending on the extent that they are able to actually achieve their policy goals (Figure 6.1). A state that is strong in the international sphere may be weak domestically and vice versa. A capable military, a strong currency, respected leadership, and possession of an export needed by the international community, such as oil, contribute to international strength. Domestically, a state's strength depends on its ability to make the rules for the whole society in the face of competition from other institutions and from local strongmen.

The trials of Gamal Abdel Nasser, who ruled Egypt from 1952 until his death in 1970, reveal some of the obstacles to building a strong state even when there is capable leadership. Under the monarchy that Nasser displaced, the large landowners held enormous regional power. Through an extensive land reform, their strength was broken, but much of that power shifted to newly wealthy middle peasants who formed their own organization to challenge the state. In addition, the officer's corps shifted its loyalties to one of its commanders, threatening Nasser's presidential control. To counteract the threat, Nasser was forced to build up the Arab Socialist Union, a civilian political party, but as soon as it gained strength and autonomy, that organization, too, assumed its own agenda.

This illustrates a common Third World paradox: a strong state requires the creation of supporting agencies and institutions, but these may gain sufficient independence and power to then challenge the state. Constantly thwarted by other leaders and by his own organizations, Nasser never did achieve state predominance, and much of his program was never realized or was dissipated on his death (Migdal 1987, 1988).

THE RULES OF THE GAME: CLIENTELISM, LEGITIMACY, AND POLITICAL CULTURE

Political actors, whether individuals or groups, work within sets of constraints. Power is based on relationships, and even the strongest leader must seek support by forming bonds with others. In addition, if governance is to be more than just a matter of repression, it needs to be justified, either by bestowing benefits or by appeal to the beliefs, values, and expectations of the people.

Clientelism — Power through Reciprocal Bonds

In 1976, a community of peasant Indians in southern Peru wanted to purchase a specific tract of land for a school, which they would build themselves. They approached the owner, a major *latifundista*, who made them an offer. When the local priest, a Maryknoll missionary from New York, heard about the offer, he was appalled. He called a

FIGURE 6.1
Strong and Weak States

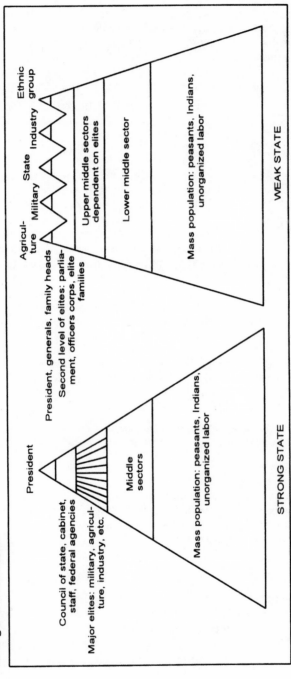

Note: The diagram on the left shows a strong state in which elites are subordinate to the government. In many Third World nations, however, the state may be one contender for power among others, such as organized tribal and ethnic groups, the military, local warlords, and various agricultural and industrial elites. In the weak state, the government may be focused on the international sphere — diplomacy, trade, warfare — but be unable to extend its control and enforce its laws over the entire populace of the country. Recently, political scientists have tended to emphasize the strong state, but weak states may be more the norm. In reality, there are degrees of strength and weakness, and few real states would fit these ideal models.

special community meeting to inform the people that not only was the price asked more than twice the going rate but also the landowner was charging for some land that was not even his. The peasants listened respectfully, assured the priest they would carefully consider his words, and then went out and purchased the land at the price asked. In a sense, they had no choice. Virtually every man in the community had established a relationship of vertical *compadrazgo* with the landowner. This is a formal, culturally enshrined bond of mutual obligation in which the richer man becomes the godfather of the poorer man's child, making the two adults *compadres* (Figure 6.2).

FIGURE 6.2
Latin American Compadrazgo

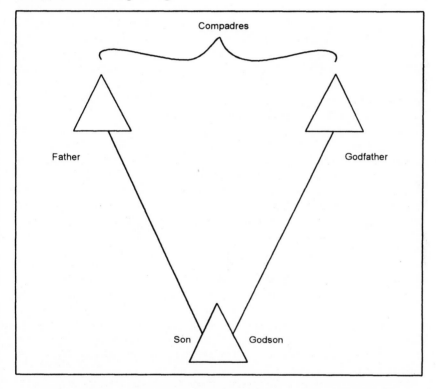

There is a horizontal form of *compadrazgo* that establishes close friendships among equals, but the vertical form is clearly exploitive. The rich *patrón* can offer legal help if the peasant finds himself in trouble with the police, may assist the child to get into a high school in the city, and essentially provides a seldom-sought but badly needed access to the non-Indian world. In return, the peasant must support the landowner politically, work for the landowner whenever asked and for whatever wages are offered, and pretty much do whatever the landowner wants.

Vertical *compadrazgo*, which was established by the Spaniards as a means of control in the New World, is a classic form of clientelism. The relationship, which is for the lifetime of those involved, is fundamentally unequal, established between a superior patron and an inferior client. It is based on the reciprocal exchange of goods and services, though what is exchanged — and when and how — may be ambiguous and open-ended rather than explicit. A sort of supply-demand logic determines the relative values of the partnership. There are always few patrons and a great many potential clients. The client desperately needs his patron, who is often his only access to the power centers beyond the closed world of the peasant or of the inner city slum dweller. The particular client, however, is of little importance to the patron; there is always a surfeit of potential clients. Herein lies the patron's power; he can take or leave any particular client, whereas the client is dependent. Although based on divisions of class or caste, the relationship is always a personal one; it is established between individuals or families. Yet, it also is impersonal in the sense that the individuals may have little to do with each other because of the difference in their statuses.

Clientelism is one of the most widespread and most enduring types of political relationship. It forms a transition between the kinship politics of village life and the more impersonal politics of the bureaucratic nation-state — though many Third World countries seem unable to progress beyond it. Some theorists believed that clientelism would die out with the emergence of the modern state, because government institutions or political parties would provide alternative access to power, thus, undermining local patrons. A peasant who could get a seed loan from an agricultural bank should have no need to borrow at exorbitant interest from a patron. However, clientelism is a relationship that flourishes in situations of extreme inequality, and, as we have seen, the initial stages of economic development almost invariably exacerbate inequalities of both income and power. In order to have any power at all, illiterate peasants must use such intermediaries to approach the government and other elite institutions upon which they are dependent.

Clientelism has not only continued to exist in modern state societies but also has flourished. The *Godfather* films of the 1970s accurately portray clientelism in U.S. organized crime. Until recently, "political machines" — in which individuals in ethnic neighborhoods were linked to public officials through a chain of local bosses — existed in Philadelphia, Boston, and Chicago. In the Third World, a multitude of forms of clientelism are normal in local politics, and some states are based on the system even to the highest levels of government (Randall and Theobold 1985:50–64; Clapham 1985:55–58).

Political Culture and Legitimacy

The number of countries that have adopted democratic governments or that are struggling in that direction would appear to validate the Western conviction that democracy is a universal yearning. The aspiration for equality of opportunity and power would seem to be intrinsic to human nature. In reality, however, there are many political cultures — that is, many beliefs about the nature of power, the ideal society, and proper forms of political leadership and secession. Contrary to the Western model of a society that is wealthy, equitable, democratic, and stable, another culture's image of the good society may be one that is austere, hierarchical, authoritarian, and martial (Huntington 1987:25). For many Islamic fundamentalists, the ideal state would be a theocracy based on the Koran and the *shari'a*, traditional law. Many Eastern Europeans are having a hard time adapting to capitalism because they interpret equality not as opportunity, as Americans do, but socialistically, as a leveling of wealth.

Political scientists, who have had little success in linking governmental types to particular cultures, have often written off the concept of culture as a "soft" form of explanation — nonquantifiable and nongeneralizable — that is adopted only when other explanations do not work (Weiner 1987a:xix). Many anthropologists, however, have found culture to be crucial to any study of human behavior; it is an integral part of a group's material and psychological heritage — its symbols, its language, its idea of what constitutes the good life, its values, its concepts of leadership and authority. Culture is what seems normal and right. For a tribal people, the belief in the justice of revenge feuding might make the state's claim to a monopoly on the use of force seem an insufferable infringement on the authority of the kin group. For others, the hereditary power of a king might be the "natural" form of politics.

There are many reasons why states do not necessarily evolve out of nor reflect the country's political culture. One reason is that there may be as many political cultures as there are ethnic groups, and these may be in conflict. The autonomy of the state may set it outside of national culture; the state may appropriate a foreign doctrine, such as communism; it may express the ideology and structure of the military; or it may conform to the whims of a dictator. In addition, states have to adapt to numerous external constraints, such as the need for foreign aid and loans, the demands of multinational corporations, the prospect of paying off huge international debts, or the need to appease a threatening superpower. Politics at the top has its own requirements that can be quite independent of national values and aspirations.

This does not mean that political culture is irrelevant. If a government is to maintain itself without the costly use of constant force, it must acquire a degree of legitimacy. In the United States, polls periodically show that a majority of people do not support the president, but no one suggests that he should be overthrown. Attainment of office through constitutional processes gives the president a legitimacy that is independent of his popularity at any given time. Political secession through the vote is such a deeply engrained part of U.S. political culture that to question it would seem less radical than simply ridiculous. Many Third World countries lack such a consensual political culture, with the result that regimes can claim little in the way of legitimacy. Democracy or dictatorship may be equally valid. If a democracy fails to bring down inflation, it might not be the party in power or the president that comes under fire, but democracy itself. After only a couple of years of even semidemocracy in Brazil and Guatemala, many were already calling for a return to the enforced stability of military dictatorship.

If a state cannot gain legitimacy through some national political culture, it may try to do so in other ways: it may provide benefits to the elites who support it or to the populace; it may try for real or illusory consent of the people by holding elections, even fixed elections; it might try to improve the economy or win a war; it might find a common enemy to arouse nationalistic passion. Or, it might not do any of these. Many governments have stayed in office for decades by the sheer repressive power of their armies and police. Legitimacy may be desirable, but it is not always necessary.

THE AUTHORITARIAN STATE

By one count, of the 175 independent states existing in the later 1980s, almost three-quarters were nondemocratic. Although there are numerous variations of authoritarianism, all have certain characteristics in common. There is limited pluralism, or, in the most extreme cases, none at all. Usually a single leader or a small committee exercises inordinate power, including control of lower level institutions like the parliament — if one is allowed to exist at all — and the judiciary. Some authoritarian systems have clearly defined ideologies; others merely legitimize themselves around such simplistic patriotic notions as fatherland, the nation, law and order, natural hierarchy, national security, anticommunism, or antiimperialism. There is usually a low level of political mobilization, though in fascist and Marxist regimes, the opposite may be the case; the government itself may attempt to mobilize the people toward state ends through rigidly controlled organizations. The limits on state power are ill-defined; the government's power may be relatively benign, or it may reach into the most intimate aspects of people's lives.

To maintain the system requires an effective apparatus of repression — armed forces, national police, secret police. Once the repression becomes routinized, often after a period of brutal state terror, there may be little open opposition for long periods. Independent organizations, whether political, economic, or social, will most likely be banned outright or co-opted by the state. Political parties will be ruled illegal; labor unions will be controlled, banned, or incorporated as state-run syndicates; peasant cooperatives will be ruthlessly suppressed. Government actors are responsible to the state rather than the people. The police and judiciary turn a blind eye to crimes committed by government functionaries. Land may be stolen; taxes may be used as personal wealth (Morlino 1990).

The Neopatrimonial State

The legitimacy of the modern state in the industrial democracies rests upon what Max Weber calls "rational-legal authority": individuals in government exercise their limited powers to accomplish public goals that are defined and accepted within the broad political culture. The system requires a strict division between public and private roles. This is embodied in the concept of "office." As long as the functionary is working in his capacity as an official, his personal life has been superseded by the impersonal duties and responsibilities of the job.

If this system is only approximated in the First World, it hardly exists in most of the Third World, even as an ideal. More common are neopatrimonial states, in which there is little differentiation between public and private roles.

In contrast to the rational-legal model, true patrimonialism is a system based on clientelism. Authority is ascribed to an individual rather than to an impersonal office. The authority is that of a father over his children, in which neither leader nor followers have well-defined functions or powers. Rather than working through a hierarchy of bureaucratic offices, the system is held together by oaths of loyalty, by kinship ties, or by other personalistic relationships. Because its goal is to secure and maintain the privileges of power, patrimonialism tends to be relatively nonideological. In its pure form, it is the political structure of feudalism, which continues to exist in some rural areas of Asia and Latin America. There can be no real corruption in such a system, because there is no separation between individual and public objectives.

When this classic patrimonialism is combined with the bureaucratic state, a curious form of neopatrimonialism evolves. The structure is based on the rational-legal model of a hierarchy of clearly defined bureaucratic offices, but these offices, far from being directed toward the attainment of impersonal public goals, are thought of as virtually the private property of the office holder. Corruption is routine, because the office holder views his position as an opportunity to expand his own wealth and power. Appointments to office are based on personal relationships with those above or as payoffs for political support. The whole system, from top to bottom, is bound together in a series of reciprocal patron-client alliances.

Although a typical neopatrimonial state might ostensibly be run by the army or a political party, it would include a single leader at the top who might be virtually deified. Journalist Henry Horowitz described Baghdad, Iraq, as "a city-wide portrait gallery devoted to a single subject," Saddam Hussein.

The traditional Islamic ban on representation of the human form had been overcome . . . in a very big way. Saddam's face perched on the dashboards of taxis, on the walls of every shop and every office, on clock faces, on ashtrays, on calendars, on billboards at every major intersection — often four pictures to an intersection. Some of the portraits covered entire building fronts. And to ensure that your eye didn't ignore the pictures from sheer repetition, Saddam appeared in innumerable guises: in military fatigues festooned with medals, in bedouin garb atop a charging steed, in pilgrim's robes praying at Mecca, in a double-breasted suit and aviator sunglasses, looking cool and sophisticated. The idea seemed to be that Saddam was all things to all people: omniscient, all-powerful and inevitable. Like God. (Horowitz 1991:107–108)

The impression of power and omniscience was not empty bluster. The secret police actually enforced article 225 of the penal code, which stated that criticism of the president, his Ba'athist party, or the government could be punishable by death. The government was extraordinarily personalized around Hussein and his circle, which included a core of key officials from his own family and clan. The Ba'athist party network was permeated by patron-client relations. Though Saddam, and, thus, all power, belonged to the minority Sunni sect of Muslims, the majority Shiites were kept in check both by severe repression and by the sharing of oil revenues with Shiite areas. Prior to the Gulf War disaster, Saddam traveled the country, constantly seen, persistently establishing personalist bonds with regional and local leaders (Mansfield 1992:404–416).

Bureaucratic Authoritarianism

In many ways, a bureaucratic authoritarian regime is the opposite of the patrimonial system. Whereas the patrimonial state is based on personalist politics, the bureaucratic authoritarian system views itself as rational and objective and may even try to legitimize itself by putting an end to patron-client corruption. Though highly moralistic, often in petty ways, their morality seldom extends to a ban on torture or extrajudicial killing, which may be employed on a large scale to crush and intimidate opposition.

As manifested in the southern cone countries of South America from the 1960s through the 1980s, military coups were not organized by an individual, a faction, or an elite within the officers' corps. Rather, the whole military ruled as an institution, with leadership depending on the normal military hierarchy. Taking over in response to perceived internal threats, the leaders legitimized themselves around an ideology of virulent anticommunism and national security (earning them the designation "national security states"). The system was especially amenable to military and civilian technocrats, who believed that the economy and society could be rationally manipulated toward developmental goals. The state, basing its economic program on "trickle-down" capitalism, worked closely with multinational corporations and banks and tried to provide favorable investment climates by imposing stiff restrictions on wages and workers' benefits. Such programs were, naturally, opposed by unions and by peasant organizations, which were ruthlessly suppressed by the imprisonment, torture, and killing of their leaders (Collier 1979).

Though often criticized as fascist by their critics, these bureaucratic-authoritarian states are very different. Whereas the fascists practiced economic nationalism, these countries clearly admit and accept their dependency within the international arena, opening their borders to foreign investment and influence. Unlike the populist ideology of fascism, there is no attempt to mobilize the masses, even for government programs; on the contrary, the popular sectors are viewed as actual or potential enemies to be suppressed. Finally, whereas fascism legitimized itself by a complex ideology, these states are largely bereft of ideology beyond the doctrine of anticommunism and national security.

Though almost exclusively applied to a set of states in Latin America, many aspects of the bureaucratic-authoritarian model can be found in Indonesia under Suharto and in various African states.

Corporatism

Corporatism is a system in which the state recognizes and deals with only a limited number of organizations that represent specific interest groups. For example, there may be a group representing the landed elite, another representing industrialists, another for urban workers, and so forth. In contrast to pluralist systems, where there may be any number of autonomous and voluntary unions, these organizations are monolithic and compulsory. If there is an organization for industrial workers, it will be the only such organization allowed or, at least, the only one recognized by the government, and all eligible workers will automatically belong to it. These organizations are hierarchically ordered, with the top leadership representing the entire group to the government (Schmitter 1974:93–94).

Corporatism is based on the idea that individuals gain their rights, their identities, and their privileges through membership in groups. Although this may be repugnant to the individualist political culture of the United States, it can be entirely reasonable in the context of the Third World, where the individual who is not embedded in an organization may have few rights and no political power whatsoever. The corporatist ideal is to give people a say in government policy through their officially recognized interest groups. Ostensibly, political demands will be siphoned up the organizational hierarchy from the bottom to the top, where they will be heard, and perhaps even acted on, by the government. In reality, of course, the system gives the state an inordinate degree of control over the crucial extragovernmental power centers of the society (Cawson 1986; Wyn 1985).

Normally, corporatism has only integrated the elites and perhaps urban workers into the governmental system, excluding peasants and the poorer laborers. The Sandinistas, a Marxist revolutionary party that ran Nicaragua from 1979 to 1990, attempted a curious populist form of corporatism that embraced virtually everyone in the society. Six "mass organizations" were incorporated (along with thirty-two political parties) into the Council of State: an urban workers' federation, a similar organization for rural workers, a union of farmers and ranchers, a woman's organization, the Sandinista youth, and the Sandinista Defense Committees. The latter, which held more seats than any other group, consisted of neighborhood committees that carried out national directives on health, education, rationing, and military conscription. As time went on, other major organizations came to prominence, such as an association of health workers, another of teachers, and the Higher Council of Private Enterprise, a virulently anti-Sandinista umbrella organization of businessmen and large-scale landowners. It is difficult to tell how well the system might have worked, because, during virtually its entire tenure, the government was involved in a civil war. As the military and economic situation deteriorated, the organizations increasingly lost their function of guiding government policy through populist input and took on a character of top-down authority. With the Sandinista defeat in the 1990 elections, these organizations abandoned their official connection with government. Some disintegrated; others continued. The Sandinista Defense Committees changed their names to Communal Movements and became almost exclusively concerned with local issues such as sewage, potable water, and electricity. Political parties took over the political functions of the mass organizations (Ruchwarger 1987; Lewellen 1991).

In the early 1930s, some scholars predicted that corporatism would replace democratic liberalism as the political-economic ideology of the twentieth century. This hardly proved true, because the two dominant corporatist states of the era — Nazi Germany and fascist Italy — hardly inspired emulation. However, corporatism can take many forms, both democratic and authoritarian, and it is found in several modern European states, such as Austria, Portugal, and Spain. Many Third World countries have adopted aspects of corporatism, though it is most common in Latin America, where it is virtually part of the political culture.

Military Regimes

The temptation for the security forces to take over the government may be an irresistible one. Although the state ostensibly holds a monopoly on the legitimate use of force, it is the military that has the guns. If the military is autonomous — that is, not under the direct control of the civilian government — it can assume power at virtually any time. The military has several advantages beside guns. For one thing, it has continuity. Civilian dictators or elected presidents may come and go every few years (in some cases, every few months), but the military may have had a continuous existence from the time of independence — decades in Africa and Asia, perhaps 150 years in Latin America. There may be rivalries among the army, navy, air force, and secret police and factions within any particular service, but, relatively speaking, the military has a cohesion and structure that civilian politics lacks.

Outside influence can play a key role. Former colonial powers helped found and staff elite officers' schools that taught not only military tactics but also economics and politics. The army often saw itself as the only force in the country with the strength, cohesiveness, and economic savvy to lead the processes of development. During the Cold War, enormous amounts of military aid and training were extended to Third World militaries around the globe by the the United States and the Soviets for the purpose of either containing communism or advancing it. Immensely strengthened, and supplied with Cold War fervor, many militaries took over, often with the explicit or implicit blessing of one of the great powers.

Military regimes run the gamut from neopatrimonialism to bureaucratic authoritarianism, often with a heavy dose of corporatism, and they may be conservative, reformist, or even revolutionary. However, most do share some common characteristics. Because they do not run for office like political parties and they do not have to put together alliances of elites as do individual dictators, militaries seldom start with much in the way of a popular support base. Even if a large segment of the populace acquiesces to a coup, there is usually a vast gap between the military leadership and the people. This may be why so many such regimes have turned to corporatism to supply linkages with civilian groups. Whatever mechanism is used, as time goes on, there is almost always an attempt to "civilianize" the government in order to give it a degree of legitimacy. However, top-down authority is intrinsic to the military's very nature, and leadership is assumed to consist quite simply in giving orders and having them carried out. In reality, bureaucracies are seldom so easily manipulated, and policy initiatives may suffer the lack of enthusiasm of lower-level functionaries (Cammack, Pool, and Tordoff 1988).

As early as the 1950s, some discouraged political scientists were abandoning their optimistic belief that liberal democracy was the end point of modernization. Without order and stability, they protested, no real progress could be achieved, and the militaries were the most likely to realize that stability. Because the officers' corps were largely from the middle class, they would represent a progressive element, displacing conservative, entrenched elites and leading the way toward greater economic development. None of this turned out to be true. Despite their moral trappings, military dictatorships were as corrupt and self-serving as their civilian counterparts. When, after a few decades of rule, a military junta returned the government to civilians, more often than not, the country's economy was in shambles.

Military dictatorships can be roughly classified into three general types:

Veto regimes seize power in reaction to some threat either to the military itself or to the socioeconomic structure that supports the military. In the 1960s and 1970s, the perceived threat was usually that of communism, with the result that the West either actively supported the coups or ignored their excesses. The taking of power is followed by a period of extreme repression with the goal of reducing political participation and wiping out opposition. Once established in power, these regimes tend toward the bureaucratic authoritarian model. Examples include recent military dictatorships in Chile, Argentina, Uruguay, and Indonesia.

Moderator regimes view themselves as guaranteeing national values and standing above political conflict. Unless an individual general develops a taste for power, such regimes are short-lived and tend to hand the government back to civilians as soon as stability is achieved. The goals of the coup are often quite specific — to change the constitution or to remove specific politicians perceived as corrupt or too radical. Even if the goals are accomplished, the underlying problems may not be solved, because they were simplistically diagnosed in the first place; militaries are not known for realistically analyzing the complexities of issues. If the basic problems are not solved, another intervention may be necessary in a few months or years. The second or third time around, the military may decide to stay for an extended period.

A *breakthrough regime* is one with a radical ideology that makes a real attempt to create new institutions and to manipulate the traditional economic and political structures, including the overthrow of the established oligarchy. For example, the Velasco regime in Peru from 1968 to 1975 initiated a massive land reform — virtually abolishing the hacienda system — and nationalized much of the mineral and fishing wealth of the nation, disposing of old elites while bringing new ones into power. Even more radical left-wing military dictatorships took over in Ethiopia in 1974 and Liberia in 1980. One problem that such regimes may create is factionalism within the military itself; the senior officers usually are loyal to the old regime and must be displaced by a new group of junior officers (Clapham and Philip 1985).

In terms of human rights, military dictatorships have appalling records. According to one comparison, military governments were three times more likely than their civilian counterparts to indulge in the "frequent" use of official violence against citizens, including torture, brutality, disappearances, and political killings (Sivard 1987:27). In the transition from civilian to military rule in Indonesia in 1966, from 500,000 to a million people were murdered by military forces in a nine-month span. During the decades of military dictatorships throughout Latin America that ended in the late 1980s, tens of thousands were murdered by their governments, and torture and "disappearances" became institutionalized. In the 1990s, the military government of Myanmar (Burma) resorted to similar tactics.

DEMOCRACY IN THE THIRD WORLD

Samuel Huntington (1985:255) defines a system as democratic "to the extent that its most powerful collective decision-makers are selected through periodic elections in which candidates freely compete for votes and in which virtually all the adult population is eligible to vote." A more detailed definition would include meaningful *competition* among individuals and groups (especially political parties), a high level of *political participation* so that no major adult groups would be excluded from organizing or voting in regular and fair elections, and substantial *civil and political liberties* to ensure the integrity of the electoral process (Diamond, Linz, and Lipset 1990:6).

By these definitions, the United States could not be considered even remotely democratic for the first two-thirds of its existence; at its inception, only about 15 percent of the adult population could vote; excluded were women, Native Americans, slaves, indentured servants, and, in some states, non-property owners. The percentage of eligible voters did not rise above 50 percent until women were enfranchised in 1920. African-Americans continued to be effectively excluded in many southern states until 1965. This is worth considering when countries only thirty years out of colonialism are held up to First World standards.

To the West, democracy seems such an obvious ideal that it would be only natural if all states were evolving in that direction. Indeed, in the

1950s and 1960s, scholars were optimistic about the democratization of the newly independent countries of Africa, Asia, and the Middle East. However, the pluralistic institutions inherited by colonialism quickly dissolved into authoritarian rule (the only exceptions were some formerly British colonies, such as India, Malaysia, Gambia, and a few Caribbean island nations). In part, this was a logical reversal; although the colonial powers often introduced pluralistic democracies at the last minute, just before granting independence, the long period of colonialism itself was thoroughly autocratic. Also indigenous political cultures were not particularly amenable to democracy. In tribal tradition, decisions are made by consensus, not by majority, and monarchs — whether of small kingdoms or of vast realms — traditionally rule by decree. In the West, there has been a high correlation between Protestantism and democracy, but there were few Protestant countries in the Third World. Historically, Catholicism has an ambiguous record, more often than not supporting oligarchic rule. Though Hinduism is relatively tolerant of all forms of government, Islam — dominant in the Middle East, much of Africa, and parts of South Asia — is actively hostile to democracy. A political culture that values hierarchy and deference to authority — which would include much of the preindustrial world — should not be expected to be particularly supportive of democracy.

Preconditions for Democracy

Democratization in the West followed a linear evolution; institutions and values evolved more or less in a single direction over hundreds of years. In the Third World, the progression has often been a cyclical one, in which despotism alternates with democracy, as is found in Bolivia and Nigeria. Also, in the West, pressures from democracy came largely from the increasing power of a growing middle class. In Third World countries, the middle class usually has been quite small and has been either quiescent or conservative, seeing themselves threatened more by the masses of impoverished below than by the elites above. In the Third World, democratization has seldom been a reaction to populist pressures; rather, it has been instituted from above by the military or the elites, invariably with a view to benefitting themselves. In a democratic system, new elites can gain a foothold of power that might be denied them under a traditional authoritarian system. In addition, revolutionary pressures derived from inequities of wealth can be dissipated through real or illusory popular participation. Democracy can legitimize vast inequities that seem intolerable under authoritarian systems.

Economic development — that is, a raising of the standard of living of the masses — aids the prospects for democracy, partially because extreme impoverishment may require authoritarian repression to keep the poor at bay. Economic development usually coincides with such social improvements as increased literacy and the expansion of mass media, which are conducive to greater political awareness and participation. However, this is a difficult and complicated issue. Although most democracies have a fair degree of economic development, there are just as many or more economically developed countries that are authoritarian. In other words, although economic development may be a necessary precondition for stable democratization, it is by no means a sufficient condition. Developing countries seem to reach a sort of zone of transition where they can choose democracy or authoritarianism, depending on their political culture, the strength and make-up of their elites, and their individual leadership.

Once established, democracies do not seem any better than dictatorships at promoting economic growth or at fostering income equality. Although Taiwan and South Korea are both democratic now, their "miracle" periods of growth and income equalization were products of repressive one-party dictatorships. Costa Rica has fared very well under democracy; India has had so-so economic success; the Dominican Republic remains one of the poorest countries in Latin America.

Pluralism — in the form of a widely differentiated social structure including social classes and well-articulated regional, occupational, ethnic, and religious groups — may be beneficial to democratization. Similarly, a rich associational life is of value. In India, for example, there are voluntary associations devoted to language, social and legal reform, education, freedom of the press, women's rights, and so forth. Dictators tend to suppress or control such groups, so, a country attempting the transition to democracy may have to create them virtually from scratch.

A faith in the fundamental legitimacy of democracy is crucial if democracy is to last. Because there is nothing particularly natural or genetic about democracy, this faith has to be earned over long periods, and incipient democracies may be incompetent at best. If democracy is only tepidly embraced within the political culture, the inevitable failure to cure all social and economic ills may bring about a call for a return to authoritarianism. Other elements of political culture conducive to democracy are a tolerance for opposing viewpoints, a willingness to compromise, pragmatism and flexibility rather than rigid ideologies, moderation in political positions and party identification, and some degree of civility in political discourse (Diamond, Linz, and Lipset 1990). These are often in short supply in revolutionary or transitory political situations.

Types of Democracy in the Third World

Formally, Third World democracies fall into two broad types, based on Western models, and various combinations of these two. Each type has its peculiar advantages and disadvantages.

The presidential system, in which the top leader is elected by the people, puts the emphasis on a strong executive. The legislature may be relatively weak and, in some countries, is little more than a rubber stamp for presidential decisions. Because elections are winner-take-all, small political parties have little chance, so, there are likely to be only two or a few significant parties, all of which may be roughly centrist. On the positive side, a strong president may be able to override party and factional divisiveness and actually get something done. This is especially important where national integration is a serious issue. On the negative side, presidential decision making is not always of the highest quality, and policies that are truly detrimental may be effected with little discussion or debate. Also, many smaller groups will find themselves with no access to power, with the result that the government will have little legitimacy for them.

In parliamentary systems, the locus of power is the legislature; the president or monarch, if there is such, will have only a ceremonial function. The prime minister is voted not by direct elections but by the members of parliament, and he or she represents the parliament, not an autonomous executive. Many parliamentary systems have proportional representation; parties are awarded seats according to how many votes they get. In contrast to winner-take-all elections, this system encourages small parties as well as large ones. Even fringe groups may have some official representation in the government. If there are more than two major parties in the legislature, it is necessary to put together a coalition in order to elect a prime minister. This forces parties to work together. However, because decisions must be made by a group, conflicts and feuding among parties and factions can bring the government to a halt.

Sri Lanka, an island nation south of India, defies easy stereotypes. Although the country is one of the poorest of the Third World, with a per capita gross domestic product of only $470 in 1990, it is one of the more stable and long-lasting democracies in Asia. The governmental system, based on that of France, is a mixture of both the presidential and parliamentary types. The president is exceptionally strong; he not only appoints the prime minister, subject to parliamentary approval, but also presides over and has the authority to dissolve parliament and call new elections. Parties are elected to parliament by proportional representation. The party system is extremely volatile. There are eight major parties as well as numerous minor ones. Because many of these represent antagonistic ethnic groups, such as the dominant Sinhalese and the minority Tamils, or factions within ethnic groups, there is often little cohesion in parliament. Only a strong presidency could override such disunity.

The Sri Lanka system is pervaded by clientelism. Legislators use their powers to gain benefits for their supporters to the extent that parliament is a virtual national employment agency, dispensing jobs to fill the bloated bureaucracy. Family, caste, and ethnicity form the basis for patron-client relations. The system is so personalistic that national leaders, including the president, are regularly referred to by their first names. The patron-client system, rooted in centuries of political culture, has merged with a bureaucratic democracy inherited from colonialism. Given its stability and its exceptionally high levels of health and education, the system seems to work. Still, human rights violations, including political killing and torture, are deplorable (this is also true of other democracies, such as Turkey and Mexico), largely because of a civil war against northern Tamil separatists (Baxter et al. 1987:395–354).

Formally, Sri Lanka approaches the ideal definition of democracy in terms of fair elections, political pluralism, and freedom of political competition. Informally, the country is more or less typical in its clientelism, political patronage, corruption, military influence, ethnic dissension, and oligarchic domination. However, there are degrees, and some countries require a further classification, especially those in transition either from or to authoritarianism.

In semidemocracies, the power of elected officials may be extremely limited; party competition is tightly restricted, as is freedom of press and speech. Although there are formal elections, they do not really represent the popular will. The governments of Senegal, Zimbabwe, and Thailand have all fallen into this category in the recent past.

In hegemonic party systems, one party holds virtually all political power. Opposition parties may be legal, but the electoral machine is so wired that they never win elections. Corrupt electoral practices are so routine that the public may be completely aware of them but powerless or too disinterested to change the system, which may be shot through from top to bottom with clientelism. This has been the form of government practiced for decades in Mexico, where the Institutional Revolutionary Party reigns virtually unchallenged.

Finally, pseudodemocracies are really authoritarian regimes. The state wears a thin mask of democracy to legitimize itself not so much to its own people, who are very well aware of the illusion, but to the international community (Diamond, Linz, and Lipset 1990:7–8). During the 1980s, virtually all power in El Salvador was in the hands of a particularly butcherous military, but fixed elections in 1984 legitimized the government to the U.S. Congress, which continued to pour in massive amounts of aid (ultimately about $6 billion). The elected president was little more than a figurehead; he was so powerless that he could not dismiss officers accused of mass killings, and when his own daughter was kidnapped, he had to beg the military for permission to ransom her.

A Decade of Democracy?

It has often been noted that regional, or even global, politics seems to follow trends. The 1990s promises to be a decade of democratization for the Third World. After a long period of bureaucratic authoritarianism, virtually all of the countries of Latin America have at least assumed the formal attributes of democracy. In sub-Saharan Africa, longstanding neopatrimonial dictatorships are giving way to political parties and elections. In the newly industrializing countries of East Asia, such as Taiwan and South Korea, one-party dictatorships have been succeeded by more pluralistic systems.

The promise is real, but political evolution does not always follow a one-way course. Most of the countries of Africa started out democratic at independence and quickly degenerated into personalistic authoritarianism. The southern cone of Latin America had a long experience with democracy before reverting, one by one, to brutal military dictatorships in the 1960s and 1970s. In few places in the Third World can democracy claim a deep foundation in the national political culture.

The conditions that give rise to authoritarianism still exist. The problems of poverty, vast inequities of wealth and power, entrenched elites, ethnic and class rivalries, rapid population growth, unemployment, and inflation have all been exacerbated by crushing international debts. So far, democracies have not shown themselves any more adept at solving such problems than dictatorships and often are less able to maintain national unity and stability.

Democracies remain fragile, but long-term successes, such as India, suggest that even the poorest, most divided, and conflictual countries may make a go of it. What we will probably *not* see is the widespread adoption of the liberal democracy taken for granted in the First World. Governments, even democratic ones, will be curious mixtures of corporatism, socialism, theocracy, authoritarianism, and clientelism.

SUGGESTED READINGS

Chazan, Naomi, Robert Mortimer, John Ravenhill, and Donald Rothchild, *Politics and Society in Contemporary Africa* (Boulder, Colo.: Lynne Rienner, 1992). This book sets African politics within its historical and social context. Final chapters focus on international relations and the future of Africa.

Clapham, Christopher, *Third World Politics: An Introduction* (Madison: University of Wisconsin Press, 1985). The title is somewhat misleading, because the author is really arguing a theory, namely, that the state is the center of the political sphere in the Third World. From this perspective, Clapham provides a good, jargon-free overview.

Diamond, Larry, Juan J. Linz, and Seymour Martin Lipset, eds., *Politics in Developing Countries: Comparing Experiences with Democracy* (Boulder, Colo.: Lynne Rienner, 1990). The authors see democracy as "the preeminent political issue of our time." This book contains ten specific examples of Third World democracies, ranging from Chile to India and Zimbabwe.

Migdal, Joel S., *Strong Societies and Weak States* (Princeton, N.J.: Princeton University Press, 1988). In contrast to Clapham, Migdal sees the state as central in only a few countries. The more normal pattern is that of a weak state in conflict with other power centers, such as the military, elites, and ethnic groups.

Weiner, Myron, and Samuel P. Huntington, eds., *Understanding Political Development* (Boston: Little, Brown, 1987). Huntington provides a concise overview of the "Goals of Development." There follow eight chapters on subjects ranging from political change in specific world regions to agrarian politics and the role of foreign capital.

Wynia, Gary W., *The Politics of Latin American Development* (Cambridge: Cambridge University Press, 1978). Much has happened since this book was published in 1978, but Wynia's game theory approach remains fresh. He delineates the "players" (business elites, the military, foreign interests, etc.) then analyses the various games that politicians play in Latin America, such as populism, democracy, and military authoritarianism.

7

So Many People, So Little Time: Population, Urbanization, and Migration

There is an old tale, told by mathematicians, about a wise man who saved the life of a very rich and powerful Chinese emperor. In return, the emperor offered a reward of anything the sage desired, whether it be half the kingdom, a treasure in diamonds, a palace, or the emperor's most beautiful daughter in marriage.

"No," said the wise man, "what I ask is much more modest. I would like you to take a chessboard and put one grain of rice on the first square on the first day, two grains on the second square on the second day, four grains on the third square on the third day, and so forth, doubling each day through all sixty-four squares."

"Done!" exclaimed the emperor, thinking he had gotten off easily — and thereupon gave away all of the rice that would be produced in China for the next five hundred years.

That is the way that exponential growth works. An exponential progression increases by doubling: 1, 2, 4, 8, 16, 32. . . . Growth may remain small for a long time then suddenly burgeons with great rapidity as higher and higher numbers double.

World population has been growing exponentially since at least 1650. Some estimates even suggest that exponential growth, broken now and then by famine and plagues, extends back to the dawn of humankind, though the numbers would not have been large enough to be particularly noticeable until the last few centuries. It is well-known that exponential systems have a tendency to collapse if they are not stabilized. The ember from a cigarette thrown carelessly from a passing car may smolder among dead leaves for hours, burning at first slowly, then surging into a conflagration that will devour the surrounding forest before dying out.

One of the earliest scholars to observe that population was increasing exponentially was Thomas Malthus (1766–1834), who countered the optimism of the time that held that social problems could be eliminated by application of reason. Although population increases at an exponential (or, in his terms, "geometric") rate, said Malthus, food increases only at an arithmetic rate (one, two, three, four, five . . .). Population would, thus, overwhelm the food supply, so that "positive checks" such as famine and epidemic would be necessary to bring human numbers back down.

Is it true that the growing world population consumes resources at such a rate that humanity itself is in danger? This was the question posed, and answered affirmatively by *The Limits to Growth* (Meadows et al.), a report published in 1972 by a group of scientists called the Club of Rome. According to this study, not only is population increasing exponentially, but resources also are declining exponentially. When these numbers are run through a computer with other systems subject to exponential growth or decline, such as pollution, food per capita, and industrial output, the result is that civilization collapses about the year 2040. "Collapse," in addition to the drying up of resources, means catastrophic decline in world population — several billion people — between 2040 and 2100. Although much less specific about outcomes, Paul and Anne Ehrlich (1968, 1990) view the population "explosion" as a crisis that is being insufficiently acknowledged by a somnolent world headed for disaster.

Computers no longer retain the mystique that they held when *The Limits to Growth* study became a bestseller and frightened a lot of thinking people out of their wits. A detailed critique of the study, titled *Models of Doom* (Cole et al. 1973), suggested that a basic doctrine of computing, "garbage in, garbage out," had been transmuted to "Malthus in, Malthus out." Though the Club of Rome group had used the best data available and one of the largest academic computers of the time, their results were preordained by their Malthusian assumptions. It really does not take a computer to show that exponential growth cannot continue indefinitely, and when several exponential systems are combined, the outcome is inevitable. Also, there were a lot of factors that were not plugged into the computer model, such as increased technology, better methods of finding and extracting resources, substitution of declining resources for those more plentiful, and so forth. Equally problematical was the assumption of a world that was more integrated than it really is. Population growth in the industrialized countries is low, and a number of Third World countries have reduced their rates of growth dramatically.

However, the original authors of *Limits to Growth* took such criticisms into account in their later book *Beyond the Limits* (1992), in which they plugged up-to-date statistics into their world model. Although emphasizing that humans still have time to alter existing tendencies and establish stability, they conclude: "If the present growth trends in world population, industrialization, pollution, food production, and resource depletion continue unchanged, the limits to growth on this planet will be reached sometime within the next 100 years. The most probable result will be a sudden and uncontrollable decline in both population and industrial capacity" (Meadows, Meadows, and Randers 1992:xiii).

If many demographers would offer a more moderate assessment and are now talking more about "problems" than "crises," the severity of those problems should not be minimized. Population growth is manifesting itself not only in diminished resources but also in the too-rapid growth of cities and the voluntary or forced migrations of tens of millions of people each year.

POPULATIONS IN TRANSITION

Estimates of world population for more than a few hundred years ago are crude, to say the least, based as they are on settlement patterns and the carrying capacity of land given certain levels of technology. It is clear, however, that relative to the modern era, populations were small and were sometimes stable for long periods. There may have been only from 275 to 345 million inhabitants of the earth in the year 1000 A.D. (it now takes about four years to *add* that many people). After the first millennia of the Christian era, populations probably increased fairly rapidly, and from about 1750, that increase became a surge. It is not clear why populations grew so fast in the past 300 years; certainly the industrial revolution can account for much of the expansion in Europe, but we also find similar increases in other parts of the world, such as Russia and China, where circumstances were very different. In any case, it is in the twentieth century that population growth really takes off. The world's first billion was achieved only in the early 1800s; by 1930, there is a second billion; a third billion is added in the next thirty years, and a fourth — by 1973 — in the next thirteen years. Despite a slowdown in the rate of growth, it still takes only about thirteen years to add a billion. The population in 1994 was about 5.6 billion, and by the year 2000, world population will be over six billion (Figure 7.1).

Because almost all First World countries and many former Second World countries have more or less stabilized their populations, virtually all new growth is taking place in the Third World. The doubling time varies greatly from country to country and region to region. Growth rate is determined on a world basis by subtracting the number of deaths from the number of live births; in specific countries, one must also include the effects of emigration and immigration. A growth rate of 1 percent will double in seventy years. (The U.S. increase was less than 1 percent in 1990, including both natural increase and net immigration.) A 2 percent increase will double in about thirty-five years, and 3 percent will double in twenty-three years. (A convenient way to calculate doubling time is to divide seventy by the percentage rate; for example, 70 ÷ 3 = 23.) A few countries, such as Kenya and China, briefly attained over 4 percent, which would double in about seventeen years. If these

FIGURE 7.1
World Population — Past and Projected to 2100

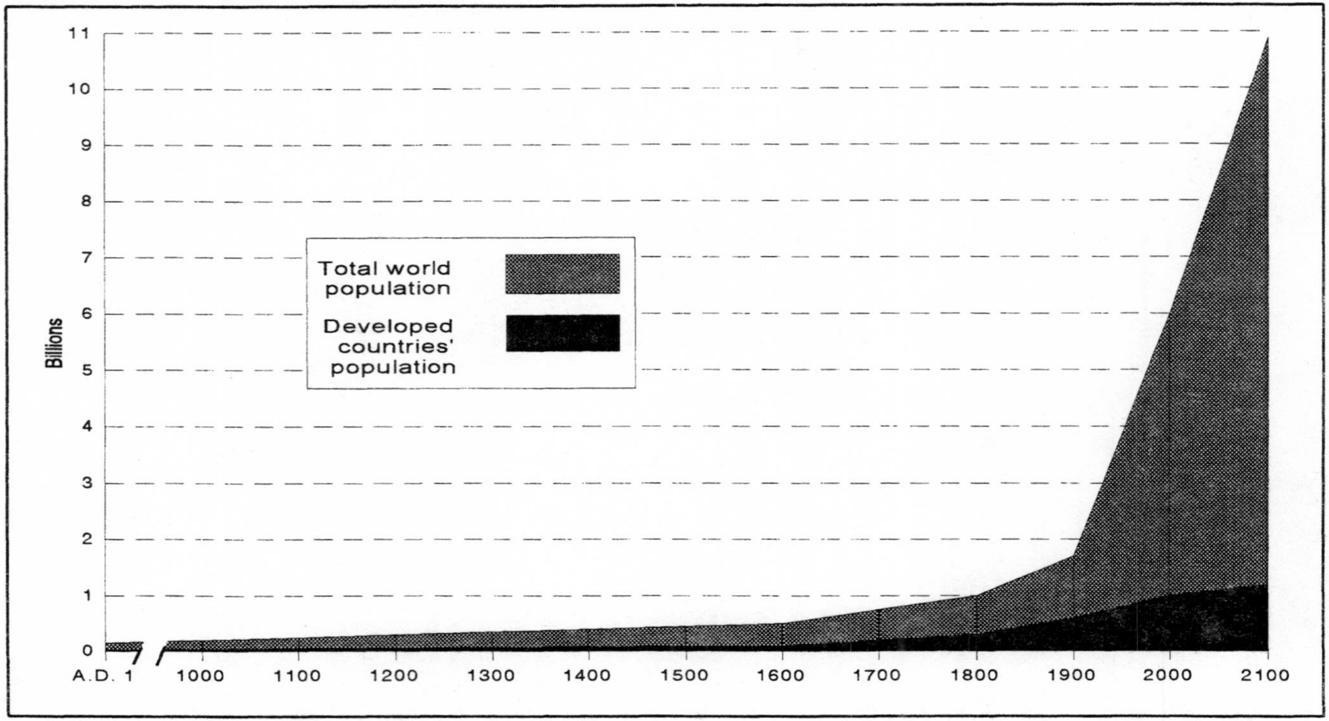

Source: World Bank, *World Development Report 1984* (New York: Oxford University Press, 1984), p. 3.

rates had been sustained, which, blessedly, they were not, the country would have had to double its food supply, jobs, schools, teachers, doctors, houses, electrical output, and so forth in just over a decade and a half just to stay even. As it is, most Third World countries need to double production and services in twenty to thirty years just to maintain present standards. Doubling time for the world as a whole peaked in the mid-1960s at a mere thirty-three years and declined to about forty years in 1990.

A major determinant of growth is the age structure of the population. In developed countries, most people are in their middle years, so they are emerging from their prime childbearing period. In countries with rapidly increasing populations, a large proportion of people will be young, as shown in Figure 7.2. In the developing world as a whole, about 40 percent of the population is under fifteen years of age; in Zambia and Yemen almost half the population are children. This means that a majority of people will be coming into their childbearing years. Even the most ambitious of family planning programs is often struggling upstream against the sheer numbers of childbearing couples.

Age structure is important in regard not only to fertility and mortality but also to productive labor. Old people and children are dependent on others to support them (though child labor, usually at very low levels of productivity, is fairly common in the Third World). In the United States, for every hundred people in their productive years, about fifty are dependent. Third World countries normally have much higher dependency ratios; in Mexico and Syria, there are about as many dependents as there are productive adults. This means that in precisely those countries where production is often lowest, each working individual must produce for more dependents than in the First World (Kammeyer and Ginn 1986; Ehrlich and Ehrlich 1990; World Bank 1984, 1992).

The effects of rapid population growth extend beyond pressures on critical resources. It has often been noted that the world can support many more people than now exist, which is true, but that assumes that food and other resources are distributed according to need. The fact is that vast maldistribution is the norm, both globally and within individual countries. Whether or not a country can feed and clothe its population depends to a great extent on the nature of its economy. Japan, which has a very high population density, thrives through exporting high-tech manufacture and importing a great deal of food. By redistributing wealth, China has, until recently, sustained a huge population at relatively high nutrition levels without importing much food. Neither of these options seem realistic for countries like El Salvador or India; the deeply ingrained economic systems of such countries assure immense inequalities in distribution of domestic resources and in the gains from exports, so that population growth at the bottom

FIGURE 7.2
Typical Distribution of Population by Age

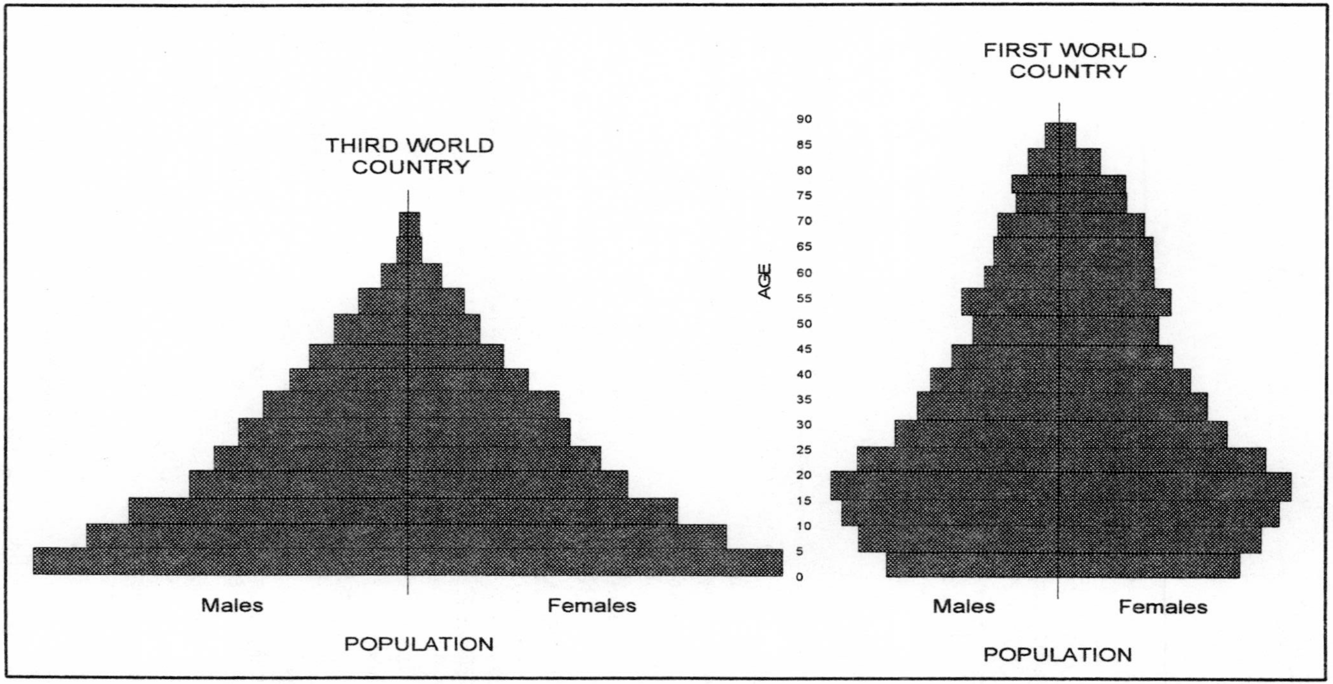

Third World countries tend to have young populations, with most of the people coming into their childbearing years. First World countries have older populations, with most people either beyond or moving beyond their prime childbearing years.

of the economic pyramid will inevitably lead to malnutrition and increased poverty.

The Demographic Transition

Why is population growing so rapidly in the Third World while it has stabilized in the First World? The answer would seem to lie in the "demographic transition," which is partially historical description and partially controversial theory. As countries modernize, they will pass through three phases. First, in the pretransition stage, both mortality and fertility will be high, with the result that population will be more or less in equilibrium. As a country starts to develop, it enters the transition stage in which fertility remains high but deaths decrease, with a resultant rapid increase in population. Finally, the posttransition period is ushered in when fertility rates fall and a new equilibrium is established. The transition is, thus, the period between the decline in mortality rates and the decline in fertility rates (Figure 7.3).

Most mortality is among the very young or the very old, so that reducing infant deaths and adding a year or two to the average life span can have great consequences. Not only do populations grow, but the dependency ratio also increases dramatically. Until recently, medical advances have not been as significant in reducing the death rate as is commonly thought. Simple improvements in the water supply, in sanitation, and in diet have been much more important. The construction of the London sewer system had a considerable impact on mortality, as did the introduction of the potato into the European diet. More recently, the spraying of DDT to kill malaria-bearing mosquitos has greatly affected death rates in tropical countries. Even improved transportation can have an effect; in the Andes, fresh fruits and vegetables can be quickly moved by truck among the various ecological zones so that diets for even the poorest are more diversified. Anything that increases a mother's nutrition will also increase the life chances of her babies. At the other end of the spectrum, life expectancy is higher in the Third World today than it was at similar levels of income in the First World, and it continues to rise.

Reduction in the death rate is relatively uncomplicated. Positive changes that make people healthier are easily embraced, and such changes seldom threaten traditional culture. Reducing fertility, however, may be difficult and complex. In order to compensate for high mortality rates, traditional cultures evolve deep-seated mores and ideologies to maintain high fertility. These cannot be changed overnight. Religious doctrines, moral codes, educational systems, laws, customs, marriage practices, and the structure of the family may all be oriented toward high fertility. In agrarian societies, the extended family is the primary social group, and wealth and power derives from having the largest families possible. Challenging such conventions may require

FIGURE 7.3
The Demographic Transition

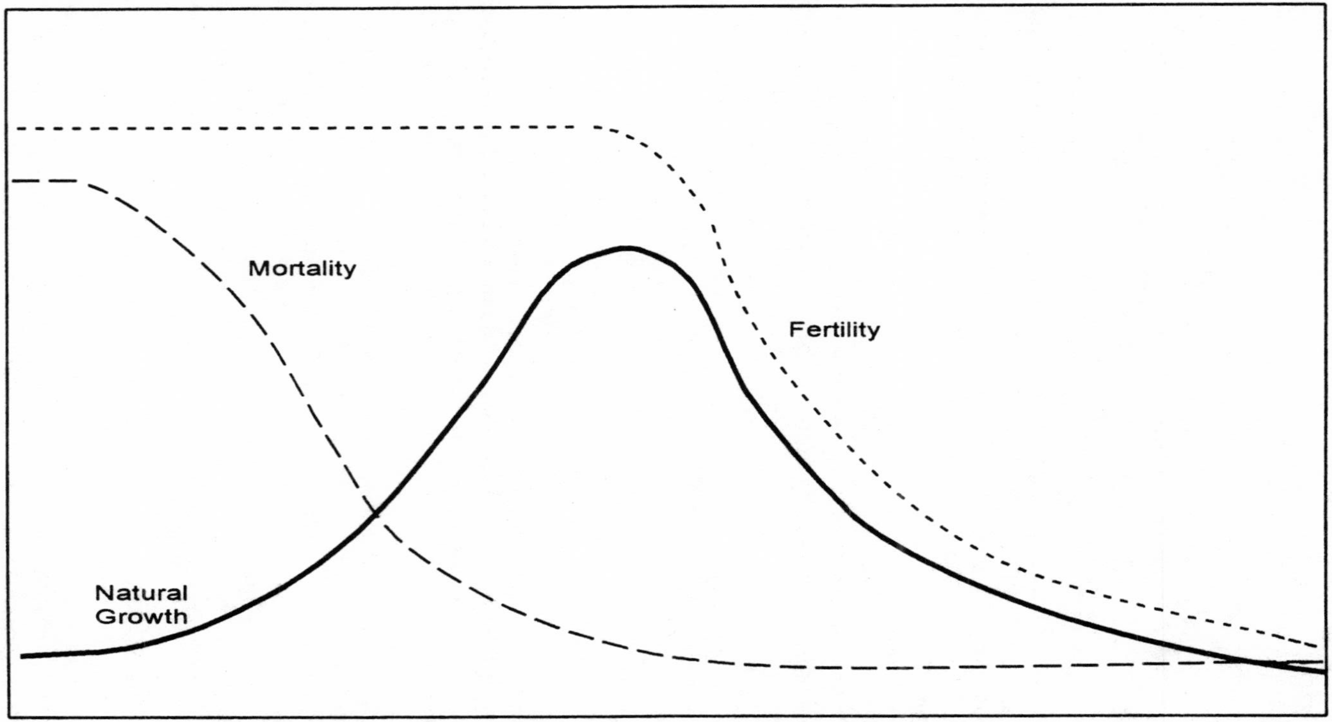

Fertility

Mortality

Natural
Growth

nothing less than the reorganization of the society. From the individual perspective, even though mortality declines, for some time, a woman may continue to have babies on the formerly accurate assumption that one out of three will die before age five.

In addition, there are quite practical economic reasons for poor people to have as many children as possible. Throughout the world, it is common for children to take care of their younger brothers and sisters, thus, relieving their mothers of a great deal of work. Children are also involved at young ages in such productive activities as cooking, washing clothes, carrying firewood and water, and marketing. Peruvian and Nepalese children as young as five or six shepherd farm animals. Indonesian teenagers in traditional communities commonly work eight to ten hours a day. In countries without pensions or social security — which would include almost all of the Third World — people must depend upon their children for survival in old age; old people without children or whose children have died may find themselves reduced to begging.

A decline in mortality can occur with no input whatsoever on the part of the individual, who is a passive benefactor if the state sprays against malaria or chlorinates the water supply. However, in order for fertility rates to decline, both cultural and individual attitudes must change. Fertility decline must be a conscious decision. Some of the things that affect that decision are a decrease in the labor value of children and an increase in the costs of raising a child, old age security, the breakdown of the extended family, increased mobility, secularization of society, an increase in individuality, and the emergence of the assumption that one can control one's fate — all characteristics of Western industrial society.

Urbanization has often been claimed as a primary determinant of fertility reduction, but cities often have very high natural growth rates. Children may continue to be perceived as economic assets — through begging, doing odd jobs, or helping at home — even in the city. Many traditional values can be brought to the city, especially if strong family networks are maintained and if people live in cultural enclaves. Birth rates are generally lower in cities than in rural areas but not necessarily for all sectors of the urban population.

It was originally assumed, based on the Western experience, that industrialization was necessary to bring about fertility decline. However, some theorist now believe that fertility decline is universal once there has been a radical reduction in mortality. According to this point of view, once mortality has decreased, fertility will follow; the question is how long will be the gap between the two. Current evidence supports this hypothesis; though declines in fertility occurred earliest in the most rapidly developing Third World countries, reductions have been registered even in countries with very low levels of industrialization or economic growth. The highly Europeanized Southern Cone countries of

Latin America — Argentina, Uruguay, and Chile — achieved decreasing fertility by the end of the nineteenth century. A few small, densely populated societies that were open to Western influences, such as Taiwan, Sri Lanka, and Puerto Rico, were already showing the first signs of fertility decline by midcentury. The decade of the 1960s was a crucial turning point when three of the most populous countries — China, India, and Brazil — started the final phase of the demographic transition. By the early 1980s, most Third World countries were either starting or well-advanced in stabilizing or reducing birth rates, though there are still a few (mainly African) countries in which birth rates continue to climb.

Though the doubling rate for population in the early 1990s was about forty years, it should not be expected that the population will actually double in that period. The world population growth rate is declining. However, the population base is now so high, with so many young people coming into childbearing age, that billions will be added before the Third World completes the demographic transition. Western Europe took as much as three hundred years to stabilize its population once its mortality had started to decline; Japan, which is quite exceptional in this regard, took less than a hundred years. Another century or two of continued growth before global stabilization may bode a dark future for a world that is already having a hard time feeding its current population (Chesnais 1992; World Bank 1984; Orubuloye 1991).

Population Policy

What should be done about population growth?

The answer depends on how critical the problem — if there is a problem — is perceived to be. Neo-Malthusians, such as the Club of Rome and Paul Ehrlich, believe that we are already in a crisis situation. Malthus himself rested his argument on two fundamental assumptions: first, that technological change could not increase the food supply faster than the growth of population; and, second, that population would ultimately be reduced by an increased death rate caused by famine, disease, and war. With some adjustment, both views still can be defended. In many countries, there has indeed been a severe decline in per capita food production (though population growth is only one factor involved), and there do seem to be places where the death rate is increasing because the land can no longer support all of the people trying to sustain themselves on it. For Neo-Malthusians, ecological catastrophe is close upon us, and every effort should be expended by governments to reduce fertility as rapidly as possible. For such theorists, who perceive the earth as a single, integrated and interdependent ecological system, *world* population growth is the issue; population within the United States and Western Europe needs to be addressed as much as that in the Third World (after all, the First World uses the vast majority of the world's resources).

At the other end of the ideological spectrum, Julian Simon (1977, 1981) argues that historical evidence reveals that people are "the ultimate resource" and that population growth leads to improvements in living conditions, not to deterioration. There is no population problem, let alone a crisis. Far from depleting natural resources, population growth increases pressure to find and extract more raw materials and to expand food production through new technology. The more people there are, the more minds there are to apply to solving social and economic issues.

Although Simon is correct that rapid population growth in the West was accompanied by even more rapid rises in income and the increased development of new technology, it makes little sense to assume these same dynamics apply to the Third World. Indeed, it should be blatantly obvious by now that population growth in much of the Third World does not coincide with economic betterment. Vast inequities of land ownership and wealth in the underdeveloped countries — not to mention large armies, amply supplied by the West, whose job is to maintain elite power — prevent the masses from effectively pressuring for more food or for a greater share of goods. Hungry people do not solve complex technological or social problems, and the well-fed educated people too often follow the "brain drain" to the United States or England. Resources are not being used by the Third World peoples but are being exported on a massive scale to the West. Despite his fringe status among demographers, Simon's views were quite popular with conservative politicians during the Reagan administration, who wanted to reduce the U.S. role in the promotion of family planning in the Third World. A few leaders in Africa, Latin America, and Asia have taken positions similar to Simon's, arguing that greater numbers provide larger domestic markets and, thus, encourage industrialization. Population reduction, from their perspective, is a U.S. and European plot to reduce the power of non-Western peoples.

Policy makers have generally assumed a middle position, holding that population growth is indeed a problem, but one that is soluble with proper intervention. One orientation, which might be called the "development-is-the-best-contraceptive" approach, starts from the empirical observation that all industrialized countries have stabilized their populations. The demographic transition can be accelerated by speeding up the rate of development. A redistribution of international wealth would not only help Third World countries develop faster but also would hasten their passage through the demographic transition. Such an approach has been amenable to Catholics, who oppose family planning programs, and socialists, who see underdevelopment and capitalist exploitation as the underlying cause of too-rapid population growth. Although this position has its virtues, many of the countries with the fastest growing populations are, realistically, the least likely to develop in the foreseeable future, because they lack the infrastructure and the political and economic institutions that promote development. Also, there is good evidence that economic development may be retarded by rapid population growth, as poor and indebted countries are forced to shift resources to feeding and housing large underemployed and minimally productive workers as well as an increasing proportion of dependent children and old people. Development-before-population-reduction policies would seem to put the cart before the horse. To simply wait for such countries to develop might be a prescription for disaster.

Another approach, which has been quite successful in some instances and a failure in others, is for the government to actively promote family planning. This involves providing knowledge about reproductive physiology and contraception, making contraceptives and sterilization available, and propagandizing to change traditional attitudes about large families. The Indian government adopted family planning as early as 1952 but did not vigorously pursue it until 1976, under Prime Minister Indira Gandhi. Unfortunately, strong incentives became coercive in the hands of local promoters; in Delhi, a couple with three or more children had to submit to sterilization in order to get a driver's license or a telephone. In one village, four hundred men were arbitrarily arrested and forcibly sterilized. Public reaction against such practices was so great that the next prime minister disassociated himself from the program. Later, a greatly moderated revision of it was revived. Despite setbacks, overall success has been impressive; the population growth rate in India was reduced from 2.3 percent to 1.7 percent. The family planning approach has been officially adopted in South Korea, Mexico, and Indonesia, with significant results. The Mexican government even hired Madison Avenue admen to assist in their promotional efforts. In order to associate contraception with masculinity, condoms were sold in the colors of favorite soccer teams, and a phallic "condom-man" in a soccer uniform adorned T-shirts sold at sporting events.

Because of the force of tradition and the continued perception of children as economic assets (even when this is not objectively true), family planning alone as a strategy is seldom successful. It must be combined with structural changes — sometimes called the "societalist approach" — that involve the education of women and the removal of the need to depend on sons and daughters for support in old age. Several studies have suggested that the education of women provides one of the most powerful tools for the acceptance of family planning. Education can give women a sense that they can control their own destinies so that they assume a greater decision-making role in the household. Educated women are more likely to know about and adopt contraception. They are more likely to delay marriage past the teen years and, if they find employment in the modern sector, to marry and have children much later than they otherwise would. Education in literature introduces Western conceptions of romantic love and companionate marriage as well as the legitimacy of small families. In Tamil Nadu, India, in the 1970s, the government started providing free midday meals for children in primary schools. The program resulted in an enormous increase in enrollment, including that of girls, because the extra meal saved scarce family resources and pupils could sometimes bring some food home. The first girls in the program began to marry in 1985, and in the next six years, the birth rate dropped more than 25 percent. Studies elsewhere have reaffirmed the importance of education for girls even at very low levels; as more grades are completed, the effect increases accordingly (Mathews 1994). Aside from the education of girls, there are many other societal changes that can help reduce the fertility rate, including raising the legal age of marriage, enacting child labor laws, and providing subsistence benefits for the elderly.

The United Nations (UN) has been a cauldron for controversies over population. A Population Commission was established in 1946 to disseminate information but with little decision-making power. At the time, the United States, England, Sweden, and India were in the forefront of the position that population growth needed to be addressed by government intervention. Catholic and communist countries either denied there was a problem or held that development was the solution (their agreement ended there, because Catholics oppose birth control while socialists are all for it). A UN-sponsored World Population Conference in Bucharest, Romania, originally sought to establish an international policy supporting family planning but split apart between two factions — the "redistributionists," who emphasized Third World development via the New International Economic Order (see Chapter 5), and the "incrementalists," who advocated active efforts by governments to reduce population. As it stands, different countries are adopting different policies or no policy at all, depending on their perceptions of population growth. Those who opt for an interventionists policy can find assistance through a number of international public and private agencies.

Population Policy in China

No large Third World country has been as successful at reducing its population growth as China, which from a peak annual rate of over 4 percent had achieved 1.3 percent by the 1990s. The feat was all the more remarkable considering the precipitous drop in the death rate: infant mortality is one of the lowest (twenty-nine per thousand live births) and life expectancy among the highest (over seventy) in the Third World. China accomplished its birth rate decline through a combination of societal changes and family planning policies. With a fifth of the world's population, China's demographic efforts inevitably have a profound effect on world statistics.

In 1949, when the communists assumed control of a rural, impoverished, and war-torn nation, Chairman Mao Zedong did not believe that there was a population problem. Several of the structural changes that were introduced, however, tended to have the effect of lowering the growth rate. The traditional patriarchal family was challenged as women were given equal rights. In 1950 the legal age for marriage was raised to eighteen for women and twenty for men. Direct action on reducing births was not introduced until 1954, with a modest family planning program that included the distribution of contraceptives and education in their use. The program was abandoned in 1958 because the population was in decline, more from food shortages caused by government blunders than from family planning. The program was resumed in 1962, but it was not until 1971 that China got really serious about its population problem. With its self-sufficient economy and only 11 percent of its land base capable of producing food, the government saw its only options as either decreasing fertility or abandoning the gains of the revolution. Through its "Later, Longer, Fewer" campaign, couples were encouraged to marry later, space their births longer apart, and have fewer children.

The famous "one-child" campaign was begun in 1979 as a policy that involved tremendous social pressures but no direct legal compulsion. It is doubtful that there ever was truly a one-child policy for the nation as a whole; administration of the policy was given to local cadres, and in rural areas where children were needed for labor, two or three children might be permitted without sanction. However, in towns and cities, the one-child ideal was often taken very seriously. In 1980, the marriage age was raised to twenty for women and twenty-two for men. Contraceptives and abortions were provided free; paid vacations and other bonuses were awarded those who were sterilized. After the first birth, a one-child certificate was issued that obligated the parents to refrain from having more children but provided numerous benefits, including a monthly pay bonus of up to 8 percent until the child was fourteen, extra housing space, preferential treatment for new housing, plus supplementary old age care above the pension provided by law. An only child was given priority admittance to nurseries, kindergartens, and schools and was exempted from tuition. When such a child grew up, he or she would receive priority in job assignments. The carrot-and-stick policy also included sanctions, such as reductions in pay, for those who had more than the allotted number of children.

Although highly successful relative to other Third World countries, the policy has not brought the population growth rate down as much or as fast as the government had hoped. Some of the negative effects include cases of coerced abortions and sterilizations, forced by local cadres competing to meet quotas, and a significant rise — strenuously opposed by the government — in the number of female infanticides by couples who want their only child to be a boy. The most telling effect may be down the road twenty or thirty years when an entire generation of only children — who have been the focal points of innumerable doting grandparents, aunts, and uncles — become politically active. Such adults may not be particularly amenable to the collectivist culture of austerity bequeathed by the revolution.

Although some of the more coercive facets of China's policy would be incompatible with less-authoritarian regimes, there are important aspects that could be emulated. The family planning part of the program would not have worked nearly so well if there were not several structural changes in the social and economic systems. A major driving force of population growth is the perception of children as economic assets; with the Chinese communal system of land tenure, a child's work is added to a pool of several hundred rather than just to the family, so the labor value from the parents' point of view is severely reduced. Support in old age, as well as medical treatment, is provided by the commune or the state, so that children are no longer necessary as the sole source of old age insurance. Reducing the labor value of children and providing security to the aged is more important to population stabilization than making modern contraceptives available.

THE THIRD WORLD CITY

The Third World, with the exception of parts of Latin America and Southeast Asia, remains predominantly rural, but cities are bearing the brunt of population growth. In 1950, only ten cities in the Third World had more than one million inhabitants; by 1990, there were 171 such cities, with nine exceeding ten million. In addition, there are hundreds of cities with populations from 500,000 to a million, as well as numerous small urban centers that did not even exist forty years ago. At midcentury, only about 16 percent of Third World peoples lived in cities, while today, the figure is close to 40 percent, and within the next three decades, as much as two-thirds of Third World people may reside in urban areas. Mexico City, which may soon top Tokyo as the largest city in the world, if it has not already done so, is growing from just over three million in 1950 to over twenty-five million by the year 2000. At that time, twelve of the world's fifteen largest cities will be in the Third World (Kasarda and Parnell 1993; Hardoy, Mitlin, and Satterwaite 1990).

If an American were to find himself suddenly set down in the middle of one of these large cities, he might assume he was still in the United States. He would be surrounded by glass and steel skyscrapers, the streets would be jammed with honking cars, many people would be dressed in business suits and ties, and there would be signs advertising McDonald's, Kentucky Fried Chicken, and Arnold Schwarzenegger movies. The sense of familiarity would be illusory. Despite the adoption of Western urban architecture and fashion, Third World cities are very different from those in the United States or Europe. They have unique histories and structures. Although cities in the West grew at a gradual pace, in the developing countries, there has been a true urban explosion; New York required 150 years to add eight million new residents, but Mexico City and São Paulo accomplished that feat in less than fifteen years. If our hypothetical U.S. observer were to leave the city center, he might find that the skyscrapers, apartment buildings, and middle class suburban homes were ringed with makeshift shantytowns, crowded with houses built of scrap lumber and tin. There might be enclaves of recent immigrants still wearing the colorful traditional dress of the countryside. Open markets would bustle with small-scale entrepreneurs selling from carts.

The disparity between the rich and poor would be even more blatant than in cities in the United States, and it would be obvious that the percentage of poor was quite large. Most large cities suffer all of the problems of too-rapid growth: underemployment, inadequate sanitation, poorly distributed and possibly contaminated water, air pollution, traffic congestion, and overpacked public transportation. Nevertheless, cities are also the focal points of much that is the best a nation has to offer; here are the museums, the universities, the monumental architecture. If you want to hear the best jazz in Africa, go to Lagos, Nigeria. Calcutta and Bombay are the capitals of the Indian film industry, the largest in the world. For dance and music, it would be hard to find a city more lively than Rio de Janeiro. In short, Third World cities are as unique as individual people, and equally complex and contradictory.

The Emergence of the Modern Third World City

Cities, often quite sizable ones, long preceded European expansion, but colonialism would put its stamp on almost all of the larger urban complexes of the Third World. Tenochtitlan and Cuzco, respectively the capitals of the Mexican Aztec empire and the Andean Incas, were both razed to the ground in warfare and rebuilt by the Spanish conquerors. Throughout the Third World, small towns were restructured and entirely new cities were built, often situated by the coast or along navigatable waterways. The distribution of cities was determined not by indigenous factors but by the needs of the colonialists and imperialists for ports for export and for access to the ores and agricultural commodities of the hinterland. In Asia, during the period of mercantilism based on private companies, Europeans established small trading settlements or enclaves within existing cities. As trade expanded, settlements grew larger to include troops needed to protect warehouses, and, gradually, companies took over the production process itself, requiring more European administrators. Though the large port was the more typical colonial city, there were also innumerable military garrisons, mining centers, and secondary trading posts.

The industrial revolution greatly accelerated the pace of colonial urbanization. The growing need for raw materials and for food for the factory workforce required more than a toehold in the supplier country. In Asia and Africa, European governments stepped in to replace private companies. The extraction and transport of raw materials on an ever-expanding scale required the restructuring of entire societies. The British, no longer confined to enclaves, built cities based on their own culture, with broad boulevards, churches, theaters, clubs, and middle class housing. Improved transportation, including railways, permitted a separation of workplace and residence. Politically and economically cities were structured on the dominant-subordinate relationship between the colonizers and the colonized. The needs and desires of a very small proportion of the population, the European administrative elite, shaped the colonial cities.

In the West, many modern cities emerged principally as manufacturing centers, drawing labor as it was needed from the surrounding countryside. In the Third World, industrialization was not the initial impetus to the growth of cities; many cities had little manufacturing. Cities were mainly administrative centers or ports for export. Their raison d'etre was overseas trade rather than the needs of the natives. Connections with the hinterland were narrowly restricted to lines of transport for trade goods, and there were few links with neighboring countries, which might be under competing colonial powers.

With the end of colonialism, indigenous people flocked into the cities. Lacking a manufacturing base, however, urban jobs were scarce. Cities maintained their colonial appearance under new rulers and, in many cases, a similar dominant-subordinate structure. The major new additions were the ever-present shantytowns and the emergence of informal economic systems (Drakakis-Smith 1987; Reitsma and Kleinpenning 1989).

The Long Road to the City

An early academic stereotype pictured cities growing almost exclusively through floods of rural migrants. In reality, natural population increase accounts for most growth. Urbanization does not of itself lower fertility; those urban factors that do effect a decline in births, such as increased education and later age of marriage, may be found just as well in the countryside. However, migration will account for anywhere from a third to a half of the growth of cities (though in some Southern Cone countries of Latin America, migration has declined to a trickle), and these new urbanites will put a tremendous pressure on overburdened administrators to supply jobs, utilities, and services. Because the majority of these migrants will find themselves settled in slums or shantytowns, eking out a bare living, it may well be asked why they come at all.

The answer seems to be that no matter how bad city poverty may appear to an outsider, things are worse in the countryside. Both "pull" and "push" factors stimulate rural-urban migration. A "bright lights" theory of migration suggests that radio advertising and soap operas reaching the most remote urban areas portray the city as attractive, fun, and exciting. This image is reinforced by reports from returning migrants and is especially appealing to young men and women. Other pull factors include the promise of education for oneself or one's children and better health facilities.

Push factors, however, are probably the more important motivators. People move mainly to improve their economic circumstances. There may be little employment in rural areas, even at the extremely low wages that are normal in agriculture. Few opportunities exist and, thus, little hope for the future. The expansion of commercial planta- tions evicts subsistence farmers from their land or forces them onto marginal lands incapable of feeding a family. Mechanization of agriculture destroys jobs. Rural poverty, by itself, however, is not a sufficient explanation. Families that move or that send their sons, daughters, or husbands to the city are seldom the most impoverished. Education and literacy are crucial factors; of those who go to the city, almost all are better educated than those left behind. Also, it is important to have contacts in the city, as well as sufficient money to get there. In addition to poverty, natural disasters such as drought or flood may impel people to seek new lives in the city. Often, political violence, whether outright warfare, ethnic conflict, or death squad activity, can drive many into the cities (Gilbert 1994; Parnwell 1993).

Early rural-urban migration in the Third World was characterized by a series of steps from towns to smaller cities to the metropolis, each new move increasing the distance from home. This was typical, for example, of the Quechua Indians of Peru moving from their mountain homes to the coastal capital of Lima. Such migration often required more than one generation before an individual or family finally settled in a major city. This pattern still exists, especially where great distances — both physical and cultural — are involved, but there are many other patterns.

Three significant themes have emerged from recent migration studies. First, urban migration is tightly embedded within social relations. Migration is a group decision, made by the family as a whole. Within the city itself, it is necessary to have a network of friends or kin. First-time migrants are often alienated and confused and may not even speak the language of the city. It is rare that someone would move to a city without contacts to provide initial shelter and orientation. Some- times an entire village or community will specialize in a particular type of migration. Thai migrants from the same village tend to live within the same area of Bangkok and work in the same professions.

Second, much rural-urban migration is only temporary. Improved transportation has not only made long-distance migration cheaper, faster, and easier, it has also accelerated the rate of return migration. Many people regularly travel to cities for short or extended periods but maintain their homes in rural areas. Such circular migration has become extremely common. If men are away for a year or more, they may set up dual households, one in the city and one in the countryside, and even have separate families in each. Another pattern is for entire families to migrate to the city for a while, then return to their rural home. The basic reason for circular migration is to earn more money than is possible in the rural area while maintaining one's home, kin, and culture. Such a family keeps a foot in two different economies, never becoming totally dependent on either.

Third, gender plays an increasing role in rural-urban migration. In many parts of the world, men are involved in mining or agricultural work, and more women move to the cities to find jobs as domestics or on assembly lines (Gugler 1993).

Primate Cities, Megacities

It is no longer true, as it once was, that each Third World country has a single large city. Most countries have two or more large cities, plus numerous smaller urban areas. However, when one city is more than twice as large as the next largest city, and when it is the cultural, administrative, and industrial center of the country, it assumes national "primacy." Many primate cities have their roots in colonialism, when virtually all important activities were centered in a single locale, ruled by Europeans, but primacy also occurs in countries that were never colonized, such as Iran. Primacy is not a unique Third World phenomenon; Copenhagen and Vienna well fit the mold. However, such cities are more common in the Third World, and their primacy is more exaggerated; Bangkok, for example, is nearly fifty times the size of the next largest city and holds almost three-fourths of the population of Thailand. In some African cities, fully 90 percent of the nation's secondary and tertiary activities take place in one city. Dakar, Senegal, would seem to be much larger than the country can support; in colonial times, it was the administrative center for all of French West Africa (Findley 1993; Drakakis-Smith 1987).

Primate cities are often accused of internal colonialism. Indeed, they may represent a severe imbalance in power, wealth, and production. In Latin America, a mere ten cities account for 70 percent of all nonagricultural economic activity, even though there are more than two hundred cities with populations above 50,000. Primate cities may inhibit the growth of smaller urban centers by drawing most investment.

Unlike First World cities, which are usually surrounded by smaller urban conglomerates, primate cities in the Third World may drain an entire region of its wealth and population. An extreme example is Lima, Peru, with its port of Callao; there is not another urban center of any size within a three hundred mile radius. The absence of a hierarchical system of urban centers deprives a country of overall development. The wealth of the primate city may be directly related to the poverty of the rest of the country (Reitsma and Kleinpenning 1989).

Some primate cities are also "megacities," urban agglomerations of more than eight million people. In the year 2000 there will be about thirty megacities globally, of which twenty-three will be in the Third World, including Mexico City, São Paulo, Calcutta, and Seoul. Such cities are usually, but not always, industrial centers. Despite the high cost of land values and infrastructure in such massive urban complexes, manufacturing operations often choose to cluster together to gain the benefits of supportive industries and transportation networks and to be near their major markets. Megacities also have the advantage of a large and varied labor force. The result may be high levels of pollution and a great deal of underemployment, because industry cannot absorb all those seeking jobs. Perhaps because of such problems, the growth of megacities seems to be slowing; Mexico City, for example, grew at a rate of over 5 percent per year in the 1950s, but this had dropped to under 4 percent by the 1980s (Richardson 1993).

Urban Employment, Unemployment, and Underemployment

The stereotype of the Third World city filled with beggars, street hawkers, bootblacks, and prostitutes is true to a certain extent, and such marginal occupations have increased with the recession and debt crisis of the 1980s and 1990s. However, the large majority of people are not engaged in such work. Many have jobs in small-scale home industries, and there are many office workers. In the post–World War II period, a middle class has emerged of perhaps 20 percent to 40 percent of a nation's population, and these live mainly in the larger cities. In a few countries, Western multinational corporations have shifted much of their manufacturing to Third World cities, where labor is abundant and cheap. The result is a growing proletariat of industrial workers. There is also considerable small-scale manufacturing in the informal economy; in India, it is estimated that nearly 80 percent of the industrial labor force is employed in the "nonmodern" sector. This does not mean, however, that there are a great many jobs in industry. The very large majority of people will be involved in commerce and services, which do not produce tangible goods. This gross inflation of the tertiary sector has led some researchers to speak of the "tertiarization" of Third World urban economies.

Official urban unemployment in cities is often under 10 percent, comparable with that in the First World, but this is highly misleading. Underemployment, not unemployment, is the real problem. In Mexico City, if an individual had worked one hour the previous week, he was considered employed for the benefit of national statistics. Because there is no unemployment insurance, no workman's compensation, and no welfare in most cities, there is little point in registering oneself as unemployed. Also, unless a person has a spouse or close relative with a relatively high-paying job, true unemployment is simply not an option. Survival requires some kind of income. As a result, many people take whatever odd jobs they can get, often moving in and out of the informal economy. However, even underemployment in the city may be more remunerative than full-time work in agriculture, which often pays subsubsistence wages and which may be available for only a few months a year (Gilbert 1994; Gugler 1993).

Many — and, in some cases, most — of those moving to the city in search of employment are women. Pay for women is normally less than for men, a practice that is falsely rationalized on the grounds that men must support their families while women's work is supplemental. The reality is that there are many women-headed households, and even in two-parent households, the woman's contribution is usually crucial. Women are funnelled either into domestic work or into jobs that are repetitive and quickly learned, such as assembly line operations. As in rural areas, women are expected to put in as many hours at home as on the job. Kusum, a typical female worker in the city of Suva, Fiji, normally rose at 4 A.M. to prepare breakfast for her children and unemployed husband and to do various household chores. She left for her job at seven. The factory did not open until eight, but employees were expected to make an unofficial start a half hour earlier. Once inside, an iron grill was locked over the entrance so no one could get out. Unrealistic production quotas were set, far higher than anyone could accomplish, so it was necessary to work rapidly until five, with only a brief toilet break in the morning and a thirty minute lunch break. The company routinely fired employees before their legally required annual paid holiday, then hired them back almost immediately. Though her pay was barely adequate for survival and she was often paid months late, she considered herself lucky to have the job. Returning home in the evening, she would prepare the evening meal and do housework until bedtime (Drakakis-Smith 1987:79).

Shantytowns and Public Housing

Housing is a critical problem in Third World cities. Although cities will have their wealthy and middle class residential districts, with paved streets lined with trees and flowers, most housing must be created for the masses of poor people. Governments often have tried to provide housing, but their attempts have been inadequate and often badly planned. With a demand for 300,000 new houses in the early 1990s, Thailand could build only 7,000 units. In order to get the most for the money and to conserve valuable urban space, much public housing is in the form of high-rise apartments that are culturally unacceptable to many people because they isolate families and break up networks of kin and friends. Such housing tends to deteriorate rapidly. Despite the severity of the problem, housing assumes a low priority in the minimal budgets of most Third World cities.

Many poor people live in slums, which are inner-city areas that are decaying through overcrowding and lack of maintenance. Space is in such demand that it is quite normal for squatter settlements to form on the roofs of slum buildings. Because land inside the city is of premium value, slum dwellers are constantly threatened with having their homes razed in order to make room for commercial buildings or middle class apartments. Redevelopment and relocation schemes are seldom successful.

Most new immigrants to the cities sooner or later try to build their own homes. Large squatter settlements — variously termed *favelas* (Brazil), *gecekondu* (Turkey), *bidonvilles* (North Africa), and *barriadas* or "young towns" (Peru) — are found everywhere in the Third World. As early as 1960, there were more than a hundred million people living in such shantytowns, and that number may soon reach half a billion (Reitsma and Kleinpenning 1989:192). In Cairo in the 1970s, over 80 percent of all new housing units were built by squatters. Many settlements, especially in Latin America, have been formed by "invasions." In Peru, for example, Indians from the mountains would settle in the center-city slums, paying rents for years, while getting organized and collecting straw and weaving it into mats. Then, in a single night, a group of perhaps a hundred families would create a community built entirely of straw on the desert outskirts of the city. They might be thrown out by the police, but if the land was uncontested or if they could gather enough public sympathy, they would be permitted to remain. The straw houses would soon be replaced by structures of scrap lumber, flattened 55-gallon drums, cardboard, and whatever else could be salvaged. Slowly, over perhaps two decades, solid, permanent houses would be constructed, brick by brick. The government might be pressured to provide electricity, sewage lines, and water facilities. The original shantytown, which might have resembled a human garbage dump, would be transformed over a generation into a stable, lower middle class community.

Susan Lobo's 1982 study of Ciudadela Chacala, a "young town" on the outskirts of Lima, revealed the inner workings of such settlements. Though stereotyped as chaotic, squalid, smelly, and dangerous, in reality, the community had very little crime, was relatively clean, and was highly organized. The *barriada* had originally been established by five founder families in 1938 rather than by invasion, and had grown by increments to over 12,000 people. By 1953, it was large enough to elect a community council that gained official recognition for the settlement, which included police protection and garbage disposal. In 1973, taking advantage of a government "remodeling" program, Chacala was able to get water and sewage systems.

The community has been highly organized right from the start, but as it grew, it established an elected community council and secretaries of sports and cultural events. The council arranges dances in its community hall and has formed a youth group. The council also has the power to regulate construction and to halt new building in overcrowded areas. Parents put a very high value on education, and a sort of parents-teachers association meets every week. The majority of young people complete primary school, about 10 percent graduate from secondary school, and a few attend the university or technical schools.

Not all squatter settlements are as organized as Ciudadela Chacala; many are indeed dirty and crime ridden. However, such settlements offer hope that is not available in slums or in public housing. Though squatter settlements take place in the informal economy and, therefore, have no legal status, more and more governments are trying to come to terms with them and even provide deeds. Some city administrations have stopped fighting squatter settlements, recognizing their value, and have adopted "enabling strategies" that involve a cessation of building public housing and a shift in resources to the informal sector. However, a major reason for building in the informal sector is to avoid paying taxes, so many people have reservations about such official government recognition. When the government of Karachi established a pilot project to legalize land tenure for a small fee, only 10 percent of the target squatter population took advantage of the offer.

Many governments are afraid that official recognition of squatter communities will encourage new settlements, at a time when land around major cities is running out. There is little public property left, and the expansion of cities outward has increased land values, so private owners are holding out for offers from developers of middle class homes or industry. In many cities, the days may be coming to an end when squatting is seen as a normal and easy strategy for the migrant (Brennen 1993).

Regulating City Growth

There are basically two theoretical perspectives that dominate Third World urban policy. The accommodationists reject the idea that cities have grown too large and unwieldy. They emphasize the positive aspects of urbanization. Megacities and primate cities are perceived not as rapacious parasites living off the rest of the country but as highly efficient centers of essential economic activities that add much to national development. The concentration of industry provides jobs and encourages commerce. Cities are centers of innovation, and far from draining the countryside of its resources, they provide markets for agricultural goods and rural crafts. Rather than being a strain on the economy, the informal sector is a thriving system of small-scale capitalism. The government's job is not to discourage growth or to halt the flow of immigrants but to make sure that the city functions well.

Opposed to this view are the interventionists who see the too-rapid growth of large cities as pathological, leading to poverty, crime, congestion, environmental degradation, and economic breakdown. The overcentralization of politics in primate cities strips the rest of the country of power, making real democracy impossible. The solution is decentralization through encouraging small and medium-sized companies, which form the largest growth sector in most countries, to relocate to other cities. Such a policy, which could be carried out through targeted tax strategies, would redirect migrants away from the already overburdened major cities and establish important urban centers throughout the country (Findley 1993).

In reality, except in the most dictatorial regimes, government policy does not seem to matter that much. Migrants continue to flood into megacities, and natural urban population growth remains high. It is true that in many countries smaller cities are growing faster than the larger ones; however, megacities are already pressing against their limits, and without a rapid reduction in national population growth, problems are liable to reach crisis proportions.

PEOPLE ON THE MOVE: MIGRANTS AND REFUGEES

The city may be a primary goal of migrants, but it is hardly the only goal. Cross-border movements are also of vast dimensions. There are presently 350 million people of African descent living outside of Africa; that is almost 65 percent as many as still live on the African continent. Twenty-two million Chinese have left their country, and nine million South Asians reside outside of that subcontinent. Many of these are citizens of other countries, often several generations removed from their homelands. The exodus continues: in 1984, the International Labor Organization estimated that there were twenty to twenty-two million active migrants spread throughout the world (Parnwell 1993:49).

Historically, world civilization has evolved out of the movement and interaction of peoples. Migration was crucial to the spread of industrialization and modernization, both through the influence of Western colonizers and through migrants returning from Europe and North America. Many countries, such as Israel, Australia, South Africa, and even the United States, have been created largely by migration. Much migration, of course, has been coerced; the slave trade and the great movements of entire populations during and after World War II testify to the immense cost in human suffering of people unwillingly displaced from their homes. Most people, however, move voluntarily to better themselves and their families.

Types of Migration

In general terms, migrations can be measured along three inter-related dimensions — the spacial, the temporal, and the motivational. The *spatial* dimension deals with distance and direction. Is the movement a few score miles, from a rural community to a small city, or thousands of miles across national borders? Is it from one Third World country to another, or from periphery to core? The *temporal* dimension considers how long the migrant will be gone. He or she may travel and return home in short-term cycles (the commonest type of movement), may spend a year or more before returning, or may take up permanent residence in a new location. *Motivationally*, we must distinguish between voluntary and involuntary movements and, when voluntary, between push and pull factors. Often motives are quite individual and complex: a young woman may move to join a favorite relative *and* seek employment *and* find excitement in the city *and* escape an alcoholic father.

The most common motive for international migration is employ-ment. A number of countries need cheap, often-unskilled labor. The potential for mass movements exists wherever there are wide differ-entials in income and economic opportunities between adjacent countries or regions. In oil-rich countries of the Middle East, such as Saudi Arabia, Kuwait, and the United Arab Emirates, indigenous populations may be relatively small, highly educated, and well-off, so that foreigners from poorer countries are brought in to do construction, domestic work, and the most menial tasks. In the 1980s, almost three million Pakistanis, Indians, Bangladeshis, and Filipinos worked in the Middle East. Western Europe after World War II required masses of workers, mainly recruited from Mediterranean countries, for recon-struction. In parts of the United States, unskilled agricultural labor is traditionally done by migrants from Mexico.

Although most international labor migration is authorized, much is illegal. Every country tries to control the flow of immigrants, but many people determined to better themselves economically are not deterred by borders. Estimates of illegal immigration into the United States range from two million to twelve million, with about five million — or 2 percent of the population — as more realistic. About half of these are Mexicans, but there are also many Cubans, Haitians, Dominicans, and other natives of the Caribbean Basin, as well as some Chinese and Vietnamese. Thousands of Chinese have invaded Hong Kong, and great numbers have left Thailand and Malaysia for Singapore. Oil-rich Libya has had an influx of illegal immigrants from Tunis and Egypt. The few relatively wealthy countries of Latin America have gotten their shares of illegal immigrants; there may be two million in oil-producing Venezuela and one million in Argentina.

Internal migration is even more extensive than international migration. A great deal of such movement is from rural areas to the cities, as has already been discussed, but other types are also common. There is a tendency for people to converge on a core region, perhaps a more affluent state or province, rather than just to a city. During colonial times, British and French administrators forced internal migration by applying a money tax to subsistence farmers. Unused to money, and unable to earn it in their home regions, tens of thousands of men and women had to travel to get wage-paying jobs in mines and on European-owned plantations. In any given year, over half the men of Basutoland (now Lesotho) were away from their homes. Though the motives are different, a similar situation exists today among the Aymara Indians of highland Peru; up to three-quarters of the men in many communities travel several hundred miles twice a year to work in planting and harvesting rice fields near the coast. Such circular migration, often based upon agricultural cycles, is extremely common throughout the Third World.

Many people return to their home communities after spending years or decades in cities or another country. Returning immigrants often bring money and innovative ideas to improve agriculture or start up new businesses. In Tanzania, for example, return migration was responsible for introducing new high-yield varieties of crops (Parnwell 1993).

Why People Move

It is a truism that people migrate in order to better themselves economically. However, such macrolevel generalizations do little justice to the complexity of human motivation. If it were simply a matter of the poor moving to richer areas, we might expect impoverished regions to be almost denuded of their populations, but that is not the case; most people stay where they are. Disparities in wealth between neighboring nations is a significant factor but not sufficient of itself to cause mass migrations. We must ask in what type of development the wealthier country is involved. Can such a country absorb new workers, or is the indigenous population filling available jobs? What is the richer country's immigration policy, and what is the outmigration policy of the poorer country? Similarly, rural-urban migration cannot be reduced to a simple formula based on higher wages in the city. The urban cost of living is often much higher than in rural areas, and many people must survive for months without wages before they find employment. Ultimately, each individual or family must make the decision based on a host of personal and economic factors, such as available networks in the target location, commitments at home, the stage of the individual in the life-cycle, and expectations for the future at home and away. All potential migrants must consider positive and negative factors at home, intervening obstacles such as the cost of a long-distance bus trip, and perceived positive and negative factors at the destination. Even if it is an individual that is migrating, the decision will invariably involve the whole family and, possibly, friends and the wider community. An individual's migration may be a family or community investment, with expected returns for the entire group.

The obvious reason for mass migration is that people are drawn from regions of relative underdevelopment to the jobs in regions of higher development. In areas that are still based on subsistence and barter economies, people who are surviving quite well may need to travel in order to earn money to purchase modern goods such as radios and sewing machines. In Latin America especially, but also throughout much of Asia, population growth combined with the expansion of large-scale land ownership and the mechanization of agriculture forces people to seek their living elsewhere. Formal education, now universal in even the most rural areas of many Third World countries, not only raises expectations about the "good life" but also breaks down barriers between rural and urban, for example, in teaching the national language to indigenous groups.

Ecological theories of migration postulate a necessary equilibrium between population size, social organization, technology, and environment. If substantial changes take place in any of these, the system must be readjusted to reestablish equilibrium. Both fertility and mortality play crucial roles, but migration is often the quickest and most efficient solution to immediate problems. A number of traditional cultures have based their entire social systems on movements for ecological reasons. Hunter-gatherers must follow the seasonal changes in the availability of vegetation and game; pastoralists must move their cattle or sheep to different ecological zones during different times of the year; slash-and-burn horticulturalists, living in tropical rain forests, may have to move entire villages when their fields go fallow. Similarly, subsistence peasants cannot increase their populations beyond the carrying capacity of the land, and commercial farmers must send away people in excess of the labor demands of the region. Ecological factors, such as floods and droughts, have often been even more directly responsible for mass migrations (Kammeyer and Ginn 1986).

Often, people have no choice but to leave their homes. Construction of the Damodar Valley dam and reservoir in India in the 1950s displaced 93,000 people; Egypt's Aswan dam forced the relocation of 70,000; and China's Danjiangkou Dam, 383,000. Governments often sponsor migrations in order to move people from overpopulated to underpopulated regions. The single island of Java accounts for only 7 percent of Indonesia's land area but has two-thirds of the country's population. Other islands are sparsely populated but have much poorer tropical soils. In the early 1970s, the government established a Five Year Plan that made migration from Java to other islands a national priority. Almost half a million families — two-and-one-half million people — were resettled at an average cost of about $6,000 per family. After several years, despite lower crop yields, most families felt themselves to be better off. Indonesia planned to expand the program, ultimately to as many as thirteen million families (World Bank 1984:99).

Women in the Migratory Stream

Women form a significant part of migration nearly everywhere. A high proportion of rural-to-rural migrants within countries are women; in India, women comprise almost 80 percent of such migrants, and in Egypt, the figure is over 60 percent. In a number of countries — such as Brazil, the Philippines, and Thailand — women also outnumber men in rural-to-urban migration. In most other regions, they make up close to half of those moving to cities.

Despite such statistics, women often have not been taken seriously in migration studies. It is accepted that one of the key determinants of migration is a better paying job, but the motivation of women has been considered to be predominately noneconomic; they tend to follow their husbands or to move as part of a family unit. Recent research has shown that both men and women are equally likely to move as part of a family and that women have more say in the decision-making process than was previously supposed. In addition, the number of women migrating on their own is increasing.

One of the reasons that women move in such numbers is that development projects often have a more devastating effect on women than on men. Women are usually the mainstays of subsistence agriculture and hold the most menial jobs in commercial agriculture, so the introduction of cash crops or mechanization can quickly displace them. In Indonesia, mechanical hullers in the milling of rice supplanted nearly eight million part-time workers, mostly women, in the 1970s. In cities, women are mainly concentrated in the service sector, especially as domestics, where they may work long hours for very little pay. This is especially true of recent migrants who are young, unmarried, and have few skills. Worldwide, women form a relatively small proportion of workers in manufacturing, though the range is from 1 percent in Bahrain to over 40 percent in Haiti. They are often found in export processing zones, where they take low-paying, repetitive jobs that lead to little skill development and have no chance of promotion.

Despite their numbers, women migrants have not been able to gain a voice in pressing for better jobs, better working conditions, and better pay because they often are considered — wrongly — as mere adjuncts to their husband or, if single, as deserving of little because they are not supporting families (Zlotnik 1993).

The Effects of Migration and Migration Policy

Mass migration has profound effects, positive and negative, on both the home communities and the places of destination.

In rural areas, migration eases population pressure without usually affecting agricultural productivity, especially if mechanization is one of the reasons that people leave. There are instances, however, such as in northwest Malaysia and the Dominican Republic, when a large-scale exodus has caused severe labor shortages in the countryside. The timing of circular migration is critical. If migrants can arrange to be home for planting and harvest, domestic production should not be affected. Unfortunately, commercial planting and harvest often coincides with that of subsistence crops, so men may be working other fields far away, leaving almost all agricultural work at home to their wives and daughters. Such sexual selection can have profound consequences, especially if migration is permanent and jobs are available for only one sex. Among Indians of Peru, many males migrate for long periods to mines or construction jobs, leaving entire communities virtually devoid of adult males in the prime of life. Skilled workers — such as doctors, teachers, and craftspersons — as well as the most dynamic and intelligent young people are the most likely to leave rural areas and the most difficult to replace. Although migration acts as an essential "pressure valve" on rural population, it is not without costs.

One of the major benefits of country-to-country migration is remittances that are sent back home. An unskilled worker from Bangladesh working in an Arab Gulf state will earn ten times as much as he could at home, and much of this will be returned to his family. Even after expenses, Pakistanis were able to save as high as 70 percent of their pay and to remit nearly 50 percent. Such remittances amounted to almost 9 percent of the gross national product of Pakistan.

On the negative side, the so-called brain drain is a severe problem for many Third World countries, because migration tends to increase with education and developed skills. In the 1970s alone, the United States admitted nearly half a million professionals and technical workers, three-quarters of whom came from Third World countries. Over 40 percent of Sudan's engineers, scientists, and medical practitioners have left the country. The Philippines sent over 12 percent of its new professionals to the United States. Although the host country undoubtedly benefits from such migration, the country of origin may rightly feel it suffers, despite remittances. In 1979, it was estimated that if the incomes of migrant professionals were taxed by the home countries at 10 percent — which, of course, they could not be — it would have brought in about $600 million. Aside from the loss of tax revenues, governments feel they have subsidized extensive educations with no payoff to the home country. More important, it is precisely the people who could be the most active in the development process who tend to leave (World Bank 1984).

Though the host country usually benefits from legal migration, tensions often have arisen when there is an economic downturn or when migrants are seen as displacing indigenous workers. Ethnic neighborhoods may become the targets of antialien hatred and even violence, as has happened recently in Germany.

Because of such problems, virtually every country has adopted policies on outward migration and on immigration. There are basically four types of policy. A *negative policy* emerges from the perception of migration as undesirable; cites may be closed to people from rural areas or tightly restricted, and excess population and "undesirables" may be forcibly relocated. China has made a concerted attempt to control its internal migration through such policies. A population registration system identified people as either rural or urban, and official permission was needed to leave the countryside. During some periods, there have been efforts to encourage large numbers of people to leave the cities, either voluntarily or under coercion. As a result, shantytowns, underemployment, poverty, and begging are less prevalent in Chinese cities, though at a cost of personal freedoms. During the 1980s, controls were relaxed as a part of a policy of rapid industrialization, with the result that urban growth is rapidly increasing, with all the attendant problems so common in other Third World countries.

An *accommodative policy* accepts migration as inevitable and, perhaps, desirable and attempts to improve migrant conditions through upgrading slums and shantytowns, passing minimum wage laws, and providing essential services such as education and modern medicine. A *manipulative policy* seeks to redirect migration, through colonization and decentralization of industry, and otherwise control migrants, as in Java's resettlement program mentioned above. Former President Marcos of the Philippines encouraged Filipinos to work abroad but passed laws forcing migrants to remit their earnings through state banks so that they could be taxed in the process. Finally, a *preventative policy* attempts to get at the root causes of migration by alleviating rural poverty through land reform and creating jobs in the home communities to make mass movements unnecessary (Parnwell 1993:131).

Refugees

In contrast to migrants, who usually move voluntarily in search of better employment, refugees are forced to move because of war, natural disaster, or persecution. Refugees may be "internal," that is, people who have been forced to flee their homes but remain within their countries, or international. Sometimes refugees are quickly resettled in new countries, but when large groups of people are involved, as is usually the case, they may be crowded into camps. A team of doctors described a camp of 60,000 Kurdish refugees inside Iraq fleeing government troops in 1961 as "a sea of thick mud." "A single latrine existed, and there was no source of clean water at the time of our visit. We heard many complaints of thirst, hunger, and cold. The supply of blankets was grossly inadequate. About ten percent of the population was barefoot; the remainder had some form of foot covering, usually rubber sandals" (quoted in Bread for the World 1992:19). In this camp, there were thirty to sixty deaths each day, mostly infants and young children.

Refugees who escape their own borders are more likely to receive international assistance, but the new countries — often themselves extremely poor and overburdened — are often reluctant hosts. No matter how much international aid is received, asylum countries must bear the brunt of the burden. Host countries differ on the extent that they will allow refugees to mix with their own populations; often, there may be potential for ethnic or religious conflict, and governments may rightly fear that refugees will take jobs or land from the country's citizens. After the communists took over Vietnam in 1975, hundreds of thousands of people left the country. Many of these escaped in flimsy boats to Hong Kong, where they were held in detention centers for years. Detention was based on a controversial distinction between political refugees, who by international law have resettlement rights, and economic migrants. Despite riots in the camps and even pledges of mass suicide, Hong Kong signed a pact for the return of the Vietnamese to their home country.

By mid-1994 there were about twenty-three million refugees worldwide (Figure 7.4). The war in Afghanistan produced 6.6 million refugees, of which over three million resided in Pakistan. Years of civil war and famine in the Sudan has created almost five million refugees, both inside the country and scattered in surrounding nations. Nearly two million fled the southern region of the Sudan for the capital, Khartoum, where they live in dwellings of cardboard and sheet plastic, sometimes erected literally on the tops of garbage dumps. In order to discourage the movements, the government prevented private agencies from assisting the people, and in 1991, many were killed in forced relocations. In 1994, the Hutu massacres of the rival Tutsi tribe in Rwanda and the subsequent takeover by largely Tutsi rebels sent millions fleeing into Burundi, Tanzania, and Zaire. In addition, there remain from tens to hundreds of thousands of refugees from Mozambique, Burma, Ethiopia, Somalia, Sri Lanka, Cambodia, Guatemala, and El Salvador.

Women and children account for 70 percent to 80 percent of international refugees, as well as a high percentage of the internally displaced. Girls and women are especially prone to suffer violence,

FIGURE 7.4
Total Refugees Worldwide

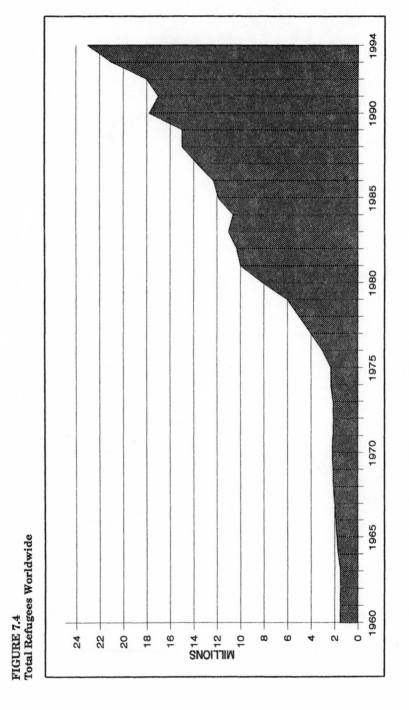

Source: The Economist Newspaper, November 13, 1993, p. 45. All rights reserved.

mostly prior to or during their flight. Muslim women fleeing Burma for Bangladesh were routinely raped by Burmese troops. A survey of Central American women living in Washington, D.C., found that the large majority had been victims of rape, injury, threats, and house bombings in their home countries.

There exists an international framework of organizations to assist refugees. Before World War I, a group of private charitable organizations headed by the Red Cross successfully pressed the League of Nations to appoint a commissioner to coordinate efforts on behalf of refugees. One result was the establishment of four basic principles: first, that refugee status was an internationally legitimate one; second, that there would be no forced repatriation where persecution was possible (non-*refoulement*); third, that the most urgent physical needs of refugees must be met; and fourth, that a coordinated policy, rather than individual efforts by various agencies, was the key to success.

Such policies were put to a test on a massive scale with the displacement of twenty-seven million people in World War II. The UN Relief and Rehabilitation Administration, established in 1943, and about sixty voluntary organizations tried to handle the overwhelming situation. In 1947, the International Refugee Organization was the very first agency created by the UN General Assembly, and, in 1950, the UN High Commissioner for Refugees was established as the principal coordinator of refugee assistance. Originally, these operations only applied to Europe, but Africa and Asia became more vocal about their plight, and the mandate of the High Commissioner was universalized to all countries. Though most countries signed various international documents supporting refugee aid, no state ceded its sovereignty in the matter; governments would be the final arbiters of who would be able to enter their countries. Thus, despite numerous conventions, the claims of refugees to international protection remains ambiguous. The principle of non-*refoulement*, however, is universal; states that refuse to take refugees are at least obligated not to send them back where there is a legitimate fear of persecution. This principle, however, is subject to interpretation; many Haitians, Salvadorans, and Guatemalans were returned from the United States on the grounds that they were economic migrants, even during the worst periods of warfare and governmental terror in the home countries.

There are many ways in which refugees can be helped. The most pressing needs obviously are emergency food, shelter, medical care, and sanitation, but because refugees often must remain in limbo for years or even decades, education, training, counselling, and job procurement may be extremely important. Most governments have agreed to allow the UN to work with foreign refugees within their countries. The UN mandate, however, does not apply to internal refugees (though sometimes a country will permit the UN to help). The main source of aid for internal refugees is the Red Cross, which has a mandate under the

Geneva Convention to help people in their own countries, and other voluntary agencies. Such groups have learned to keep a low profile within politically sensitive situations and have established a well-deserved reputation for courage under fire.

The primary goal of refugee policy is repatriation, and most refugees do return to their homeland when the crisis that drove them out has passed. If political persecution continues or an ecological catastrophe has destroyed the productive capacity of the land, return may not be a viable option. Settlement in place may be possible. Numerous Palestinian refugee camps in Jordan have become thriving towns, and the Palestinians continue to make a significant contribution to Jordan's economy. In Africa, where artificial colonial boundaries split tribes and ethnic groups, many refugees fleeing to neighboring countries have been welcomed among their own people. A recent phenomenon is a growing number of "jet people," refugees who travel by plane from one country to another in search of permanent asylum. Most come from Africa and Asia to Europe and North America, often by tortuous routes. Tamil refugees from Sri Lanka traveled first to Singapore, then to Berlin, and from there spread out into Sweden or Denmark.

Unfortunately, the assimilation capacities of host countries seem to be reaching their limits as once-welcoming nations succumb to "compassion exhaustion." Meanwhile, the conditions that create refugees show no signs of abating (Smyser 1987; Bread for the World 1992).

POPULATION CRISIS OR DISTRIBUTION CRISIS?

In the past, migration has been a key means by which regions and countries dealt with problems of overpopulation. Today, although not all countries are, by any means, overpopulated, neither are there very many that are underpopulated enough to invite extensive immigration. Migration — whether to megacities from rural areas or from one country to another — can no longer be considered a way to solve demographic difficulties.

The problem, however, is not merely too many people on too little land. The population growth rate is already declining and will continue to decline as more and more countries progress through the demographic transition (though it will be a very long time before any sort of population stability is achieved, and then at a very high level in absolute numbers). The issue of economic *distribution*, however, is not being solved and in most cases is not even recognized. On the international level, despite great increases in productivity, huge amounts of agricultural goods are flowing from the Third World to the First World, from the poor to the rich. Within Third World countries, vast inequities condemn the majority to lives of poverty. The "population problem" must not be viewed simplistically as a matter of increasing numbers of people but also, and perhaps fundamentally, as a structural issue that will be solved only through extensive social and economic reform.

SUGGESTED READINGS

Chesnais, Jean-Claude, *The Demographic Transition: Stages, Patterns, and Economic Implications* (Oxford: Clarendon, 1992). This study of sixty-seven countries covering the period from 1720 to 1984 is perhaps the most extensive analysis yet of the pattern in which populations pass from stability to high growth to stability.

Drakakis-Smith, David, *The Third World City* (London: Methuen, 1987). This brief, well-written overview of urban growth in developing countries provides interesting case studies and is illustrated with numerous maps and charts.

Ehrlich, Paul R., and Ann H. Ehrlich, *The Population Explosion* (New York: Simon and Schuster, 1990). The Ehrlichs are neo-Malthusians who see the world as on the verge of ecological and social collapse because of exponential population growth. One need not completely agree with their crisis perspective to be alarmed by the implications of their data.

Kasarda, John D., and Allan M. Parnell, eds., *Third World Cities: Problems, Policies, and Prospects* (Newbury Park, Calif.: Sage, 1993). The various articles deal with megacities, urban housing, labor migration, and transnational investment in cities. An introductory chapter by Sally Findley provides an excellent overview of the subject.

Lobo, Susan, *A House of My Own: Social Organization in the Squatter Settlements of Lima, Peru* (Tucson: University of Arizona Press, 1982). This anthropological study of a *barriada* goes beyond stereotypes to reveal the high degree of structure in many shantytowns.

Smyser, W. R., *Refugees: Extended Exile* (New York: Praeger, 1987). The author was UN Deputy High Commissioner for Refugees from 1981 to 1986, so he speaks with authority about the problems of refugees and what various agencies can do about them.

World Bank, *World Development Report 1984* (Oxford: Oxford University Press, 1984). Each annual report, aside from providing valuable statistical tables, focuses an a particular issue of international importance. Though the tables and examples are somewhat dated, the 1984 *Report* on population provides a wealth of valuable information.

8

In Search of Sustainable Development: The Threatened Environment

In 1944 the government of Canada introduced twenty-nine reindeer on St. Matthew Island in the Bering Sea. Under favorable climatic conditions, the herd expanded to six thousand by 1963. This large number, in a confined area, overgrazed the lichens, which were their main source of winter forage. A severe winter crashed the population, leaving only fifty animals — a decimation of more than 99 percent in a single year.

The reindeer had overgrown the carrying capacity of the island. "Carrying capacity" is simply the largest number of a certain species that a habitat can support indefinitely. When the maximum number is reached, pressures on resources must force a population decline (Postel 1994). As we have seen, Paul Ehrlich (1968) and the authors of *The Limits to Growth* (Meadows et al. 1972) and *Beyond the Limits* (Meadows et al. 1992) believe that the human species is already pushing against the carrying capacity of its global habitat and if something is not done — and done fast — rapid population decline through the Malthusian checks of war, famine, and disease is inevitable.

Human carrying capacity is much more difficult to determine than that of reindeer, because humans radically alter their environments in much more complex ways than other animals. Not only are food and climate important to humans, but so is their technology, their levels of consumption, and the ways that they handle their waste. Theoretically, at least, humans have the capacity to foresee the results of their actions and take measures to prevent disaster. The problem is that there is considerable controversy about the present and future effects of air and water pollution, deforestation, and the degradation of agricultural land. Politics, national sovereignty, and ideology play more of a role than objective, scientific analysis. The First World has often accused the Third World of not restraining its population growth, while the latter rightly points out that the overconsumption of the average person in a developed country is responsible for twenty times more water and air pollution than that of an average Third Worlder. However, it is increasingly recognized that — ideology and self-interest aside — the Earth is in serious trouble.

Humans have been altering the Earth since they first set foot upon it. In Plato's dialogue *Critias*, written three hundred years before the Christian era, the philosopher complained that deforestation and overintensification of agriculture had left the plains of Attica looking like "the skeleton of a body wasted by disease." Similar protests were voiced by critics of Rome. What is new is not environmental degradation but its sheer scale after the mid-twentieth century. Not only has the world population more than doubled since 1950, but there also has been a quintupling of economic output. Meanwhile, the gap between the rich and the poor has consistently widened, fostering overconsumption at the top and mass poverty at the bottom.

Already, numerous tribal peoples have been wiped out or forced to migrate by the ecological destruction of their environments. In the Amazon region, scores of Indian groups have disappeared as their forest homes have been razed for ranching or their water has been polluted. Africa has the most environmental refugees, as pastoral range and marginal agricultural areas have given way to desert. The idea that the world is — slowly or rapidly — committing "ecocide" no longer seems far-fetched.

Only recently has the situation been sufficiently recognized by governments that serious measures are being taken to achieve "sustainable development," that is, development that does not destroy the resources that will be needed for the future.

THE SCOPE OF THE PROBLEM

Protecting the environment too often seems a luxury for the rich. Even in the developed countries, it was only after industrialization had been fully achieved and only at the point of crisis — dead Great Lakes in the United States, killer smogs in London, mercury poisoning in Japan — that governments began to take the environment seriously. It is doubtful that the Earth could sustain a similar waiting period while the Third World develops. The assault on the environment is too all-encompassing, including air, water, agricultural land, and forests.

Polluting the Air

In the 1970s, the Union Carbide company established a factory to produce and store chemicals in Bhopal, a city of 800,000 in central India. Though there were several accidents and cases of leakage, these warnings were not taken seriously. On December 2, 1984, a leak emitted a gas of methyl isocyanate, a chemical used in pesticides, over a large area. About 200,000 people were affected. They fled in panic, coughing and unable to breathe. Most of those who could find a place on the jammed busses or who could escape by scooter, bicycle, or car survived, but thousands of those who stayed behind or tried to flee on foot died in agony. The hospitals were crowded with 25,000 new patients the next day. Thousands suffered long-term effects so severe they were unable to continue earning a living.

Union Carbide and the city government were censured for allowing people to settle near such a dangerous plant. Repeated portents of disaster had been ignored, and once the leak occurred, the public alarm was not immediately sounded. Information on the type of gas and its antidote reached doctors and hospitals too late to save many who might otherwise have survived (Gupta 1988). The Bhopal catastrophe was exceptional in its short-term intensity, but, over the long run, normal levels of toxic pollution are also proving deadly.

In many places throughout the Third World, a poisonous air pollution spews from factory smokestacks on a daily basis. As countries develop, their requirements for power increase rapidly. These burgeoning needs are often met with the cheapest fuel available — low-grade sulfur-bearing coal. Emissions lead to acid rain that destroys vegetation and damages buildings. Even without sulfur impurities, large power stations emit numerous toxins. The Taj Mahal, the famous mausoleum in Agra, India, is being severely damaged by acid corrosion from a petroleum factory about twenty-five miles away. Sulfur oxides and nitrogen oxides from the burning of fossil fuels also lead to respiratory ailments and eye and throat irritation.

Particulates from coal combustion, motor vehicle emissions, and waste incineration can cause serious respiratory diseases and lung and stomach cancer. Carbon monoxide, which comes from incomplete combustion of carbon in car exhausts and petroleum refining, affects the nervous system by reducing the ability of blood to carry oxygen; people with emphysema and heart disease are especially vulnerable.

Such pollution remains a problem in the First World, despite regulation of industry and restrictions on auto emissions. In Third World countries, antipollution laws are, more often than not, minimal, ill-enforced, or nonexistent.

One result of using the world's air as a huge reservoir for waste disposal may be the "greenhouse effect." In order for the Earth to maintain its normal climatic parameters, energy absorbed from the sun must be balanced by the outgoing radiation of heat. If atmospheric gasses build up to the extent that such radiation is blocked, climates will gradually get warmer. There can be no doubt that humans have been altering the chemical make-up of the atmosphere since the beginning of the industrial revolution. Though vast amounts of carbon dioxide are emitted naturally by soil, plants, and water, the human contribution from burning fossil fuels and from tropical deforestation increases every year. Another major greenhouse gas is methane, which is emitted by natural gas production, the burning of forests, and coal mining. The average surface temperature of the air has increased from 0.3° to 0.6° centigrade over the past hundred years. It is unclear if this is part of a normal climatic change or the result of greenhouse gasses. There is considerable controversy among scientists about the long-term effects of the buildup of atmospheric pollutants. Some believe that agricultural regions may shift and that water from melting glaciers may inundate coastal cities and settlements. In any case, the governments of the world are finally taking the greenhouse effect sufficiently seriously that the United Nations is discussing means of curtailing atmospheric emissions.

Despoiling the Earth's Water

The Aswan High Dam has been considered an enormous success for Egypt. Built on the Nile in 1971, with extensive assistance from the Soviet Union, the huge construction created a large reservoir that stretches south into the Sudan. The dam, which increased Egypt's arable land by about a third, is important in maintaining the country's self-sufficiency in wheat and its export of rice and also provides a large hydroelectric capacity. Agricultural areas that depended on annual flood irrigation can now be irrigated all year long. However, there are problems. The large lake, in a desert environment, loses much of its water to evaporation. Much of the fertile silt that Nile valley farms depended on for thousands of years no longer reaches past the dam, forcing dependence on expensive commercial fertilizers. With less water reaching the Mediterranean, there has been a great increase in coastal erosion, and the lack of nutrients reaching the sea has severely diminished the once-rich schools of sardines. Some of the irrigated land has become salinated, and parasites, such as that causing schisto-somiasis, have invaded irrigated lands.

Water — with air, the most precious of nature's commodities — does not come free. The large-scale management of water dates back at least 6,000 years, when the people of Mesopotamia built a civilization on the storage and distribution of the seasonal flow of the Tigris and Euphrates Rivers. In the past, there was little damage to the hydrologic cycle, the natural recirculation of water. The enormous increase in water use in the twentieth century, however, has led to pollution and disruptions in the natural water cycle.

About 97 percent of all water is in the oceans, which comprise two-thirds of the world's surface area, and most nonsaline water is frozen in Antarctica and Greenland or is at considerable depth underground. Only a small percentage of the Earth's fresh water is accessible to humans through rain, rivers and streams, and lakes.

Farming accounts for about 70 percent of water use. Each year an amount equivalent to six times the annual flow of the Mississippi is removed from rivers, streams, and underground aquifers to irrigate crops. Only about 40 percent of this is actually absorbed by plants, so the remaining 60 percent is lost through evaporation or runoff. In some places, waterlogging is a problem; without adequate drainage, the capacity of roots to absorb oxygen can be impaired. In dry regions, the subsurface water table may be lowered through intensive agriculture. In parts of north China, an important wheat-growing region, groundwater levels are falling up to three feet a year. In the Indian state of Tamil Nadu, subsurface water levels have dropped more than seventy-five feet in a decade. Many countries face serious water shortages. Countries utilizing more than 10 percent of their annual renewable water resources will sooner or later encounter problems of scarcity. In the Third World as a whole, twenty-five countries are now using more than 20 percent of their water. It is estimated that by the year 2025, two-thirds of the population of Africa will face water shortages (Gupta 1988; Postel 1990).

Israel has taken the lead in water-efficient agriculture, reducing water per acre by over a third since mid-century. Innovative techniques include drip irrigation, in which water is applied only when needed, based on optimum amounts for each crop. In Africa, age-old techniques have been revived, such as building lines of stones across slopes to reduce erosion and to maintain soil moisture.

Pollution is often a worse problem than water scarcity. The Ganges, India's holiest river, is annually the recipient of the untreated sewage of 114 cities, at least 10,000 unburned corpses and 60,000 animal carcasses, plus thousands of tons of industrial effluents. In the city of Kanpur, only three of 647 factories have treatment facilities; the rest pour their wastes directly into the river. Aside from being used for drinking and for clothes washing, six million pilgrims each year immerse themselves in the Ganges, which is a carrier of bacteria for cholera, dysentery, and typhoid.

The largest water pollutant by weight is sediment; about a third of this is natural, and the rest comes from man-made erosion. Fertilizers and pesticides, the use of which is increasing in the Third World at a rate of over 10 percent per year, are the next largest causes of water pollution. Along with sewage and detergents, fertilizer runoff contributes heavily to eutrophication — a process by which the growth of plants and algae is stimulated by nitrogen and phosphorous in water. In many Latin American countries, over half of all lakes and reservoirs are eutrophic, and globally, up to 40 percent of standing fresh water is affected.

Millions of tons of industrial wastes, toxic to humans, animals, and fish, are dumped into rivers and streams each year. The oceans ultimately receive much of these effluents. Eutrophication is a serious problem for coastal areas, causing "red tides" of phyloplankton that damage fisheries and poison seafood. In addition, between six million and seven million tons of industrial waste were dumped directly into the world's seas every year between 1975 and 1985 (Harrison 1992:197–203).

Pollution combined with overfishing has had a severe effect on catches throughout the world. In South America, the anchoveta industry collapsed in the 1970s, and much of the North Atlantic fishery suffered the same fate in the 1990s. Almost all stocks of bottom-dwelling fish and crustaceans are already fully utilized or overexploited. The world fish catch — both inland and ocean — has expanded five times since 1950, peaking above one hundred million tons in 1989 and now declining. Mechanized hauling gear, bigger nets, electronic fish detection, and other technologies have led to serious declines in over half of the world's seventeen major fishing areas, and the rest are already being fished to their limits.

Pressures on Agriculture

Primitive agriculture seldom abuses the land. When people are few and land is plentiful, plots may be farmed for only a year or two, then left fallow. In time, fertility will be restored, as forest or bushes reclaim the land and microbes and rain distribute dissolved nitrogen. Tree roots reach deep into the earth to bring nutrients to the surface, while decaying leaves add their fertilizer. Nature does the work of rejuvenation.

As population densities increase, the exploitation of the soil must be intensified. Larger areas are cleared and allowed little, if any, fallow time to regain their nutrients. Such soils are subject to many types of degradation.

The United Nations Environmental Programme estimates that over eighteen million acres of cropland are lost each year to soil erosion. Tropical forest land that has been farmed is especially vulnerable. Rainforests appear to be extremely fertile, but, in reality, almost all nutrients are in the trees and bushes, not in the soil. When deforested, such land can deteriorate quickly. With the canopy of leaves and branches destroyed, hard tropical rains fall directly on the ground, washing away whatever topsoil there might be. The estimated 370 million absolute-poor farmers that have been forced to eke out bare livings on marginal lands suffer most from the effects of erosion. The cultivation of steep slopes in the Himalayas, the Andes, and the East African highlands has led to massive loss of topsoil. Great amounts of sediment have been washed into valley-bottom river beds, choking off streams, clogging waterways, and killing fish. It is possible to minimize erosion through such techniques as terracing, mulching, planting different crops in alternate rows within the same field, and allowing long fallow periods. When populations are high and outputs are low, however, such time-consuming and expensive inputs may be neglected. Salinization has also destroyed much cropland. If there is an elevation in groundwater levels because of flooding or irrigation, the water table may come to within a few yards of the surface. Capillary action raises ground salt so that when surface water evaporates, a thin layer of salt covers the earth. Waterlogging is also a serious problem for insufficiently drained irrigation; roots in too-moist soil are starved of oxygen. Even without such difficulties, unless regularly fallowed or fertilized, land can be denuded of its nutrients through normal processes of agriculture; rice farming, for example, removes significant amounts of nitrogen, potassium, and phosphorous from the soil. It is estimated that, since 1945, 62,000 square miles of cropland has become degraded beyond recovery, and as much as 17 percent of the world's vegetated area has suffered serious productivity loss (Harrison 1990:116–118).

Air pollution can also have a detrimental effect on agriculture. Sulfur dioxide and other byproducts of fossil fuel combustion in cities accumulate on fields directly from the air or are deposited by rain, fog, or snow. Even lower concentrations of acids reduce yields, and high accretions severely damage plants and put soils at risk. Ozone, produced by photochemical reactions of urban air pollutants, can reduce the amount of sunlight reaching crops. Fluorides emitted from brick and steel works damage fruit and can accumulate in forage, affecting livestock (Hardoy et al. 1992).

In the past, degraded land and declining yields have been more than compensated by new lands being brought into production and by the application of more intensive technology, such as irrigation, tractor farming, or high-yield seeds. It is often claimed that there is plenty of land that still can be farmed. Though true, such optimism is misleading, because available land is not evenly distributed; most is in a few countries of the Americas and some parts of Africa. The Sahel has reached its limits, and many of the countries of Asia — including India, Pakistan, Bangladesh, and the two Koreas — are already utilizing 95 percent or more of their good farmland. Between 1957 and 1990, China's arable land diminished, because of soil degradation, by over 90,000 acres, equal to France, Germany, Denmark, and the Netherlands combined. Worldwide, newly cultivated areas increased only half as fast in the 1980s as in the two previous decades. With limited or even declining land, maintaining per capita production requires increasing yields on existing lands. Asia has performed particularly well in this regard, but per capita cereal production has been falling in Latin America, the Near East, and Africa. Between 1978 and 1989, food production lagged behind population growth in sixty-nine of 102 developing countries for which data are available (Harrison 1992:43). Green Revolution agriculture undoubtedly will help, but not without cost;

high-tech, high-yielding crops deplete the soil, require expensive fertilizers and pesticides that poison fish and wildlife, and encourage monocultural production. World projections suggesting that greatly increasing numbers of people can be fed ignore the massive maldistribution of land and wealth and assume that fertile land is used to grow food for local populations, which, as we have seen, is often not the case.

The Demise of the Forests

At one time, 90 percent of El Salvador was tropical forests; today, there is almost none left. Much of Haiti, once known as "the Pearl of the Antilles" because of its vast forests, is now barren wasteland. Africa has already lost over 60 percent of its forest cover. There remain only three large regions of rainforest left in the world — in the Amazon region, equatorial Africa, and southeast Asia — and, each year, thousands of square miles of trees are lost. By some estimates, within ten or twenty years, there will be almost no forest left (Figure 8.1).

Deforestation is hardly new. By classical times, much of the Mediterranean region was denuded of trees to create croplands, provide fuel, and furnish timber for building ships, houses, and military camps. At the end of the nineteenth century, the region contained no virgin forests. What took hundred of years in earlier periods has now accelerated to decades. World deforestation peaked in the 1970s and has slowed considerably. Unfortunately, this slowdown is almost entirely confined to the West; in the Third World, deforestation continues to accelerate. Central America is losing more than 3 percent of its remaining forest each year, and Benin and Nigeria, close to 4 percent. Every week, an area the size of the Netherlands is cut down.

Statistically, the primary correlation with deforestation is population: the greater the population density, the less forest there will be. This is certainly the case in countries like India and Pakistan, where the sheer number of people needing agricultural land and firewood explains most of the near-total deforestation. In Latin America, a primary factor is the structure of land tenure. Because the *latifundistas* own most of the fertile land and use it for export crops, poor peasants are forced to cultivate forest lands to survive. The shifting cultivation of such marginal farmers leaves wide swaths of nutrient-robbed plots where there was once rainforest.

The commercial destruction of forests is rampant. In Latin America, ranching is the single greatest cause of deforestation, amounting to over a quarter of the total. The constant decline in grass productivity requires that more and more trees must be cut down just to maintain a herd; at first, it takes less than three acres to feed a single animal, but after five years, that same animal will need almost eleven acres. Much ranching has been encouraged in Brazil through state subsidies. The

FIGURE 8.1
Remaining Tropical Rainforest

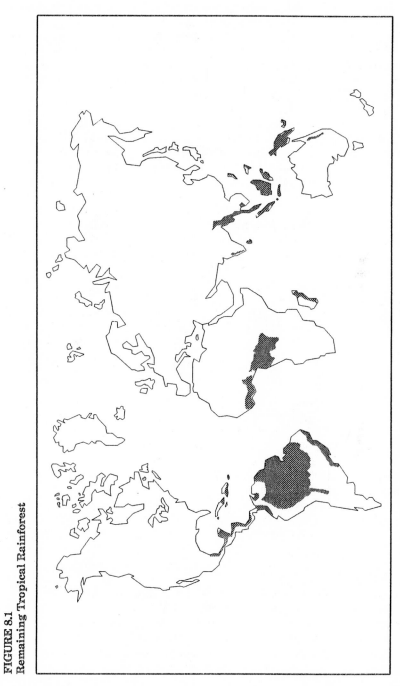

Source: Avijit Gupta, *Ecology and Development in the Third World* (London: Routledge, 1988), p. 4.

problem is less in Africa because the tsetse fly, which carries a disease fatal to livestock, is endemic to jungle areas.

The demand for tropical hardwoods in the West has led to massive timber extraction in Indonesia, Malaysia, and the Philippines. Even if only select trees are targeted, the entire forest may be laid bare; when large trees fall, the surrounding vegetation is also destroyed as vines and creepers tear down adjacent trees and bushes are crushed. In Malaysia, only 3 percent of trees are actually harvested, but more than half are severely damaged in the process. The web of roads necessary to commercial lumbering also takes its toll on the forests. These roads attract farmers and ranchers, who add their own deforestation.

Though logging will almost always destroy the original biological diversity of a forest, proper management can prevent deforestation. If clear-cutting is avoided and seedlings are replanted, forests can regenerate. Unfortunately, in tropical regions, only about a fifth of logged forests is actively managed, and then at minimal levels. Most logging companies purchase only short-term concessions from the government, so they have little motive to interest themselves in the forest regrowth.

Deforestation has had a cruel effect on peasants in Asia and Africa who must depend on firewood for fuel. In the Himalayan foothills of Nepal, where wood accounts for almost all fuel, the journey to gather firewood required only an hour or two a generation ago; now, because of the retreating woodlands, the job takes an entire day. Some areas have been so stripped of wood that people must depend on weeds and shrubs and dig roots to burn. This has led to major changes in eating patterns; people must rely on less nutritious foods that can be eaten raw or require little cooking.

One major result of deforestation is soil erosion. Large areas have been permanently denuded of anything more than scrub grass. The effect is amplified if heavy equipment is used, as in road building, mining, and lumbering; machines pack the dirt so that rain cannot infiltrate the soil. The clearing of hillsides and mountain slopes is ruinous, not only for the soil but also for rivers that are blocked by sediment and landslides.

There has already been a significant loss of biodiversity. Tropical forests supply oils, gums, rubber, fiber, dyes, resins, tropical fruits, and even the ingredients for drugs for leukemia and Hodgkin's disease. Plant, animal, and insect species have been dying out at a rapid rate, never to be replaced. As a diverse gene pool is lost, remaining forests and animals become less adaptive and more vulnerable to extinction. In Africa and Asia, over two-thirds of wildlife habitat has been lost.

The huge Amazon Basin, along the 3,900-mile Amazon River, overlaps six countries. The two-thirds of the basin in Brazil has been under relentless attack from commercial timber interests, rubber tappers, ranchers, migrating farmers, and miners of gold, uranium, manganese, and iron. Several large multinationals have attempted to exploit the area. Between the mid-1920s and 1940, Henry Ford tried to institute a large rubber plantation there, and, more recently, U.S. shipping executive Daniel Ludwig established a timber, wood pulp, and agricultural project over a vast area. Because of the fragility of the soil, such attempts have been unsuccessful and have left large areas deforested.

The Transamazonian Highway and a web of connecting roads have themselves devastated thousands of acres of forest, while stimulating settlement. Brazilian policy toward its richest resource has been erratic, alternately encouraging massive despoliation through subsidized ranching, lumbering, and mining, then trying futilely to introduce managed forestry techniques. The Amazon region is believed to contain at least 30,000 plant species, including unique varieties useful in the manufacture of drugs, many of which are already becoming extinct. Once a home to between six million and nine million Indians, the indigenous forest population now numbers less than 200,000. Buildup of sediment in the Amazon — the largest river in the world — has killed fish and aquatic animals and threatens to alter the discharge pattern into the sea (Pearce et al. 1990).

Atmospheric effects of deforestation around the world are not entirely understood. It is possible that the decrease in soil moisture in eroded areas may reduce rainfall over entire regions, and denuded areas can reflect more sunlight, leading to increases in local temperatures. On a global scale, the burning of forest adds to the greenhouse effect by elevating atmospheric levels of carbon dioxide.

The Spreading Deserts

When environmentalist Paul Harrison (1992:140) returned to the once-verdant Yatenga plateau in Africa's Burkino Faso after an eleven-year absence, he found that "former fields and grassy fallow had been reduced to bare crusted wasteland, scattered with a pavement of mauve pebbles. It was as if the soil had leprosy. The bushes were dry and brittle, and the dead trees held out their lopped branches, pleading for moisture from the sky." What he was witnessing was the process of desertification — the degradation of soil and vegetation within a semiarid zone that leads to desert-like conditions. The process, which is largely man-induced, includes the severe crusting and hardening of the earth, erosion to gullies, and the incursion of sand dunes. A United Nations study estimated that over eleven billion acres around the world — home to some 850 million people — were in some stage of desertification. Worldwide, deserts claim over sixteen million acres each year. Some 135 million people live in areas of severe desertification (Bread for the World 1992:68).

Growing populations are a major cause of the deterioration. When populations of arid and semiarid regions are relatively small, peasants and pastoralists maintain a balance with the environment, often routinely migrating in search of more productive land or better pasture. As populations grow, all the land is taken up, making migration difficult or impossible. People must overplant in order to survive. Crops become thinner, with meager roots to hold the debilitated earth in place, so that more topsoil washes away. Cattle and sheep chew grass down to the stumps, and goats eat seedlings and the leaves of bushes and trees before they can produce seeds. Wells — which provide water for people, animals, and crops — must be dug deeper and deeper as the water table drops a little more each year. Rain washes silt and clay into the interstices that permit water to permeate the ground; blocked from soaking in, rain flows along the surface, washing soil into gullies. Cash crops for export, introduced during colonial times, often exacerbate the problem in two ways: first, the crops themselves may leach the soil and use up too much precious water, and, second, because such plantations invariably utilize the most productive soils, small-scale farmers and pastoralists are forced onto the most marginal lands.

A series of studies by a Swedish research group questioned this accepted sequence for the most afflicted area of the world, the Sahel region in Africa. Using a variety of methods — including remote sensing, agricultural statistics, interviews with farmers, and climate data — the researchers concluded that the primary cause of the spread of desert was a decrease in rainfall over much of the region. Over the past two decades, areas along the southern edge of the Sahara that once supported crops are no longer capable of doing so (Toulmin et al. 1992). Also, it is not always easy to determine whether desertification is actually taking place, because in normal circumstances, deserts tend to expand and recede, often over extensive areas. Whatever the cause — probably a complex of climatic and human-induced changes — there can be no doubt that many regions are severely affected.

The burdens of desertification tend to fall most heavily on women. Men often depart the area in search of wage labor, leaving women behind to work fourteen hours a day or more carrying water and gathering fuel, often over great distances, and working fields and grinding grain. Because of their key role, women supply up to 85 percent of unskilled labor — mostly unpaid — in national and international antidesertification projects (Monimart 1991).

A disastrous five-year drought in Africa starting in 1968 led to over 100,000 deaths, and later droughts have also taken a toll in the tens of thousands (Figure 8.2). Famine, however, is not a simple matter of drought or of overgrazing and overplanting; there is almost always a political component. People may be prevented from escaping along traditional migration routes because of national borders, revolutionary activity, or overpopulation. Food prices may be kept artificially low by government edict, so that farmers reduce their output. Land tenure and profit play significant roles; often, the export of cash crops continues undiminished even during the worst periods of famine. Hunger may

FIGURE 8.2
Repeatedly Drought-Affected Areas of Africa

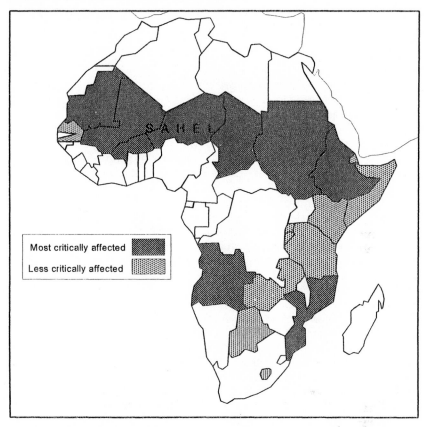

Source: Avijit Gupta, *Ecology and Development in the Third World* (London: Routledge, 1988), p. 24.

result when governments or banks choose to provide all loans and aid to cities or industry, ignoring the needs of marginal agricultural areas. The devastating Ethiopian famine of 1984 and 1985 was caused largely by government actions, such as the confiscation of grain and livestock through excessive taxes, labor conscription that took farmers away from their crops at crucial times, and an ill-conceived land-redistribution program (Clay and Holcomb 1985).

Attempts to transfer Green Revolution crops, so successful in Asia, to Africa have generally not fared well. Marginal farmers have been thwarted by the high cost of such crops, and uncertain rains compound the risk of losing everything. High-yield grains require irrigation, which is difficult or exorbitantly expensive in arid regions, and, even in good years, the low level of production may not justify the cost.

Whatever the causes of desertification and famine, the hundreds of millions of people living in arid regions remain at risk.

Cities and the Environment

Because they concentrate so many people, industries, and vehicles in relatively small areas, cities have a profound effect on regional, national, and global ecosystems. Third World cities, with their exceedingly high rates of growth and minimal environmental protections, tend to be worse offenders than cities of similar size in the West. Historically, most major cities were ecologically sound when founded. Over the centuries, and especially in the past fifty years, many cities have overgrown their original sites, spreading outward onto fragile or even hostile land — steep hillsides prone to erosion, plains susceptible to flooding, and marshes. It is usually the poor — those who have the least money to spend on environmental improvements — who must live in such areas, with the result that deterioration continues unchecked. Even when wealth is expended on urban expansion, the effect may be devastating; hills are razed, valleys and swamps filled in with rocks and waste, and river patterns changed.

There are four basic ways that cities threaten the environment. First, the regional climate may be altered as reflected sunlight from roofs and pavement is trapped by air pollution, creating islands of excessive heat. Second, natural water configurations are disrupted or altered as construction increases erosion and waste and sediment block streams. Because streets are impervious to water, flooding in the lower levels of cities is common, or massive runoff from concrete drains may cause flooding of surrounding areas. Third, geomorphological changes result from bulldozing hills or from settlement on steep slopes, where inhabitants may be in danger of man-caused landslides, and the effects of earthquakes may be devastating. Finally, all forms of pollution are found in high concentrations in cities.

Two types of dangerous smog occur in large metropolitan areas. The so-called London smog complex results from the smoke of burning coal and heavy oil. The air becomes filled with sulfuric acid, sulfur dioxide, and suspended particulates, leading to a reduction in the ability of the lungs to function, immediately increasing deaths and, in the long run, inducing respiratory diseases and lung cancer. The Los Angeles smog complex is caused mainly by traffic and other emissions of carbon dioxide, nitric oxide, nitrogen oxide, and ozone. Carbon monoxide alone can lead to central nervous system disorders, and all together the chemical soup increases respiratory disease in children and asthma in adults. London and Los Angeles have improved their air quality through stringent city laws and ordinances, but both types of smog remain common in the Third World, where industries and motor vehicles are unregulated. In Shanghai, seven power stations, eight steelworks, eight thousand industrial boilers, a thousand kilns, a million cooking stoves, and tens of thousands of cars and trucks pour their toxic emissions into the air, resulting in a content of suspended particulates four times the minimum recommended by the World Health Organization (Hardoy et al. 1992).

A city in a valley or basin is particularly susceptible to thermal inversion, when a mass of warm air traps pollutants in the cooler air underneath. Mexico City, which increased its emissions almost 50 percent just between 1972 and 1983, is perfectly situated for thermal inversions. Entrepreneurs sell brief puffs of oxygen at booths along the streets. In China, lung cancer is four to seven times greater in cities than in the country as a whole, and, in Calcutta, three-fifths of the population suffer from respiratory ailments caused by air pollution (Harrison 1992:175).

Sewers and waste disposal systems have not been able to keep up with growing urban populations, with the result that severe water pollution is common in Third World cities. In Manila, only a tenth of the population is served by sewers; road gutters, open ditches, and canals must suffice for the rest. In Accra, Ghana, a central sewage system exists, but only a third of the households are hooked up to it because of the high connection charges. Only 2 percent of the population of Bangkok is connected to the sewer system, and public water is so inadequate that a third of the people must purchase water. The problem of water is even worse in Jakarta, Indonesia, where two-thirds of the population must purchase their water from vendors at prices up to fifty times that of households served by the municipal water supply. Jakarta has no central sewage system at all, and less than 10 percent of the population have formal toilet facilities.

Garbage and industrial waste are also severe problems. Rural areas produce relatively little refuse, and most of that tends to be biodegradable. In cities, everything comes in packages that must be disposed of and include plastics and metals that will not soon decompose by natural processes. Garbage pickup is normally highly inadequate; it is estimated that for the less developed countries as whole, from 30 percent to 50 percent of urban solid wastes goes uncollected, giving rise to hordes of rats, flies, and mosquitoes. People dump wherever they can — in fields, along roadsides, in canals, and in rivers.

Only in the past two decades has the problem of hazardous and toxic waste from industries been recognized as a severe problem in the Third World. Lead, mercury, asbestos, petroleum by-products, cyanide, and arsenic are often dumped indiscriminately, possibly entering the water and food supplies. The people of Ambivali, a village near Bombay, India, are slowly being poisoned as toxic heavy metals dumped by 150 urban industries into the Kalu River enter food through irrigation and cattle browsing on the river banks.

Poor people tend to bear the brunt of such problems. The wealthier live in sanitary suburbs, while the poor are confined to unhealthy inner-city slums or squatter settlements. In one city in Indonesia, the wealthiest fifth of the population benefitted from 80 percent of public services, such as garbage collection and sewage disposal. Third World cities are normally not very densely populated, but shantytowns are an exception; in Nairobi, Kenya, the average population density is less than ten people per acre, but in one area of squatter settlements the figure rises to nearly two hundred an acre. One result of such crowding, combined with poor sanitation, is endemic disease.

Urban environmental problems are not confined to cities; they affect entire regions. Towns and cities usually develop, not in forests or desert, but in the heart of agricultural land. As cities expand, prime cropland is destroyed, and farmers are forced to push on to marginal land or into forests, leading to widespread erosion and deforestation. Cities are also major users of fuel wood, so, even without the spread of farms, deforestation may be severe. Often demands for fuel wood can reach long distances; in the early 1980s, railways emanating from Delhi, India, were bringing in over six hundred tons of wood a day from distances over four hundred miles away. Often such far-off sources of wood for cities are barred to locals, or prices are so high that rural people must forage elsewhere or do without. Naturally, rural populations far from major cities suffer from polluted rivers and other environment degradations. A 1983 United Nations study of a vast area surrounding Jakarta, Indonesia, found extensive water pollution, the loss and deterioration of farm land and forests, and the degradation of the coastline. The extraction of groundwater for city use intruded sea water ten miles inland.

Problems are not confined to large or primal cities. Small towns and cities have been multiplying rapidly, often in fragile environments and in previously uninhabited or sparsely settled regions, such as the interior of Brazil or the southern mountains of Argentina. Smaller cities are even less likely to have the basic amenities than large urban complexes, because they are often poorer and of more recent origin. In India, a study of three thousand towns found that only 7 percent had sewage systems. On a world basis, 18 percent of cities with populations from 200,000 to 500,000 lacked any piped water at all, and 60 percent lacked sewage facilities. Often, smaller cities grow up around a certain industry, or group of industries, with predictable results. Cubatao, a small city near São Paulo, Brazil, boasts twenty-three large industrial plants, each contributing its air pollution, with the result that there are extremely high levels of tuberculosis, bronchitis, asthma, and pneumonia (Gupta 1988).

The global effects of cities are profound. They provide the locus for the emission of greenhouse gasses and chemicals that contribute to the depletion of the atmosphere's ozone layer.

Cleaning up industrial pollutants is very expensive, but many of the city's environmental problems can be alleviated at relatively little cost to money-strapped urban governments. Pour-flush toilets require little water, and ventilated pit latrines can help in the problem of sewage disposal. Waste is often naturally recycled by poor people; in Calcutta, as many as 40,000 people earn their livings recovering and recycling thrown-away materials, and in Mexico, 10,000 search the garbage dumps, recycling a quarter of all waste. Nonrecyclable waste often can be used for compost. One *favela* in Olinda, Brazil, built a small plant for separating recyclable materials and composting the rest. Such efforts must be done by individual neighborhoods or communities but need to be encouraged by the city governments (Hardoy et al. 1992).

TOWARD SUSTAINABLE DEVELOPMENT

In 1992, more than 1,600 scientists, including 102 Nobel laureates, signed a "Warning to Humanity" that stated in part: "No more than one or a few decades remain before the chance to avert the threats we now confront will be lost and the prospect for humanity will be immeasurably diminished. . . . A new ethic is required — a new attitude towards discharging our responsibility for caring for ourselves and for our earth" (Quoted in Postel 1994:19). That "new ethic" has assumed the label "sustainable development," a complex concept that implies the integration of three systems: the biological, the economic, and the social. The "goals" of the biological system — meaning all that lives on the Earth — are genetic diversity, productivity, and the resilience to thrive under changing conditions. The economic system ideally strives toward increased production of goods and services, the satisfaction of basic needs, the reduction of poverty, and increased equity. Social system goals might include cultural diversity, social justice, popular participation in politics, and increased gender equality. Previously, the three systems have been kept distinct, but this no longer can be condoned if the improvement of human living conditions in this generation is to be conjoined with the maintenance of natural wealth for future generations.

Integrating biological, economic, and social goals will require trade-offs, many of which will be politically difficult. Economic growth is too often the single aim of government policy. Growth means a simple increase in goods and services with no regard to distribution or side-effects. Development, on the other hand, refers to the realization of potentialities, the movement not toward *more* but toward *better*. The current emphasis on growth may have to give way to a "quality over quantity" principle in which effects on the environment are a primary and integral consideration. Ultimately, "progress" must be measured in holistic terms, in which biological and social goals are given at least equal, and sometimes greater, weight than immediate economic goals (Holmberg and Sandbrook 1992).

Such thinking requires a radical break with the past. Some analysts are even speaking of sustainable development as a "third revolution," on a par with the invention of agriculture about 10,000 years ago and with the industrial revolution. The major difference is that the two previous revolutions are accomplished facts; the third has not happened yet — and there is no certainty that it will.

Many of the most entrenched systems in the world today are diametrically opposed to such a revolution. Capitalism historically has been growth oriented. It is true that the capitalist First World has gone farthest in making environment a priority, but this may be more an effect of wealth than of the logic of the economic system. Throughout the world, millions of people's livelihoods have become dependent on despoiling the environment — through agriculture on marginal lands, deforestation, mining, and commercial fishing — and such people cannot give up their jobs or reduce their incomes without threats to their very survival. Powerful elites in Latin America are not about to voluntarily allow their lands to be redistributed out of a sudden realization of the morality of social equity. National sovereignty and vast differentials in power have prevented a concerted international attack on environmental problems. Systems that have been generations or even hundreds of years in developing do not change overnight.

Nevertheless, the outlines of what must be done are already clear. True sustainable development would require minimizing the use of fossil fuels and minerals and other nonrenewable resources, relying more on renewable resources (and making sure they *are* renewed, such as replanting lumbered forests), and keeping within local, regional, and global capacities for waste. Population growth rates in the Third World must be reduced in the short run, and population must be stabilized in the long run. The supply of food and other goods and services must be more equally distributed, both within countries and internationally.

At a national level, many government policies encourage environmental degradation, for example, through subsidizing carbon-intensive energy plants, such as those using low-grade coal. One suggestion, more appropriate for developed than underdeveloped countries, is to eliminate all subsidies for energy and instead impose energy taxes. Although such a policy would inevitably reduce energy consumption and, thus, pollution and resource depletion, the effect on the poorest people might be to eliminate their chances of having electricity at all. However, a mixture of graded taxes along with subsidies for the poorest (who use the least energy, in any case), might be helpful. The First World can play a major role by providing credits for energy-efficient power plants and by exporting the latest technologies in wind and solar power.

National governments can do much to slow deforestation by removing subsidies for loggers and ranchers, by classifying different types of forest according to potential for regeneration and establishing separate policies for each type, and by setting aside those forests that are particularly fragile or have a high value for their natural diversity. Nonwood substitutes have been found for making paper, such as bamboo (a grass), hemp, jute, and kenaf. The latter is a fast-growing plant that produces two to four times more pulp per acre than southern pine. In China, 80 percent of paper is already made from nonwood products. In addition, instead of clear-cutting forests for agriculture, both subsistence and profit can be realized through shade-tolerant crops such as cocoa, cassava, maize, and some green vegetables. In India, individual farmers and entire communities have been subsidized by the government not to destroy woodland but, rather, to plant trees. In one very successful program, schoolchildren were encouraged to plant seedlings and look after them as they grew to trees.

Garret Hardin (1974) argued that the "tragedy of the commons" explains much environment degradation. If a pasture is held in common by an entire group, so that all can forage their animals on it, each individual will be encouraged to overuse it and no one will have responsibility for maintaining it. The pollution of the air and the overfishing of the oceans are similar. Such a situation exists with some socialized collective agriculture, which has proven inefficient and destructive to the land. Squatter settlements and squatter farming might have a similar effect. Clarifying property rights can be a significant factor in reducing environmental degradation. In Thailand, providing land titles reduced damage to forests, because farmers were willing to take care of their own land rather than constantly seek new land by burning down trees. In Kenya, providing title to farm land led to greatly reduced erosion.

The private-property solution has its limits, however. Lands traditionally held in common by Indian groups in Latin America often have been cared for with devoted attention for centuries. On the other hand, private companies have been quite willing to destroy the environment for short-term profit, and private markets provide little or no incentive to curb pollution or to get rid of wastes responsibly. In fact, market prices very seldom reflect ecological values; the costs of pollution are not included in prices, forcing the taxpayer to bear the costs of cleanup and reclamation. Ultimately, the government must step in not only to prevent air and water pollution but also to assure that market prices include necessary costs to the environment.

The World Bank (1992:22) suggests seven important ways that national governments can promote sustainable development. First, environmental considerations must be built into the policy-making process. Second, reduction in population growth should be a priority. Third, in keeping with the slogan "Think globally, act locally," local problems should be attacked first. Fourth, administrative costs of environmental protection should be minimized by setting realistic goals and enforcing them. Fifth, the need for trade-offs between the economic, social, and biological spheres cannot be avoided, but such trade-offs should be enacted only after a careful analysis of both short- and long-term effects. Sixth, governments need to conduct research on environmental problems and assure that the results reach administrators and the public. Finally, the old adage that "prevention is cheaper than cure" should be kept in mind; it is much easier and cost efficient to protect the environment in the first place than to suffer the consequences of irreparable damage or of cleaning up.

The Road to — and from — Rio

Worldwide attempts to protect the environment have a relatively short, but not undistinguished, history. The Stockholm Conference of 1968 brought together representatives from 113 countries and four hundred environmental groups. The resulting "Action Plan for the Human Environment" called for conscious environmental management on the part of policy makers, a global assessment of problems, and education and training. Though weak and lacking any legal status, the Action Plan did promote the development of some national environmental policies and, more importantly, stimulated the creation of the United Nations Environmental Programme. Other conferences followed, including those leading to a Law of the Sea, completed in 1982, which, among other things, included ordinances relating to marine pollution. The Montreal Protocol of 1987 set target dates for the complete phasing out of chlorofluorocarbons, which are responsible for the diminishing ozone layer. Both measures have the status of law and show that the international community can really act as well as talk. Also in 1987, the World Commission on Environment and Development issued a report titled *Our Common Future* — known as the Brundtland Report after the Norwegian Prime Minister who headed the project — that developed and popularized the idea of "sustainable development."

In June 1992, the largest environmental conference up to that time was held in Rio de Janeiro, Brazil. With over 20,000 participants representing thousands of organizations from 171 countries, plus 9,000 journalists and 450,000 visitors, the whole enterprise threatened to collapse into a huge media circus. The hype did not, however, detract from the seriousness of 350 formal meetings as well hundreds of substantive discussions over a period of two weeks. The primary result emerged as Agenda 21, consisting of five hundred pages of recommendations on issues of development, the role of groups, problems related to specific resources, and the implementation of environmental programs.

Key among its themes was an emphasis on a bottom-up approach, utilizing communities and nongovernmental organizations both to protect and to restore the environment. There should be a complimentarity between market mechanisms and regulation, so that trade is encouraged, but without environmental degradation resulting from the drive for profits. The importance of adequate research and the dispersal of information was emphasized. In order that the achievements of the Rio Conference not be lost, it was recommended that a "Commission on Sustainable Development" be created within the United Nations (the United Nations quickly complied). Though Agenda 21 did not have the binding force of law, it did have more authority than a mere report (Table 8.1).

One agreement to emerge from the conference — the Convention on Biological Diversity — *was* legally binding. This committed signatory nations to conserve biological diversity through the protection of species and established terms for uses of biological resources and technology. The United States, fearing threats to its growing biotechnology industry and to the protection of patents, was not among the 155 signers of the document.

Though in many ways a success, the Rio Conference exposed some fundamental conflicts between the First World and the Third World. Many developing countries came to the conference apprehensive that they would suffer limits on their development and that the West would come up with new constraints on foreign aid. The industrialized North tended to perceive population growth as the primary cause of environmental degradation, whereas the poorer countries pointed to the First World's exorbitant consumption patterns, noting, for example, that the United States with 5 percent of the world's population uses a quarter of nonrenewable resources. Issues important to the developed countries, such as the greenhouse effect, often got more attention and more publicity than issues of prime importance to impoverished countries, such as fresh water and debt relief. In pressing for more aid and limits on consumption, the Third World often showed little understanding of First World political realities and budget constraints. Ultimately, however, everyone got a hearing. Agenda 21 committed the developed countries to 0.7 percent of their gross national products in official development assistance. Population growth was faced, but with compromise wording; because of Catholic opposition, "family planning" became "reproductive health techniques," and the emphasis was on child mortality and economic security over contraception (Grubb et al. 1993).

Perhaps the most important result of the Rio Conference was to irretrievably put the environment on the table, so to speak — to assure that, from now on, the Earth must be a consideration in national or international policy decisions.

TABLE 8.1
The Seven Worlds of Agenda 21

The main outcome of the 1992 Earth Summit in Rio de Janeiro was Agenda 21, an environmental action plan for the 1990s into the twenty-first century. It includes:

A Prospering World — the integration of environment and development
  Growth with sustainability through a market economy, in which prices of natural resources reflect resource depletion and costs of maintaining the environment
  International support for developing countries to make the transition to sustainability

A Just World — sustainable living
  Need to reduce and ultimately eradicate poverty worldwide
  Rich need to change lifestyles to less reliance on nonsustainable consumption
  National policies must integrate population growth, environment, and development
  Basic health needs must be met, with a focus on especially vulnerable groups such as infants, women, and indigenous peoples

A Habitable World — human settlements
  Management of human settlements to raise quality of shelter, water supply, energy, and transportation
  Special attention to problems of urban areas, such as pollution and solid waste

A Fertile World — efficient use of resources
  Need to address soil erosion, salinization, waterlogging, desertification
  Develop and employ techniques of sustainable agriculture
  Protect forests and other fragile ecosystems, such as coastal areas
  Conserve biological diversity

A Shared World — management of global and regional resources
  Protect the ozone layer, and protect the atmosphere from greenhouse gasses and other pollutants
  Address the problems of overfishing and the degradation of the oceans
  Necessity for international cooperation

A Clean World — managing chemicals and waste
  Reduce the production of toxic waste, and improve its safe handling and disposal
  Minimize the dangers of radioactive wastes

A People's World — participation and responsibility
  Involve all groups in sustainable development, including women, youth, farmers, labor unions, business and industry, and the scientific community
  Reorient education toward sustainable development and promote public awareness

---

Source: UNCED 1992

The Role of Grass-roots Organizations

One of the major points to emerge from the Rio Conference was that sustainable development must begin at the grass roots. Governments have not fared well in protecting the environment; entrenched interests, corruption, and extremely limited budgets have prevented effective policies or implementation if such policies have been enacted. Local independent groups are often much better acquainted with environmental problems and much more motivated to confront them. There are two basic types of nongovernmental organizations. More than 30,000 "grassroots support organizations" are nationally or regionally based and usually staffed by professionals. They are concerned with the environment, development, the role of women, and primary health care and often work with local indigenous organizations, funneling money to them from international sources. The true grass-roots organizations are locally based and dedicated to improving their own communities. Often, they have restricted memberships, such as farmers or women.

There are probably hundreds of thousands of grass-roots organizations with a collective membership of millions. In Africa alone, thousands of groups devoted to development and environmental improvement have emerged over the past decades. In one study of five hundred households in Zimbabwe, over half belonged to local agricultural associations. In Kenya, grass-roots organizations proliferated from 5,000 in 1980 to 26,000 in 1991. The pattern is similar throughout the Third World. In Brazil, there are 4,000 rural unions and 100,000 Christian Base Organizations, which devote themselves to community improvement. In São Paulo alone, there are 1,300 neighborhood associations that plant gardens, recycle garbage, and have built more than twenty miles of street gutters. Such groups are in the front line in the battle against environmental degradation (Fisher 1993).

The Greening of the World Bank

Until recently, the World Bank had established a long reputation for financing large-scale projects with little trickle-down benefit to the poor. In addition, in the early 1980s, nongovernmental organizations uncovered and publicized numerous examples of World Bank projects that degraded the environment. One development scheme increased deforestation in the Amazon from under 2 percent to almost a quarter of one large region. A coal mining and power plant project in Singrauli, India, became one of the greatest sources of carbon emissions on Earth. Also in India, five power plants, twelve open-pit mines, and eight cement plants funded by the World Bank displaced over 200,000 natives.

The U.S. Congress responded to such reports by passing legislation in 1985 making U.S. contributions to the World Bank dependent on environmental reforms. Two years later, the World Bank announced substantive changes, including the screening of projects for environmental impact. In 1993, the bank committed nearly $2 billion to twenty-three projects specifically targeted at protecting the environment, including $1.3 billion for pollution control, $500 million for projects designed to protect natural resources, and $140 million for building environmentally protective institutions. In 1991, a Global Environment Facility was created as a partnership between the World Bank and the United Nations Development Programme to make grants to cover the additional cost of environmental protection during development projects.

The new "green" image of the World Bank has not been universally accepted, however. Many environmentalists still feel that their concerns have not been taken seriously enough. For example, loans to commercial loggers continue to encourage deforestation without — say the critics — adequate consultation with affected natives or sufficient guarantees of replanting. Despite such reproofs, there can be little doubt that the World Bank has come a long way in recognizing the centrality of environmental concerns in project planning (French 1994).

A PROMISING BEGINNING — AND A LONG WAY TO GO

For decades, the transfer of toxic wastes from the First World to the Third World went unchallenged. Taking advantage of less stringent environmental and health controls, U.S. industries that manufactured asbestos routinely sent their carcinogenic by-products to Brazil and Mexico for disposal. Bangkok's main port became the storage area for large quantities of chemical waste from developed countries. Italian companies paid a Nigerian landowner about $100 a month to dump thousands of tons of European chemical wastes (Hardoy et al. 1992).

Such practices have come to a halt. In March 1994, over the objections of the United States, Japan, and Germany, the industrialized nations agreed at a United Nations conference in Geneva to stop the practice of toxic waste exports. Though this agreement is but a footnote in the history of environmental policy — and it remains to be seen to what degree it can be enforced — it does demonstrate two important points: first, that the global community *can* work together to tackle environmental problems and, second, that this can be accomplished even against the wishes of the most powerful nations on Earth.

The number of international agreements and actions on the environment is relatively small but impressive. The Montreal Protocol put a stop to ozone-depleting chlorofluorocarbons; the Law of the Sea protected the oceans from some types of pollution; Agenda 21 of the Rio Conference provided a blueprint for sustainable development; and the World Bank has integrated ecological considerations into its planning policy.

Despite such promise, the barriers to sustainable development are — so far — much greater than the accomplishments. After more than a decade of sharp declines in population growth rates, such rates have leveled off, and population continues its exponential climb. Not only is population growing exponentially, but so is industrial production, carbon dioxide and other greenhouse gasses in the atmosphere, energy usage, and the consumption of metals; at the same time, rainforest is in exponential decline, as are nonrenewable resources in general (Meadows et al. 1992). Per capita agriculture is no longer expanding and, in many places, especially Africa, is diminishing. There has been little success in making sure food actually reaches the billion or so people who need it most desperately. As long as rural people are hungry and the most fertile properties are held by large-scale landowners for export crops, the devastating attack by the poor on marginal lands will proceed undiminished. The gap between the rich nations and the poor nations continues to widen, meaning that about 20 percent of the world population will persist in using an inordinate amount of the Earth's limited resources. Elites that benefit from despoiling the environment are reinforced by the profits of their efforts, giving them the power to block environmentally protective legislation. One of the greatest contributors to environmental degradation is the international debt, which pressures countries to reduce pollution controls, remove logging restrictions, promote cattle ranching, and expand export cropping in order to service their loans.

In other words, the attainment of sustainable development is not merely a matter of international conventions or of ecologically sensitive World Bank loans but is closely intertwined with the very structure of local, national, and international systems. Such systems are notoriously difficult to change. However, recent successes on behalf of the environment suggest that "sustainable development" may be more than just a catch phrase for the 1990s.

SUGGESTED READING

Brown, Lester, ed., *State of the World* (New York: W. W. Norton, annual). This annual series provides up-to-date articles on various aspects of the global environment.

Grubb, Michael, *The "Earth Summit" Agreements: A Guide and Assessment* (London: Earthscan, 1993). The United Nations Conference on Environment and Development in Rio de Janeiro in 1992 was part media hype and part substantive. This book provides a critical overview and analysis of the conference and its results.

Harrison, Paul, *The Third Revolution: Population, Environment and a Sustainable World* (London: Penguin, 1992). A balanced approach to global environmental problems that provides extensive empirical data to support the argument that a crisis is impending. Five village case studies are interspersed with more general analysis.

Holmberg, Johan, ed., *Making Development Sustainable* (Washington, D.C.: Island Press, 1992). The eleven articles in this book define "sustainable development" and show how it can be achieved in agriculture, industry, forestry, and energy.

Meadows, Donella H., Dennis L. Meadows, and Jørgen Randers, *Beyond the Limits* (Post Hills, Vt.: Chelsea Green, 1992). In this sequel to the famous *Limits to Growth*, the authors plug current data into their computer model of the world and reaffirm that we are headed for real trouble if we don't amend our ways — fast!

Sontheimer, Sally, ed., *Women and the Environment: A Reader* (New York: Monthly Review Press, 1991). Women are often portrayed — if they are mentioned at all — as passive victims in the Third World, but this book shows how they have taken the lead in many countries in fighting desertification, land degradation, and deforestation.

World Bank, *World Development Report 1992: Development and the Environment* (New York: Oxford, 1992). Each World Bank annual report focuses on a different subject. This edition analyses environmental problems with an emphasis on policy options. The book contains the usual charts, diagrams, and examples that make this series so outstanding.

9

Death Squads and
Disappearances: Human Rights
in the Third World

They sit me down, clothed, and tie my arms behind me. The application of electric shocks begins, penetrating my clothing to the skin. It's extremely painful, but not as bad as when I'm laid down, naked, and doused with water. The sensation of the shocks on my head makes me jump in my seat and moan.

No questions are asked. Merely a barrage of insults, which increase in intensity as the minutes pass. Suddenly, a hysterical voice begins shouting a single word: "Jew . . . Jew . . . Jew!" The others join in and form a chorus while clapping their hands. . . . It seems they're no longer angry, merely having a good time.

I keep bouncing in the chair and moaning as the electric shocks penetrate my clothes.

— Argentine journalist Jacobo Timerman (1981:60–61)

[An eleven-year-old girl and her twenty-two year old aunt, picked up for a curfew violation, were compelled] to spend the night with the soldiers. The older one was raped by six soldiers, while her niece was first raped twice by the unit commander and then by seven soldiers taking turns.

— Eyewitness report in Myanmar, formerly Burma
(Amnesty International 1991:20)

In the beginning . . . only officer's families were killed. At the beginning of 1976, however, the families of common soldiers were also killed. One day at Choeung Prey, I cried for a whole day on seeing women and children killed. I could no longer raise my arms. Comrade S__ said to me: "Get on with it." I said: "How can I? Who can kill women and children?" Three days later I was arrested.

— Testimony of a Khmer Rouge cadre in Cambodia
(Amnesty International 1986:155)

Such atrocities, sometimes institutionalized as a hidden part of state policy or routinized within the prison system, are an ongoing problem in many Third World countries. Although there has been sporadic improvement in human rights because of an increased world awareness and international pressures, violations by states against their own citizens continue at an appalling level.

The concept of human rights is of recent origin. However, the idea of "natural law" — a fundamental, inborn morality that was rendered by God or is apprehended by correct reason — is found in the Old and New Testaments and was developed by Greek philosophers who, in turn, influenced such Christian scholars as St. Thomas Aquinas. The Magna Carta of 1215 set a strong precedent by formally limiting the powers of the British monarchy. During the European Enlightenment of the seventeenth and eighteenth centuries, philosophers such as John Locke and Jean Jacques Rousseau held that there were "natural rights" that were antecedent to government, from which governments drew their legitimacy. The U.S. Declaration of Independence includes reference to "inalienable rights," and the French Revolution proclaimed that "liberty, equality, and fraternity" should belong to all.

World War II was the primary impetus to the contemporary concept of human rights; the Holocaust and other Nazi atrocities could not go unpunished merely because they had been legal under the German system. In introducing the novel concept of "crimes against humanity," the Nuremberg war crimes trials of 1946 and 1947 provided a basis for international standards. However, the nature and source of these standards remains controversial.

THE MEANING OF "HUMAN RIGHTS"

According to the Preamble of the United Nations (UN) Universal Declaration of Human Rights, such rights are "equal and inalienable" for "all members of the human family." In other words, they are prior to and transcend the laws of nations and are not circumscribed by state boundaries. The right to life and security, freedom from slavery, torture, or arbitrary imprisonment, and freedom of opinion or association are central to the definition of what it means to be human.

Nearly all members of the UN have ratified the Universal Declaration, yet at any given time, most states in the world fail to live up to the ideal. If such standards are so commonly breached, can they truly be "real"? And, if so, from where do these rights come?

Relativism or Universalism?

Two views predominate: the relativist and the universalist. A radical relativist would hold that humanity-wide values do not exist; culture is the sole source of morality. The extreme universalist, on the other hand, would see cultural variation as irrelevant, arguing that certain principles are inherent to human beings and, thus, outside of culture. Most theorists would assume a position between these extremes.

The American Anthropological Association took a relativist stance in a letter to the UN Commission on Human Rights in 1947, when the Universal Declaration was being composed. Everyone, it argued, is socialized into a specific culture, and, thus, the standards and values of each person will depend on his or her culture. Because there is no scientific or accepted technique for qualitatively evaluating different cultures, the principle of respect for cultural variation must predominate over universal prescriptions.

In the eyes of critics, cultural relativism is unconscionable, because it would seem to condone mass human sacrifice by the Aztecs or Nazi atrocities. Anthropologists retort that such criticism misunderstands cultural relativism, mistaking an "is" for an "ought," description for prescription. The variety of morals over time and place is a fact that has been established by cross-cultural research, but recognition that such practices exist does not imply approval. One can, and must, take a moral stand, but it should be recognized that such a stand is based on the individual's own culture and beliefs and not some abstract universal system of values.

Adamantia Pollis and Peter Schwab (1979) argue that the very idea of human rights is a Western concept, growing out of the specific history and culture of Europe and the United States. A key part of Western culture is an emphasis on the individual, whereas in traditional societies, as well as many contemporary countries, the group has priority over the individual. Whether that group is a family, a tribe, a community, or the state itself, many cultures view it as much more important than the individual. In fact, the individual gains his very nature and being from the group. Another ethnocentric aspect of Western values is the assumption that political and civil rights have priority over economic rights. Is freedom of speech and association really more important than the right to a decent-paying job and health benefits? In justifying communist China's record of persecuting landlords, rich peasants, "bourgeois revisionists," and counterrevolutionaries, one official observed that such people comprised only 5 percent of the population and that they must be repressed so that the other 95 percent could enjoy human rights, such as guaranteed food, housing, and medical care (Huang 1979).

One possible way of resolving the conflict between relativism and universalism is to search for commonalities of values through comparison of cultures around the world. Among the "human universals" found by anthropologist Donald Brown (1991:138–139) is "law" in the sense of rules, rights, and obligations. Everywhere, such law forbids violence, rape, and the unjustified taking of human life (though proscriptions usually only apply to the in-group). Cross-cultural analysis by Alison Renteln (1990) suggests that "retribution tied to proportionality" is a universal value. Everywhere it is recognized that punishment must be in proportion to the crime, and this imposes strong limits on what can be done. Even in feuds and the payment of blood money for murder in traditional societies, the rule of proportionality is strictly followed. In law, *lex talionis* is the principle that punishment should correspond in degree and kind. If the principle of proportionality were made a basis of human rights, Renteln argues, it would be culturally acceptable to all peoples. However, such a lowest-common-denominator approach is difficult to elaborate into a modern canon of universal human rights. For one thing, individual cultures might view proportionality very differently; in some societies, torture might seem appropriate for a traitor. A Biblically literal "eye for an eye" would seem barbaric to most people in both the First World and the Third World.

Jack Donnelly (1985a, 1985b, 1993) rejects cultural relativism. A cross-cultural approach runs into many problems; despite a modern tendency to romanticize traditional cultures, there are numerous examples of societies based on rigid hierarchies, siavery, the execution of dissidents, torture, and the denial of political participation. If, as facts seem to show, there are as many or more countries that use torture than not, what can we conclude about cross-cultural norms? In any case, cultural relativism is based on an erroneous view of the persistence of traditional societies. Although such societies do exist, they are no longer centers of power. All such societies are now embedded in states. In prestate societies, the social conditions for human rights did not exist, but with the emergence of the state, human rights have become essential. Human rights are basically the individual's claims against the state. Unlike a tribe or a clan, a state is not some sort of in-group that has priority over the individual; it is, rather, a complex, multilayered structure that exists through the consent of the individuals of which it is composed. Inalienable human rights focused on the individual are, indeed, universal. Yet, there may be many variations in the ways that such rights are institutionalized; for example, both multiparty and single-party regimes may provide freedom of speech and political participation (Howard and Donnelly 1987).

The strength of Donnelly's argument lies in its merging of both relativistic and universalistic perspectives. Human rights are not viewed as eternal Platonic ideals but as evolving out of the real conditions of human existence. However, lacking an empirical or testable basis for human rights concepts, the controversies will persist.

The United Nations Defines Human Rights

Whatever one's philosophic position on human rights, in international law, it has been the UN that has led the way with a series of pivotal documents. Article 1, Section 3, of the UN Charter of 1945 specifies that one of the purposes of the organization is "promoting and encouraging respect for human rights and for fundamental freedoms." This was the first international agreement in which countries of the world made human rights a serious commitment at the national level. However, specific rights were not spelled out, and the wording was vague. The incipient UN established a Commission on Human Rights, with Eleanor Roosevelt as its first chair, to create an international Bill of Rights.

The result was the Universal Declaration of Human Rights, which was ratified in 1948, with forty-eight countries approving, none against, and eight abstentions, including the Soviet Union, South Africa, and Saudi Arabia. The preamble declares the document's universality "as a common standard of achievement for all peoples and all nations." The thirty "articles" of the declaration guarantee the "right to life, liberty and security of person" and numerous other rights (Table 9.1).

There is no doubt that the Universal Declaration is the single most important document on human rights, but there is debate over its legal standing. Eleanor Roosevelt did not seem to think of the handiwork of her commission as a legal statement. The Universal Declaration, she said, "is not a treaty; it is not an international agreement; it is not and

TABLE 9.1
The Universal Declaration of Human Rights

Article 1 of the UN Universal Declaration states that "All human beings are born free and equal in dignity and rights. They are endowed with reason and conscience and should act towards one another in a spirit of brotherhood." Specific guarantees among the 33 articles include:

3. "The right to life, liberty, and the security of person."
4. Prohibition of slavery.
5. Prohibition against "torture or . . . cruel, inhuman or degrading treatment or punishment."
7. Equal protection before the law.
9. Freedom from arbitrary arrest, detention, or exile.
11. Presumption of innocence before the law.
12. Freedom of movement, both within and outside the borders of the state.
16. Right to marry and found a family; freedom of choice in marriage partner.
17. Right to own property; freedom from arbitrary deprivation of property.
18. Freedom of "thought, conscience, and religion."
19. Freedom of opinion and expression.
20. Freedom of organization.
21. Right to participate in government; periodic elections.
23. Right to work and free choice of employment; equal pay for equal work.
24. Right to rest and leisure, including reasonable working hours and paid holidays.
25. Right to an adequate standard of living, including food, housing, medical care.
26. Right to education — free through elementary school.
27. Right "to freely participate in the cultural life of the community."

does not purport to be a statement of law or of legal obligation" (quoted in Pollis and Schwab 1979:4). Over the decades, the document has assumed considerable authority so that the dominant view today, at least among Western nations, is that it constitutes the definitive interpretation of human rights for the UN Charter and, therefore, is, indeed, legally binding on member nations. Also, its nearly half-century of existence has established it as "customary" international law, which is obligatory to all countries whether or not they have ratified the document. The lack of enforcement mechanisms, however, as well as the fact that some of the guaranteed rights and freedoms are routinely ignored by a great many of its ratifiers, consigns the Declaration to a peculiar legal ambivalence.

Some Third World theoreticians see the Declaration as intrinsically flawed by its Western bias. In its formation, eighteen drafts of the Declaration were submitted, all by European or North American countries, and all except two originated in England. The primacy of political over economic rights and the individual over the group represents a distinctive Western tradition. Of the thirty articles, only three — one dealing with private property — are economic, and these were included in the final text only at the insistence of a Canadian representative. The document was created with virtually no Third World input and ratified at a time when colonialism was still dominant and most new independent states did not exist. There can be little doubt that if the Declaration were written today, with input from the full General Assembly, it would look very different. Among the articles that some Third World countries find ethnocentric are Article 1 on the equality of individuals (many societies are based on hierarchy), Article 16 on the free choice of marriage (arranged marriages remain norma- tive in many parts of the world), Article 18 on freedom of religion (sev- eral Middle Eastern countries are effectively theocracies, and the Koran proscribes leaving Islam), and Article 17 on the ownership of private property (communal ownership is normal in some traditional societies in Africa, and socialist countries claim state ownership).

The Universal Declaration was reinforced with the much more detailed International Covenant on Civil and Political Rights, which elaborated on freedom from slavery and arbitrary arrest, freedom of travel, and freedom of conscience and religion. Objections that the Uni- versal Declaration overemphasized political rights were answered with an International Covenant on Economic, Social, and Cultural Rights, which covered such topics as fair wages, freedom to form unions, paid maternity leave and paid vacations, the right to an adequate standard of living including food, clothing, housing, and education, and so forth. These two Covenants were approved by the General Assembly in 1966 but were not ratified until ten years later. The Universal Declaration and the two Covenants comprise The International Bill of Human Rights. Numerous other more specific documents have emerged, so that, by the early 1990s, the UN had ratified over sixty treaties, declarations, protocols, and conventions on human rights, covering national self-determination, racial discrimination, war crimes, genocide, slavery, imprisonment, refugees, freedom of information, employment, women and families, children, social welfare, and cultural development.

As with the Universal Declaration, these other documents lack a means of enforcement. A Commission on Human Rights, and several specific bodies, can take complaints, investigate violations, and make reports, but there are few other means of redress.

Although the UN has been a pacesetter on human rights and has been a major actor in the struggle against racism and colonialism, in many ways, its own human rights record is deeply flawed. A quantitative study of UN pronouncements and actions on human rights found a tendency to focus on a few "pariah" regimes, such as South Africa, Israel, and Chile, while countries with equal or worse violations were ignored. According to this study, "human rights violators are selected for or exempted from public criticism largely on the basis of political considerations other than the nature, extent, and severity of their human rights violations" (Donnelly 1988:296).

THE DEADLY CORE: KILLING, TORTURE, POLITICAL IMPRISONMENT

The nature of human rights can vary according to one's ideological position. Freedom of the press and multiparty elections may be primary to many, but others might ask what freedom of the press means in a country in which three-quarters of the people are illiterate and the elite owns all of the media. Formal elections, even if not tainted by fraud, may signify little if they merely legitimize vast inequities of wealth and power. Dependency theorists have often used the term "structural violence" to refer to the malnutrition, sickness, and death that results not from war or systematic repression but from unnecessary poverty. Many would claim that economic rights are prior to political rights — that without food and guaranteed health benefits, other freedoms mean little. It might even be argued that Third World development requires that some freedoms be suppressed in favor of law and order, a position taken by many U.S. political scientists during the 1980s.

Despite such controversies, there is a common consensus on the three most basic human rights. Political killing, arbitrary imprisonment, and torture comprise a core of violations specified in numerous international documents that have been endorsed by virtually every country in the world. Added to this deadly core, and overlapping all three categories, is the practice of "disappearances" — the kidnapping of political opponents or ill-defined "subversives" who may never be seen again. There is no state that would openly support such practices, and though these violations are widespread, they are done in secret and denied by the responsible governments. When a government relies on such methods in order to survive, the result is "state terrorism," in which brutality becomes institutionalized.

There are many specific causes of state terror, but, in most, a situation exists in which the state or the oligarchy views itself as threatened. Often, a rigid ideology forms around the sometimes real, sometimes highly exaggerated threat so that communists, "counter-revolutionaries," a specific ethnic group, or just "subversives" in general may be repressed by the most extreme means. In the "national security states" that emerged throughout Latin America from the 1960s through the 1980s, virtually any opposition was seen as part of an international communist conspiracy that had to be stamped out at any cost. Jacobo Timerman (1981:101), who was himself arrested and tortured, notes that "The Argentine military tapped their vast reservoir of hatred and fantasy so as to synthesize their action into one basic concept: World War III had begun; the enemy was left-wing terrorism; and Argentina was the initial battleground chosen by the enemy." Argentina's professional killers and torturers saw themselves as an enlightened elite, defending the besieged system against a world threat that other countries were too obtuse to recognize. The only answer to such a danger was all-out war, with no mercy and no rules. "First we will kill all the subversives," proclaimed General Iberico Saint Jean, military governor of Buenos Aires in 1976, "then we will kill their collaborators; then . . . their sympathizers; then . . . those who remain indifferent; and finally we will kill the timid" (quoted in Donnelly 1993:45). Often, disease was used as a metaphor; subversion was a cancer that had to be surgically rooted out before it could spread and kill the society.

Behind such rhetoric, one will sometimes find anachronistic economies ruled by elites that will do anything to remain in power. In El Salvador and Guatemala, the authoritarian alliance between the military and the oligarchy was structurally incapable of the reforms that would redistribute wealth or political power. Institutionalized terror became a peculiar form of adaptation by which the system protected itself from the results of its own inner dynamics. In other cases, such as in Brazil or Chile, state terror gets mixed up with economic development, so that a military that conceives of itself as "enlightened" feels that only it has the knowledge and power to lead the country into the modern world.

Whereas in the national security state, it is the traditional elites and the existing structures that are being maintained through repression, in revolutionary countries, it is the old order that must be destroyed. Elites from the old regime must be killed, driven to exile, or "reeducated" in internment camps. Anything associated with the old system, including traditional religions, may be perceived as the enemy. In the ideological fervor that accompanies revolution, entire classes — not only the wealthy but also the educated — may be targeted, along with ethnic groups associated with the old ways. In such revolutionary situations, there may be a second wave of terror that occurs a decade or two after the first. When bureaucratization sets in, against the ideals of the revolution, or when the government fails to live up to its own goals and, thus, sets itself in opposition to many of the original adherents, the new elite may turn upon itself, devouring its own in factional struggle, as we see in Stalin's purge trials and in the Cultural Revolution in China.

State terror may erupt as a relatively brief outburst of violence that fades as soon as the perceived enemy is eradicated or when a dictatorship is transformed into a democracy. In such situations, brutality may become indiscriminate, leaving even the apolitical with no place to hide. On the other hand, repression may be a normal, long-term aspect of the state machinery of rule. People get used to it, in the sense that the limits are clearly known. Political imprisonment, killing, and torture may last for decades with little opposition.

The State as Mass Murderer

Over the past half century, more people have been killed by their own governments than have died in wars. According to figures gathered by Barbara Harff and Ted Gurr (1988), between 1945 and the late 1980s, about 5.5 million people perished in all international, civil, and colonial wars; during that same period, between seven million and sixteen million people died as a result of terror by states directed against their own citizens. These figures include the direct consequences of state policies, such as the starvation of millions of Cambodians, as well as outright murder. The large majority of the victims have been ordinary people — men, women, and children — whose only offense was to be associated with the wrong communal or political group. The forty-four instances of mass killings since World War II average to about one a year, and a typical episode lasted for five years. Of these, in four cases, over one million people died, and, in eleven cases, between 100,000 and one million were killed (Table 9.2).

Although there is a particularly heavy concentration of episodes associated with the decolonization process in Africa between 1961 and 1966, such killings are endemic to almost every region of the Third World. As late as 1993, Amnesty International was recording political killings in more than sixty countries. In China, between 800,000 and three million landlords, rich peasants, and members of the ousted Koumintang party were killed in the initial flush of victory by the communists in 1950 and 1951, and two decades later, another half million or so died in the Cultural Revolution. In Pakistan, up to three million Bengali nationalists were killed in the process of state formation. Tens of thousands have been killed in Ethiopia, El Salvador, Guatemala, Chad, Sri Lanka, Uganda, Angola, Afghanistan, Iraq, and

TABLE 9.2
Genocides and Politicides since 1945 — A Small Sample

Country	Year(s)	Victims	Number Killed
China	1950–1951	Kuomintang cadres, rich peasants, landlords	800,000–3 million
Sudan	1952–1972	Southern nationalists	100,000–500,000
Indonesia	1965–1966	Communists, Chinese	500,000–1 million
China	1966–1975	Cultural Revolution victims	400,000–850,000
Guatemala	1966–1984	Indians, political opposition	30,000–63,000
Uganda	1971–1979	Karamojong, Acholi, Lango tribes, Catholic clergy, political opposition	100,000–500,000
Pakistan	1971	Bengali nationalists	1.25 million–3 million
Kampuchea	1975–1979	Old regime loyalists, urbanites, disloyal cadre, religious groups, intellectuals	800,000–3 million
Indonesia	1975–present	East Timorese nationalists	60,000–200,000
Afghanistan	1978–1988	Old regime loyalists, rebel supporters	1 million
El Salvador	1980–1992	Political opposition	40,000
Rwanda	1994	Tutsi tribe and Hutu political opposition	500,000–1 million

Notes: Actual numbers of victims are seldom known; figures represent a range of best estimates. Victims include all civilians who have died as a direct result of regime action, including outright execution and massacre, but also bombings, starvation, and exposure. (Adapted from Harff and Gurr 1988: 365 and news sources.)

many other countries. More recently, systematic genocide has taken place in Bosnia and Rwanda.

On April 17, 1975, the Khmer Rouge guerilla army entered Phnom Penh, the capital of Cambodia (then called Kampuchea), after years of civil war. At that time, the city's population was over two million. Basing their decision on a bizarre ideology of agrarian communism, the army ordered the capital — as well as other towns and cities — to be evacuated. The process was accompanied by the killing of members of the previous government and military and their families. Soon the purges extended to merchants and the intelligentsia, including teachers and students. Ethnic minorities and religious clergy were also targeted. Thousands more were executed for minor infringements of work discipline. Nearly 20,000 were killed, often after severe torture, in one detention center alone. Altogether, about 300,000 were directly murdered, while another one to two million starved to death. The process ended only when the Khmer Rouge was overthrown by an invasion from Vietnam.

In terms of systematic murder by a government, few episodes top that of Indonesia during 1965 and 1966. After an abortive coup attempt, General Suharto turned his army against the legal Communist Party, at that time the largest political party in the country and one that sought change through democratic means. The goal was to exterminate not only party members but also their entire families. In the single town of

Kediri, seven thousand were killed; on the small island of Bali, fifty thousand died. Also targeted were the ethnic Chinese, who formed a merchant class (much as the Jews in Europe in the 1930s). It has been conservatively estimated that half a million were murdered in about nine months; the army itself estimated a million deaths. In addition, 750,000 were arrested without charge; many were still in prison a decade later.

Harff and Gurr classify such atrocities as *genocides* and *politicides*. In genocides, the victimized groups are defined primarily in terms of their communal characteristics, such as ethnicity, religion, or nationality. Killing is invariably accompanied by demonization of the target group, which is defined as somehow alien and threatening. In politicides, victims are the political opposition to the regime or to the elites. This may be an opposition party or faction, a previously dominant group that is being punished for ostensible past abuses, an heretical faction of the dominant revolutionary party, or an ethnic group engaged in political opposition. Of the forty-four episodes of mass killing, six fell into the category of genocide and thirty-eight were politicides.

Not all killings are aimed at easily definable groups. Excessive force is often used by police in crowd control situations, and peaceful protest can result in killings of both demonstrators and bystanders. Such were the cases in the infamous Tiananmen Square massacre in Peking in 1989, when Chinese troops killed at least a thousand demonstrators, and on the island of East Timor in 1991, when Indonesian troops opened fire on a funeral, killing two hundred. Rural civilians are in special danger during counterinsurgency operations, when the military may lash out at anyone available in revenge for their own losses. In 1992, the bodies of at least 794 people, including many children, were dug up from a mass grave in El Mazote, El Salvador, where they had been thrown after being massacred eleven years earlier. In Myanmar, formerly Burma, part of army strategy is to move peasants to "strategic hamlets" and declare large areas as "free-fire" zones; anyone found in such areas during army operations is subject to torture, rape, and killing.

Killing is not always directed against groups. Individuals are often targeted, such as social workers, priests and nuns, labor leaders, peasant organizers, and human rights activists. Sometimes, "social undesirables" will be killed; in Brazil, thousands of homeless children have been murdered because of the begging, petty thievery, and prostitution they must practice to survive.

Governments routinely deny any knowledge of such killings, blaming them on mysterious "death squads" over which officials claim they have no control. Such groups first emerged in Guatemala in the mid-1960s and within two decades had spread throughout Latin America and are today found in many countries of Asia and Africa. In the large majority of cases, death squads are official security forces in civilian clothes. "Early in 1980 I volunteered to join what is referred to in El Salvador as a death squad," reported a former Salvadoran soldier (Amnesty International 1993a:34–35). "However, in my experience the death squad has no independent existence outside the Salvadoran military and security forces. It is simply a form of duty which the military personnel are ordered to carry out while not in uniform. Within the military, these operations are not referred to as 'death squads' but simply as 'missions.'" Death squads get their target lists from high-level officials or military officers. In the early 1980s, death squad activity in Guatemala was centered in an annex to the National Palace; pickup trucks full of armed men in civilian clothes would leave the gates at night in search of specific victims. Sometimes death squads are made up of nongovernmental paramilitary units, but these, too, are under government or military control. In the Philippines, since 1987, the government has authorized and encouraged a network of semiofficial groups, such as the Citizen Armed Force Geographical Unit, which is responsible for numerous killings.

Political or arbitrary killing is not always done outside the law. In revolutionary Iran, thousands have been brought before religious courts on the flimsiest of charges and are sentenced to death with little or no defense. In China, sixty-five crimes — one-third of all criminal offenses — are punishable by death. In addition to murder and robbery, capital crimes include prostitution, trade in relics, organizing secret religious societies, and a host of "counterrevolutionary" offenses. One man was executed for making and selling liquor, basically a crime of patent infringement. In 1993, at least 1,411 prisoners were executed, an average of four a day, by a shot to the back of the head (Sun 1994).

Little is ever done about even the worst violators. Despite the magnitude of the killings in Cambodia, Indonesia, and Rwanda, the international community did nothing to stop them. In Halabja, Iraq, around five thousand Kurdish men, women, and children were massacred by chemical weapons in 1988, but the United States and Europe continued to trade openly, including military hardware, with the oil-rich nation until it invaded Kuwait. During the early 1990s, the world turned a blind eye to the extensive "death squad" killings in Sri Lanka.

Even when the culpable government or military is replaced, seldom is there any punishment for even the worst offenders. In Argentina, where over nine thousand were murdered by the military, amnesty laws were passed in 1986, 1987, 1989, and 1990 to restrict prosecution and give immunity to the torturers and murderers. Similar amnesties have been granted in Uruguay, Chile, Guatemala, Nicaragua, Benin, and the Congo. In March 1993, a UN "Truth Commission" issued a scathing report on ten years of butchery in El Salvador, during which seventy thousand people died, including forty thousand civilians murdered by government forces; less than a week later, the president ratified a sweeping amnesty law exempting all from prosection (Amnesty International 1993a).

Torture

Despite a near-universal revulsion against torture, it continues to be widely practiced and is often part of the "package" of atrocities that includes political imprisonment, disappearances, and political murder. Torture is seldom the independent action of a sadistic individual (though the very existence of the practice filters sadists into official positions where they can exercise their perverse predilections). Rather, it is a component in the state-supported machinery to suppress dissent. It may be justified with the "moral" argument that it is practiced for the greater good, say, in rooting out subversives. The reality is that the vast majority of victims have no knowledge of any importance to national security. In any case, there is no assurance that information gained by pain or threat of pain is true. Names of innocent people may be offered just for a moment's respite, and when they are arrested, new names may be given, so that more and more are drawn into the net and the paranoid fantasies of the accusers become a self-fulfilling pseudoreality.

In many cases, interrogation is not really the point of torture. It may be used to elicit false confessions, to break down a prisoner, or to force renunciation of beliefs. Torture is often used as a punishment in addition to prison sentences; in Pakistan and Mozambique, severe public floggings are common. Often the very existence of torture is used to intimidate the political opposition; it is a way of saying, "If you dissent, this is what will happen to you." In Turkey, one of several democracies in which torture is routine, dissidents may be picked up, tortured, and released so that they can tell their compatriots what they experienced. Often torture precedes killing, as in the secret prisons of the Argentine dictatorship in the early 1970s. Death squads routinely torture; in El Salvador and Guatemala in the 1980s, when bodies were being left in parks and beside roadways for the maximum intimidation, almost all revealed signs of torture.

Article 1 of the UN Declaration Against Torture, adopted unanimously in 1975, defines torture as "any act by which severe pain or suffering, whether physical or mental, is intentionally inflicted by or at the instigation of a public official." Methods include almost anything that can be thought up, such as *falanga* (beating on the soles of the feet), quicklime inside a hood made from a tire inner tube, and a heated electrical skewer inserted into the anus. Electrodes are perhaps the most common tool of the torturer's trade, and, like pain-causing drugs, they leave few marks and make verification difficult. Isolation is often employed as psychological torture. In Rwanda, prisoners were locked in small *cachet noirs*, or "black cells," devoid of light, where they might be held for a year or more. In Cuba, prisoners were placed in morgue-like drawers for days. Though no experience is typical, the process is often routinized within a given prison or interrogation center.

No one is safe. In El Salvador, children were tortured. In Iran, children were sometimes forced to watch the tortures of their mothers. In Syria, relatives of dissidents were held as hostages and tortured to force the fugitives to turn themselves in. In Argentina, entire families were taken into custody and tortured in front of each other.

Despite official claims of ignorance, torture exists when states let it exist, and it stops when governments say it should stop. Preconditions for torture often include emergency or special legislation that give the police and military forces wide powers of arrest and detention. Often, there is a period of days and weeks when a prisoner can be held incommunicado. This is the most dangerous period, when a prisoner's whereabouts may not be known and he or she has no access to family, friends, or lawyers. Often there are secret detention centers or areas of prisons that are off-limits to inspection. The process is especially encouraged when trial procedures legally permit evidence taken under torture, a practice that has been specifically condemned by the UN.

Trials of torturers in Greece after a period of military dictatorship between 1967 and 1974 revealed the processes by which normal individuals may be recruited into such practices. After basic training, young conscripted soldiers from right-wing families were chosen for special units, and further screening produced a select few who were most amenable to brutality. These were given the use of cars, noncommissioned officer rank, extra pay and time off, and other privileges, such as the guarantee of a government job after military service. A large part of the training for this "elite" included beating and being beaten by fellow conscripts. Following a long period of ideological and psychological indoctrination, they were inducted into the process of torture. Competition among each other for brutality was encouraged, and hesitation resulted in ridicule, beatings, and threats to families.

A prisoner's agony does not end when the torture stops. Studies of victims reveal that nearly all suffer from long-term mental and physical aftereffects. Adriana Vargas Vásquez, a factory worker in Chile, was tortured with electric shock and the "parrot's perch" — suspension for long periods upside down from a metal bar; two years later, she still suffered constant pain and ill health, including headaches, difficulty in concentrating, dizziness, nightmares, suicidal depressions, and anxiety attacks. Suicide is common either during torture or after release (Amnesty International 1984).

The UN Commission on Human Rights established a special rapporteur on torture in 1985, and there is a UN Voluntary Fund for Torture Victims that provides financial assistance, establishes support groups, and researches ways to help victims and their families. The International Rehabilitation and Research Center for Torture Victims in Copenhagen helps those who can escape their countries to heal and readjust, and there are similar institutions in Canada, Norway, and other countries. UN declarations against torture are unusually strong and include the provision that orders from superiors cannot be used as a legal defense.

Unfortunately, despite the proscriptions of international law and a universal abhorrence, the practice of torture continues.

Disappearances

Adolf Hitler, believing that trials and executions created martyrs, in 1941 ordered his infamous *Nacht und Nebel* (Night and Fog) program. Those arrested for "endangering German security" would simply vanish. The authorities would deny any knowledge about them. About seven thousand individuals fell victim to the Night and Fog program.

Twenty-five years later, the practice would reappear in Guatemala. In 1963, dictator General Peralta suspended the constitution and established the "Law for the Defense of Democratic Institutions." The new law would be implemented by a special security force, the Judicial Police, who had the power to detain without warrant and hold prisoners incommunicado for an extended period. In rural areas, "military commissioners" were given almost unlimited license. At first, only a few people disappeared, to turn up beaten a few days later. Soon, people began to vanish for longer periods and were severely tortured. By 1966, a new term was entering the Spanish language, *los desaparecidos*, the disappeared ones. At first, it was unclear to relatives and human rights advocates what was going on. It was assumed that those detained were being held in incommunicado detention. Relatives and human rights workers dutifully filled out *habeas corpus* petitions, only to have them dismissed in the courts. The police and military denied knowing the whereabouts of the victims, even when witnesses had seen them arrested by uniformed security forces. Most victims were never seen again. Since then, tens of thousands have disappeared.

The practice quickly spread to other countries of Latin America. The advantage over openly killing or imprisoning people is that governments can claim ignorance. The police do not know where these people are. Perhaps they have joined the guerrillas or gone into exile. Perhaps they have been murdered by the opposition. In reality, of course, nearly all disappearances are attributable to the governments themselves, their security forces, and protected paramilitary squads.

One of the worst outbreaks of disappearances came in Argentina during the "dirty war" after the military coup of 1976. In the previous years, the security forces had established a sophisticated intelligence network and had received extensive training in counterinsurgency techniques. By 1973, several unofficial death squads had been formed with names like the *Alianza Anti-comunista Argentina* and the *Comando Libertadores de America*, the latter being composed of junior-ranking army officers. The death squads preferred open terror and public killings, but, by 1976, these methods had garnered so much domestic outrage and international condemnation that more subtle methods were adopted. Disappearances became common, virtually replacing imprisonment, formal arrest, and even death squad killings. Over the following years, more than nine thousand people disappeared. The victims — including students, lawyers, trade unionists, and journalists — were dragged from their homes at night by men identifying themselves as agents of the police or armed forces. They were taken to secret prisons, where they were severely tortured, often for months, before being "transferred," that is, taken away and executed. Some of the bodies were buried in mass graves; others were dropped by plane or helicopter into the sea.

In Iraq, entire Kurdish families have disappeared from their villages; one wave of arrests known as Operation Anfel led to the disappearance of over 100,000 Kurds, mostly within a single four-month period. In Sri Lanka, many disappearances are attributable to a police commando unit called the Special Task Force (Amnesty International 1981). Well into the 1990s, disappearances were reported in at least twenty countries, including Indonesia, India, Zaire, the Philippines, and Turkey.

Disappearances can be devastating to family and friends, who never know the fate of the victim and are continually rebuffed when they approach authorities for information. Even seeking information may be dangerous; a wife or mother might also be targeted for disappearance. Families may be left without a breadwinner and denied rightful pensions, social security, or insurance on the grounds that death has not been legally certified.

Though there are numerous international laws covering disappearances, redress is particularly difficult. Governments routinely take refuge behind a wall of claimed ignorance.

Political Imprisonment

Although killings and disappearances most often occur during times of war or crisis, political imprisonment may be a standard part of state policy even in periods of peace and security. Many long-term prisoners are convicted for their peaceful opposition to the government under laws that are contrary to the letter and spirit of the Universal Declaration. Amnesty International has popularized the term "prisoner of conscience" to refer to such prisoners who are detained "because of beliefs, color, sex, ethnic origin, language, or religion, as long as he or she has not used or advocated violence" (Kaufman 1991:343). The definition is subject to interpretation and to accusations of ethnocentrism. Should conscientious objectors to military conscription be considered prisoners of conscience? Or those accused of adultery or homosexuality in religiously conservative countries? Despite such complications, most cases are clear-cut. Tens of thousands of people are imprisoned merely because their governments perceive them as a threat.

In Uruguay during the 1970s and 1980s, sixty thousand people — about 2 percent of the entire population — were incarcerated, giving the country the highest per capita prison population in the world. Almost all new prisoners were tortured before being transferred to official prisons, where attempts were made to psychologically break them. After the Indochina war, tens of thousands in Vietnam were sent to "reeducation camps." The government did not think of this as punishment but as indoctrination into the new society. Before the end of apartheid in South Africa, political imprisonment against blacks was virtually normative; many spent decades behind bars on trumped-up or trivial charges. In the 1980s, Cuba had some of the longest-term political prisoners in the world, many of them sentenced shortly after the revolutionary government came to power in 1959.

Though the UN declaration on the "Protection of Persons Subjected to Detention or Imprisonment" clearly spells out minimum standards, in reality, few countries observe such international statutes. In a Chinese labor camp in Manchuria, where temperatures drop to 0° fahrenheit in the winter, no heat was provided, and bedclothes had to be supplied by families. During one extended period, the food ration dropped so low that prisoners were forced to eat leaves, dead birds, and field rats. "Official prisoners" — those considered counterrevolutionary — were beaten and provided with less food than others. All prisoners were required to work fourteen to sixteen hours a day, mainly digging ditches (Amnesty International 1986:33).

If prisons are not subject to effective external oversight — and few are — atrocities such as torture and rape may be practiced with relative impunity. Rioting, often stimulated by wretched conditions, may be used as an excuse for guards and police to kill prisoners at random; hundreds have been massacred in such outbreaks in Peru and Bolivia.

ATROCITIES AGAINST WOMEN

Women as well as men are subjected to political imprisonment, torture, killing, and disappearance, but they are particularly vulnerable to offenses specifically based on sex, such as rape, sexual humiliation, and domestic violence. In addition, women are forced into prostitution, pressured to commit infanticide, and suffer numerous cultural and legal discriminations.

Rape is often used as a form of torture. Women are particularly vulnerable between the time of their arrest and their arrival at an official detention center, though rape is also common during interrogations and in prison. Sometimes, rape is routinized as an amusement for guards, the police, or the military. In Chad, a woman arrested in 1987 reported that she was taken with ten other women prisoners — none of whom had been charged or tried — to a military post, where they were forced to perform as prostitutes for the troops. During the civil war in former Yugoslavia, hundreds, perhaps thousands, of Muslim and Croat women were compelled to work in houses of "prostitution," where they were repeatedly raped by Serb forces. Such violations are common during civil wars and in government counterinsurgency operations, when peasant women may be raped at will.

In India, a thousand cases of rape are reported against police each year. This is probably a mere fraction of the actual number, because women often are reluctant to recount such episodes. Charges may never be investigated, and, if they are, it is by the police themselves, rather than by independent bodies. According to an inquiry by *The Times of India*, 97 percent of rape cases are cancelled or dismissed as "untraced" by the police (Amnesty International 1991).

Rape carries severe social consequences for the victim, who may be divorced by her husband or expelled from her household on the culturally condoned assumption that she was consenting or that she had become contaminated. Bangladeshi women who suffered rape during the war with Pakistan were often killed by male relatives to preserve "family honor" (Bunch 1990:491).

Pregnant women who are arrested are especially vulnerable to torture or to detention in harsh and degrading conditions. The special needs of pregnant women are spelled out in the 1949 UN Standard Minimum Rules for the Treatment of Prisoners, but these are commonly ignored. Detained women risk miscarriage, bearing an injured or malformed child, or separation from the child after it is born. A former prisoner in Argentina's secret detention camps reported, "The fact that a woman prisoner was pregnant never led to her getting any sort of consideration under torture. Those who did not lose their babies on the torture tables, having survived the interrogation stage, were thrown into the cells under the same conditions as the rest" (quoted in Amnesty International 1986:146). Babies were taken from their mothers and adopted to couples who did not know the source of their child.

Forced prostitution is a widespread problem, but in many cases, there is little difference between that which is coerced and that which is "voluntary." A study by the United Nations Educational, Scientific and Cultural Organization found that the majority of women who work as prostitutes had been victims of rape, incest, or violence that "resulted in the destruction of a women's identity, an essential step in subsequently transforming the human body into a sexual item of merchandise for commercial purposes" (quoted in Reanda 1991:13). In Southeast Asia, sexual tourism, much involving children of both sexes, is a multibillion-dollar industry that employs hundreds of thousands of prostitutes. In Thailand alone, it is estimated that two million women, including 800,000 children under the age of sixteen, are involved in prostitution. In Pattaya, Thailand, a center of sex tourism, girls under the age of puberty are forced to publicly dance naked and must service any man who can pay the fee (Wetzel 1993:45). In another Thai town, several women died in a brothel fire because they were chained to their beds. Given normal birth and death rates, there should be an equal number of women and men in any given country. In Bangladesh and Afghanistan, however, there are only ninety-four women for every hundred men; in India, ninety-three; in Pakistan, ninety-two. Some of this discrepancy results from underreporting to census takers because families are ashamed to have more daughters than sons, but much results from female infanticide. In cultures that idolize sons, to be born female is close to being born less than human. In India, where infanticide is largely a rural phenomenon, a survey of 1,250 women concluded that half had killed baby girls (Anderson and Moore 1993). In China, a campaign promoting one child per family has reportedly increased the number of female infanticides.

Domestic violence against women is normal and culturally condoned in many countries. In Peru, 70 percent of all crimes reported to the police involve women beaten by their partners. Where recorded, domestic battery against women ranges from 40 percent to 80 percent; in most cases, women are beaten repeatedly, so that the home becomes a place of ongoing torture. Domestic violence often results in the wife's death, and, in many countries, the husband is not subject to serious prosecution. In India, a woman must pay a dowry to her husband's family; if the dowry is unpaid or considered insufficient, the wife may be killed, often by being set afire. In 1991 alone, 5,157 dowry murders were recorded (Bunch 1990).

The UN considers offenses against women in several documents, such as The Convention for the Suppression of the Traffic in Persons and of the Exploitation of Prostitution of Others (1949) and the more general Convention on the Elimination of All Forms of Discrimination against Women (1985). In addition, women's rights groups and women's support groups are emerging in numerous Third World countries. Nevertheless, the problems are ongoing and severe and remain deeply embedded in patriarchal cultures.

INDIGENOUS PEOPLES — FIVE HUNDRED YEARS OF VICTIMIZATION

Few people have undergone such levels of death and ruin as the indigenous peoples of conquered nations. The term "indigenous peoples" is often used in place of "Indian," "native," "aboriginal," and so forth to refer to groups that have a historical continuity reaching back before conquest and colonialism. Though many are fully modern today, these groups share common ancestry, culture, and language and usually reside together in definable areas.

Historically, and even today, two polar stereotypes have dominated perceptions of indigenous peoples: they are either noble or ignoble. Both stereotypes represent an act of self-criticism on the part of the ruling culture rather than a realistic assessment of the people themselves. If "civilization" is extolled and life "in a state of nature" is conceived as "nasty, brutish, and short" — as philosopher Thomas Hobbes put it — then native peoples will be portrayed as ignorant and bloodthirsty savages with few redeeming qualities. Such a perspective legitimizes their extermination, uprooting, and forced assimilation. On the other hand, if the mass warfare, alienation, and pollution of civilization's darker side becomes philosophically accentuated, indigenous peoples will be viewed as peaceful and communitarian and as natural environmentalists. This image tends to reduce them to romantic and primitive anachronisms, who need to be "protected" like figures in a museum diorama. Either stereotype portrays them as helpless. The reality, of course, is that they are very complex people who do not fit easily into neat typologies (Tennant 1994).

The spread of a world economy in the sixteenth century brought about a clash of two fundamentally different cultural systems: tribes and states. For the mercantilist and capitalist countries of Europe, exploitation of raw materials was the basic purpose of expansion, and effective exploitation required two things, land and labor, both of which were possessed by the indigenous peoples. Whereas tribal peoples must live in a symbiotic relationship with their environment, producing for their own subsistence while maintaining ecological balance, the European culture of consumption was based on mass production for export. The Industrial Revolution enormously accelerated this process. Rationalized by the assumption of European superiority, lands were confiscated and natives were conscripted as export laborers if they were not killed outright. The weapons of the conquerors were so technologically superior that "wars" were often little more than extended massacres. Diseases also took a large toll, as did starvation resulting from the massive disruption of indigenous social and economic systems.

As a result, in both North America and lowland South America native populations declined by 95 percent. In Africa, the Congo alone lost eight million individuals. In Tasmania, the population diminished from five thousand to 111, a decline of 98 percent in only thirty years. The South Pacific, including Australia, suffered an 80 percent decline. In all, it is estimated that the colonized countries suffered a depopulation of almost twenty-nine million (Bodley 1982:40) (Figure 9.1).

Death and destruction moved with the frontier, the undeveloped area adjacent to European colonization. A common element of the frontier even today is a near-total disregard for the natives. In mid-nineteenth-century California and Canada, it was considered meritorious, even sport, to kill Indians. The Dutch Boers in South Africa killed

FIGURE 9.1
Depopulation of Selected Regions as a Result of Contact

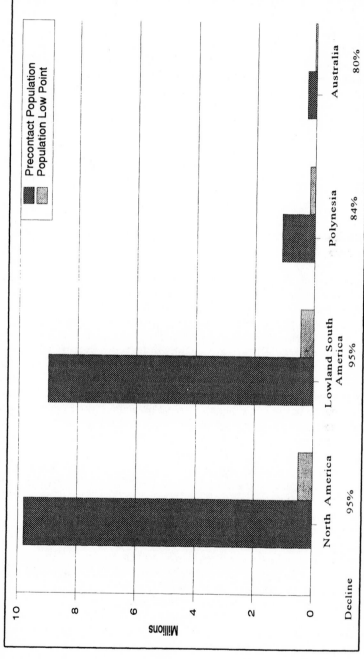

Based on John H. Bodley, *Victims of Progress*, 2d ed. (Menlo Park, Calif.: Benjamin/Cummings, 1982), p. 40.

indigenous peoples with the same indifference they would kill animals; one settler boasted personally killing three hundred natives. In Australia, tattooed Maori heads from New Zealand were offered for sale as curiosities.

The killing continues. Over the past decades, tens of thousands of Guatemalan Indians have fallen victim to government troops. The so-called *Montagnards* — diverse groups of natives — were used as cannon fodder by both sides in the war in Indochina. Iraq has been carrying out a systematic genocide against the Kurds, who also suffer arbitrary arrest, torture, and disappearance in Turkey. Atrocities remain common in the Amazonian Basin where ranchers, farmers, and prospectors invade Indian lands. In Brazil in 1963, prospectors and gunslingers were hired to clear the Cintas Largas Indians off their lands; methods included hiring a plane to strafe and bomb a village during an important tribal ceremony, with numerous lives lost (Davis 1977).

The kidnapping of millions of Africans for slaves may have been the largest-scale practice of its type in history. However, many forms of economic servitude, just short of slavery, have been employed against indigenous people. In South America, Siberia, and India, commercial agents have taken advantage of native unfamiliarity with money to entrap workers into permanent dependency. In situations of classic "debt bondage," natives are given credit for overpriced necessities in exchange for furs, rubber, lumber, fish, or labor; because the debt can never be paid, workers become totally dependent on the company. In the South Seas during the late nineteenth century, "blackbirding" was a common practice to fill the labor needs of farmers in Australia and Fiji. Agents masqueraded as missionaries to get islanders onto ships or convinced them they were signing on for three months of recreation when the actual contract was for three years of hard labor. Thousands died of malnutrition or disease during passage. Once at a plantation, recruits were sold to the highest bidder and had to work up to twelve hours a day six days a week for wages only 5 percent of those of the lowest-paid European worker (Bodley 1982:35).

Survivors have often suffered "cultural genocide," the systematic destruction of native life ways. Europeans almost invariably assume the inferiority of indigenous cultures, considering the materialism of industrial civilization to be a universal value. In reality, most tribal peoples prefer their own cultures and are not eager to embrace the dubious benefits of civilization, which for them usually means eking out a bare living as second-class citizens in slums and shantytowns. Government administration agents have attempted to force assimilation into the dominant culture by attacking or banning indigenous religions, languages, and marriage customs. Well into the twentieth century in the United States, Indian children were literally kidnapped and taken to distant "away schools," where they were indoctrinated in white ways and corporally punished for using their own language.

The plight of indigenous people, and their special need for human rights protections, has been long recognized by international bodies. In 1982, the World Council of Indigenous Peoples was formed in the UN. In addition, numerous tribal political organizations have been formed to fight for rights in their particular countries. For example, in Ecuador, a group of Jivaro-speaking Indians formed the *Federacíon de Centros Shuar*, which claims twenty thousand members and has been effective in resisting encroachment by white settlers on ancestral lands (Stamatopoulou 1994). A number of nongovernmental organizations have been formed to aid indigenous peoples in their struggles. Cultural Survival, for example, was established in 1972 by a group of Harvard anthropologists. The Aborigines Protection Society and Survival International, both based in London, have also been effective in fighting for indigenous rights.

The major demand of indigenous peoples is for self-determination, that is, the ability to decide their own lives, practice their own cultures, and assimilate — if they choose to do so — at their own rate. The fight for restitution of lands and resources, for fair compensation for losses, and for government compliance with treaties is ongoing. In many areas of the Third World — as well as the First World — indigenous peoples have found a powerful political voice and are refusing to be victims any longer.

THE UNITED STATES AND HUMAN RIGHTS IN THE THIRD WORLD

No First World country has such an important effect on the Third World as the United States, and its attitudes, policies, and actions on human rights are extremely significant. The United States has largely taken a unilateral stance and has ratified only a half-dozen or so mostly minor treaties on human rights. Though a major promoter and signer of the Universal Declaration of Human Rights, the United States has never ratified the large majority of UN human rights treaties, including the Covenants on Civil and Political Rights and on Social, Economic and Cultural Rights. The Genocide Convention, which was approved and proposed for ratification in 1948, was not passed by Congress until almost forty years later. Though a founder of the Organization of American States, the United States has never officially endorsed that body's Convention on Human Rights.

Except for the sanctity of private property and religion, U.S. political culture does not recognize the economic and social sphere as embodying "rights." In contrast to many European nations, the United States does not deal with freedom from hunger as a right. Income inequality, poverty, lack of access to modern medicine may be important economic issues, but they are not "rights" in the way that freedom of press or religion are. No country has ever been sanctioned by the United States for its malnutrition or exceptional death rates.

Official policy on human rights after World War II has varied from administration to administration. From 1949 until 1990, the Cold War dominated foreign policy. Until the early 1970s, if human rights was considered at all, it was defined simply as a matter of opposing communism. In the bifurcated world view of John Foster Dulles, secretary of state under President Eisenhower, any country that allied itself with the United States against the monolithic evil of communism was exempt from further moral considerations, and any means was justifiable in the struggle against Soviet expansionism. Presidents Kennedy and Johnson openly promoted democracy while providing massive military aid and training to armies — such as those in Brazil, Uruguay, Laos, and Indonesia — that quickly assumed power and instituted reigns of terror. Support for dictatorial regimes — such as the Shah of Iran, Somoza in Nicaragua, or Marcos in the Philippines — went virtually unquestioned. The Nixon and Ford administrations actually seemed to favor human rights violators; a statistical study of the period concluded that "it is clearly evident that U.S. aid . . . tended to flow disproportionately to those Latin American countries which tortured their citizens" (Schoultz 1981). During the Vietnam war, the Phoenix Program, which involved the torture and killing of thousands of civilians, was headed by the U.S. Army and the Central Intelligence Agency (CIA).

The situation changed dramatically between 1974 and 1978, when Congressional assertiveness on foreign policy embraced human rights. The Harkin Amendment of 1974 asserted that "No assistance may be provided . . . to the government of any country which engages in a consistent pattern of gross violations of international human rights." Taking its cue from Congress, the Carter administration also emphasized human rights but was inconsistent in implementation.

Under the Reagan administration, human rights was again put on the back burner. In a 1979 article, Jeane Kirkpatrick, later to become ambassador to the UN, argued that the United States was obligated to uphold "authoritarian" regimes (i.e., U.S. allies) in order to keep them from becoming "totalitarian" (i.e., socialist or communist). In El Salvador, the United States would support, to the tune of $6 billion, a military-dominated government that murdered, tortured, and "disappeared" its own civilian citizens on a massive scale. The administration also made overtures to Guatemala, at that time one of the most butcherous countries on earth, and sponsored the Contra invasion of Nicaragua, which was responsible for thousands of civilian killings. The United States maintained strong relations with Indonesia despite its invasion of the island of East Timor and the ongoing killings and torture there.

A country's human rights record is revealed not only in its overt foreign policy but also in its secret operations. In his book *Presidents' Secret Wars*, John Prados (1986) details twenty-four major covert CIA actions. Eighteen of these, all directed against communist countries, were complete failures. The only six "successful" operations he describes were against democracies or noncommunist constitutional governments. Actually, this is just the tip of the iceberg. The United States has been directly involved in the successful overthrow of democracies in Iran (1953), Guatemala (1954), Lebanon (1957), Laos (1960–1962), British Guiana (1961), Zaire (1962), Ecuador (1963), Brazil (1964), Indonesia (1965), the Dominican Republic (1965), Greece (1967), and Chile (1973). The CIA blocking of country-wide elections in Vietnam, mandated by a Geneva Peace Conference for 1954, was a primary cause of the Indochina War. In nearly every case, a government with a relatively benign human rights record was replaced by a government that introduced state terror. The CIA also helped create and was closely involved with Iran's secret police, SAVAK, which ran torture prisons and carried out numerous extrajudicial killings under the Shah (Lewellen 1988, 1990). During the slaughter of a half million or more people in Indonesia in the 1960s, U.S. officials supplied the perpetrators with 5,000 names of "subversives," which were checked off on a list as they were killed or captured (Kadane 1990).

Given Congressional legislation and periodic State Department pronouncements on human rights, it might seem that the United States has had a somewhat ambiguous record on the issue. The reality is that throughout the Cold War, there was a surprising consistency; aside from routine condemnation of socialist states, human rights was always subordinated, first, to perceived national security concerns and, second, to economic interests. It remains controversial whether such U.S. policy was really necessary to U.S. self-preservation against international communism. What is indisputable is that literally hundreds of thousands of people were murdered, tortured, "disappeared," and imprisoned by authoritarian governments that were either helped into power or strongly supported by the United States through military training, foreign aid, and CIA interventions.

The end of the Cold War may have made such blatant disregard for human rights a thing of the past. Though of questionable value, U.S.-involved UN interventions in Somalia and Bosnia and U.S. unilateral support of the Kurds in Iraq suggest it is possible for states to act for largely humanitarian reasons. These imply that the decline of the threat of communism may make it a little easier to inject human rights into foreign policy. However, politics and economics will always hold priority; in 1994, the United States renewed "most favored nation" trading status for China, despite that country's dismal human rights record.

NONGOVERNMENTAL ORGANIZATIONS AND THE STRUGGLE FOR HUMAN RIGHTS

The UN has taken the lead in international human rights law, but given the need for some consensus among scores of divergent nations and lacking strong provisions for enforcement, it has often proved itself impotent. It is difficult to reconcile national sovereignty with human rights implementation; states obviously will not report their own violations, and they are hesitant, for diplomatic reasons, to report the violations of others. When states do lodge complaints, more often than not, they are politically motivated.

Nongovernmental organizations (NGOs) have no such reticence. Their private status permits them to operate without state control and free from political considerations. Prior to 1970, there existed only a small group of human rights NGOs, such as the Red Cross (established in 1863), the International League for Human Rights (1942), the International Commission of Jurists (1952), and Amnesty International (1961). After 1972, a burgeoning human rights awareness stimulated a profusion of NGOs, many of them specific to a certain population of victims. P.E.N., for example, focuses on violations against writers, and the American Association for the Advancement of Science has formed its own group to fight for the rights of scientists. In addition, there are a number of NGOs, such as the Asia Watch Committee, that concentrate on specific regions.

London-based Amnesty International, which won the Nobel Peace Prize in 1977, is the largest of all human rights groups, with hundreds of thousands of members throughout the world. Though originally concentrating on "prisoners of conscience," Amnesty International's mandate has extended to torture, disappearances, extrajudicial killing, and the death penalty (which it opposes everywhere, in all circumstances). Recently, members have voted to include not only state offenses against human rights but also violations by guerrilla armies and other opposition forces. Amnesty International works mainly through letter-writing campaigns in support of specific, named prisoners and victims. Local groups "adopt" a particular incarcerated individual and stick with the case until he or she is freed, sometimes a matter of decades. Amnesty International high school and college groups lack the continuity for long-term adoptions, so they focus on "Urgent Actions," letter-writing campaigns in support of people undergoing torture, suffering incommunicado detention, and disappearance. The research department of Amnesty International provides some of the most authoritative data on human rights and has earned the organization consultative status with the UN and the U.S. Congress.

Although Amnesty International eschews political battles, other groups have no hesitation in condemning specific governments or policies. During the Reagan administration, the Americas Watch

Committee and the Washington Office on Latin America were openly critical of U.S. policy and provided Congressional opposition with facts refuting administration claims.

Indigenous human rights groups have emerged in virtually every Third World country where they are allowed, often at great danger to the participants. During the military dictatorship in Argentina, a group of women calling themselves Mothers of the Plaza de Mayo gathered each week for a public demonstration to force the government to respond to their requests for information on disappeared husbands and sons. Several of the protesters also disappeared. Similar groups have courageously formed in even the most dangerous of countries.

Religious groups have often effectively interceded on behalf of human rights, despite the targeting by terrorist states of pastors, priests, nuns, and religious organizers. In El Salvador, the Catholic legal organization *Tutela Legal* provided the best data available on killings and disappearances. In Chile, the Catholic Church became virtually the sole voice for human rights during the worst years of the Pinochet dictatorship, providing legal assistance for targets of repression, denouncing government crimes, and pressing for change. The Protestant Geneva-based World Council of Churches has intervened for human rights in scores of countries.

It is difficult to evaluate the effectiveness of NGOs, because they do not act in isolation. There will be many reasons why a prisoner is released or a government decides to abandon torture as a method of interrogation. However, there can be no doubt that their overall impact has been significant. Human rights violations thrive in darkness and secrecy. Publicity about violations can have a positive effect on countries that care about their international reputations. Lobbying by NGOs has been effective in promoting human rights legislation in all Western countries; it was only under pressure by such groups that the United States finally endorsed the Genocide Convention. Equally important, these groups have educated the public at large about the extent of violations and the necessity of human rights considerations in the foreign policy of any country that claims to be civilized.

THE FUTURE OF HUMAN RIGHTS

The collapse of the Soviet Union marked a critical juncture for human rights in the Third World. For forty years, mutual fear and hostility resulted in support of terrorist states by both sides in the Cold War. The UN was rendered impotent partially because opposition to a country's practices by one faction within the Security Council and General Assembly would automatically lead to support by the other faction. Freed from such knee-jerk divisiveness, the UN has been able to act as arbiter or even to intervene, albeit often in an irresolute and bumbling manner. The end of the Cold War was crucial to peace settlements in Central America, Angola, Israel, South Africa, and Mozambique, bringing about immediate improvements in human rights.

However, new dangers loom large. The *Pax Sovietica* held rivalries in check in Eastern Europe, and no sooner had the Union of Soviet Socialist Republics broken up than various ethnic groups fought for land and dominance. The end of apartheid and the movement toward democracy in South Africa pitted black factions against each other in a bloody struggle for power. By 1994, all of the nations of mainland Latin America had popularly elected governments (though some were only marginally democratic), yet the conditions for a return to state terrorism — poverty, hunger, massive inequalities in wealth and power — continue to exist. In Africa and parts of Asia, there have been few improvements in human rights over decades. Indeed, the 1994 massacre in Rwanda rates among the worst atrocities of the twentieth century.

Nevertheless, human rights has become, for the first time in history, an accepted and legitimate part of the international agenda. Though violations will inevitably continue, they will never again go unchallenged.

SUGGESTED READINGS

Amnesty International, *Getting Away with Murder: Political Killings and Disappearances in the 1990s* (London: Amnesty International, 1993). One is tempted to believe that the collapse of communism and the democratization of Latin America resulted in a significant improvement in human rights. This book sets the record straight, detailing state terrorism in the 1990s. Chapters on "Why the Terror Continues" and "How to Stop the Terror" go beyond mere description.

Amnesty International, *Report* (New York: Amnesty International USA, annual). This yearly country-by-country report is the authoritative document on human rights around the world.

Bodley, John H., *Victims of Progress*, 2nd ed. (Menlo Park, Calif.: Benjamin/ Cummings, 1982). An excellent historical overview of the plight of indigenous peoples, from their massive decimation by war and disease after the European conquest through the land grabbing and cultural genocide of the 1970s.

Donnelly, Jack, *International Human Rights* (Boulder, Colo.: Westview, 1993). One of the top scholars in the field provides a comprehensive overview of human rights theory and practice. One section is devoted to state terrorism in the Southern Cone countries of Latin America, and another details U.S. human rights policy.

Donnelly, Jack, and Rhoda Howard, eds., *International Handbook of Human Rights* (New York: Greenwood, 1987). Scholars on particular countries provide historical and contemporary overviews of human rights, with an emphasis on causes and underlying structures.

Forsythe, David P., *Human Rights and U.S. Foreign Policy: Congress Reconsidered* (Gainesville: University of Florida Press, 1988). This detailed analysis of Congressional action on human rights reveals the politics involved. Appendices provide data on the relationship between human rights and foreign aid.

Timerman, Jacobo, *Prisoner Without a Name, Cell Without a Number* (New York: Vintage, 1981). The author was imprisoned under hellish conditions and severely tortured during the "dirty war" in Argentina of the late 1970s. His examination of the totalitarian mindset of his oppressors is perceptive and frightening.

10

Toward the Twenty-First Century: The Third World in the New World Order

In the mid-1960s, a strange war was fought by Cubans against Cubans — in central Africa. Ever since the Central Intelligence Agency's (CIA's) early attempts to assassinate Patrice Lumumba, first president of the Congo after it gained independence from Belgium, the United States had been intensely involved in the region. The CIA had on its hands a number of well-trained and eager Cuban troops left over from the failed Bay of Pigs invasion of Cuba in 1961. Many of these men were brought to the Congo in early 1964 to bomb railroads, bridges, and other targets in a civil war that was interpreted as a struggle between communism and capitalism. In response, Fidel Castro dispatched several hundred of his troops under the personal command of his closest lieutenant "Che" Guevara. "So there, in the remotest corner of central Africa, 8,000 miles from the small Caribbean island where it started," writes Jonathan Kwitny in *Endless Enemies* (1984:84–85), "the Cuban civil war resumed. At one point . . . U.S. taxpayers even launched a Cuban-manned navy, composed of several ships, on Lake Tanganyika. . . . Whether Cubans actually engaged in naval combat with each other on Lake Tanganyika is unrecorded, but the mere possibility boggles the mind."

This incident reveals how downright loony the Cold War could get. The Congo — now Zaire — was hardly a hotbed of communism, or capitalism either, for that matter; virtually the entire population was illiterate and, thus, not particularly well-versed in either Marx or Adam Smith. The real conflicts were tribal or between nationalists and former colonizers. This mattered little to policy makers in Washington and Moscow, who interpreted internal struggles everywhere as part of the U.S.-Soviet rivalry. For forty years, polar ideologies dominated national policies in the Third World, as dictators and would-be dictators learned to play the "communist game" — inveigling military aid and covert CIA support from the United States by accusing their domestic enemies of plotting the world overthrow of capitalism. Alternatively, socialist dictators could place themselves under the umbrella of Soviet protection and receive military aid, Cuban troops, and possibly a hydroelectric dam or two in the bargain. The Cold War may have been positively icy in terms of East-West relations, but it was certainly hot enough in the South; unable to confront each other directly, the two nuclear superpowers fought their proxy wars in places like the Philippines, Indonesia, Angola, El Salvador, and Nicaragua, not to mention the use of Soviet troops in Afghanistan and direct U.S. troop involvement in Korea, the Dominican Republic, Lebanon (twice), Vietnam, Laos, Cambodia, and Grenada. Despite almost universal claims of nonalignment, only a few countries, such as India, were able to maintain even a shaky neutrality. Alignment was often essential for survival, and even if a government was not fighting off a revolution, the realities of the period required that policies be shaped to U.S. or Soviet blueprints in order to receive aid.

The collapse of the Soviet Union promised to be the most important single event for the Third World since the breakdown of colonialism. With the drying up of Soviet aid, either for existing regimes or rebel forces, numerous long-running conflicts subsided into negotiated settlements. During the late 1980s and early 1990s, wars over contested socialism ended in El Salvador, Nicaragua, Angola, and Mozambique. South Yemen abandoned its Marxist policies and united with its capitalist other half to the north. China and Vietnam, while maintaining their communism, opened themselves to as much trade with the West as they could get. The two remaining communist die-hards, Cuba and North Korea, fell into severe economic difficulties. The demise of the Soviet Union ended the nearly automatic communist veto of any Western proposal in the United Nations. The United States, which had been fighting its wars in the Third World unilaterally for decades, was able to put together a coalition front, including long-time anti-U.S. enemies such as Russia and Syria, to kick Iraq out of Kuwait. This alliance, unthinkable only a few years before, prompted President Bush to proclaim a "New World Order" no longer based on the struggle between superpowers. As Julie Fisher (1993:1) wrote, "The end of the Cold War has loosened the paralyzing grip of ideology on the world's resources and imagination. There is an emerging awareness that now the real problems confronting humanity can and must be addressed."

The New World Order would be one of increasing democracy, open trade among all nations, and reduced conflict. The United Nations, freed of its antithetical ideological constraints, would assume a more active role in promoting peace and helping nations in need. One of the earliest tests of this orientation was the United Nations occupation of Somalia, which had fallen into anarchy and mass starvation. In reality, many of the defining qualities of the New World Order had been in the works for some time. The democratization of Latin America, after decades of military dictatorship, was mostly accomplished through the

1980s, before the disintegration of the Soviet Union. Majority rule in South Africa and self-rule in Palestine were only peripherally related to what was going on in Russia, as was China's and Vietnam's opening to the West.

The New World Order was not without its problems. In Yugoslavia and other areas of the former Second World, ethnic rivalries that had been held in check by communist domination erupted with great violence. In the Third World, ethnic conflict was unaffected by the Soviet demise — as exemplified by the horrendous slaughter in Rwanda. Some peace pacts inspired by the changes in the Union of Soviet Socialist Republics quickly disintegrated; Angola resumed its civil war, and North and South Yemen started fighting again. Developmental aid, which had never been excessive in the first place, began to dry up; the United States lost its motive to use aid as a weapon against communism and began to redirect its funds to Russia and Eastern European nations. Despite good intentions, UN efforts proved weak and, to a great degree, ineffective in Somalia and Bosnia, with the result that member countries began to rethink their humanitarian and peacekeeping commitments. The Rwanda massacres went unchallenged by the United Nations, and North Korea's dedication to building nuclear bombs was contested more by rhetoric than by action.

Most importantly, the structures of global wealth and power had not really changed for Third World countries; the gap between the rich and the poor continued to grow, and there was no attempt to enact the New International Economic Order. The end of the Cold War should have given Third World countries more freedom of action, but, in reality, the developmental options of the countries most in debt were reduced to that prescribed by the International Monetary Fund. The more integrated global economy based on the ideology of comparative advantage is similar in many ways to the colonial period of the 1930s, when certain countries earned their keep through exporting raw materials and importing finished goods. A difference now is that colonizers are no longer "mother countries" but multinational corporations and financial institutions. So far, there is little evidence that this increasingly globalized economy will lead to development for the poorest countries or even for middle range Third World countries.

In purely practical terms, for the developing countries, the New World Order is looking not much different from the Old World Order.

PROGRESS AND LOSS

Today, the Third World remains a paradox, in which considerable progress contrasts with equally substantial deprivation. For example:

During the past three decades, life expectancy in the Third World has increased by over a third, yet only 20 percent of those over the age of sixty have any form of social security.

More than 70 percent of people have access to at least minimal health services, yet, each year, seventeen million people die from infectious and parasitic diseases, such as diarrhoea, malaria, and tuberculosis. Eighty percent of all HIV-infected people are in the Third World.

Between 1965 and 1990, the number of countries that meet, on average, the daily caloric requirements doubled, yet about 800 million people — nearly as many as existed on earth two hundred years ago — are still malnourished.

Primary school enrollment has increased substantially in the past twenty years and secondary school enrollment has doubled, but 35 percent of adults are still illiterate; two-thirds of these are women.

Over the past three decades, infant and early childhood mortality declined by half, but each day 34,000 young children still die from malnutrition and disease (UNDP 1993:12).

As this brief listing shows, there are many positive trends in the Third World. In addition to increased life expectancy, better nutrition, and more widely available schooling, there has been a significant emergence of democracy. Though many of these democracies are in their infancy and remain personalistic, oligarchic, and corrupt, the trend toward greater political participation seems firm, at least in Latin America and Southeast Asia. There has also been an enormous growth in the number and kinds of grass-roots organizations; throughout the Third World, people are taking more control of their lives and communities. Along with this, there has been an increasing recognition on the parts of both governments and nongovernmental organizations that ecological problems must be faced and the environment must be protected. On the international level, there has been, if not a decline in sovereignty, at least a greater willingness to work together for the betterment of all. International treaties, such as the Law of the Sea, General Agreement on Tariffs and Trade, and the Montreal Protocol (against expelling chlorofluorocarbons into the atmosphere) promise greater interaction among nations and a trend toward solving problems by negotiation rather than by edict. Finally, the population growth rate has significantly declined since its peak in the late 1970s.

On the negative side, the decline in the population growth rate has slowed and, in many places ceased, so that populations will continue to rise rapidly, especially in some of the poorest countries of Africa and Asia. Meanwhile, environmental degradation continues apace, as marginal farmers overuse fragile lands and industries flood the soil, rivers, oceans, and air with toxic wastes. Despite the global effects of pollution, deforestation, and agricultural decline, the First World has shown little inclination to share the financial burdens of conservation and cleanup with Third World countries beyond considering environmental issues in World Bank loans. Of all the problems facing the Third World, those of population and environment may be the most intractable — and, ultimately, the most dangerous.

Though the percentage of people living in absolute poverty is declining in some regions of the Third World, the real number is growing. This trend is exacerbated not only by population growth and declining agricultural land but also by the international debt, which has shifted already inadequate resources from development to interest payments. Meanwhile, the gap between the First World and the Third World widens rapidly. That gap is not merely one of economics but is increasingly one of technology. As North America, Europe, and Japan move into a postmodern era, no longer based mainly on industrial production but rather on information processing via computer, technologically, the Third World falls farther and farther behind. If the demise of the Second World left us with two worlds rather than three, those two are growing farther and farther apart economically and technologically.

Yet, this is something of a distortion, because the gap is widening not only between the First World and the Third World, but also within the Third World itself. The newly industrializing nations, such as Taiwan, South Korea, Brazil, and Mexico, are closing in on the First World and have already moved from a dominance of primary exports to industrial goods. However, outside of a few countries in Southeast Asia and Latin America — countries that tend to favorably distort global statistics — most Third World countries are progressing only very slowly, are stagnant, or are in decline. As we have seen, the gap between the world's top fifth and the bottom fifth has more than doubled, from thirty to one to over sixty to one, since 1960 (Postel 1994:5).

MODERNIZATION AND DEPENDENCY — A REPRISE

As we saw in the chapter on theories of development, scholars have been divided on the primary source of underdevelopment. Those of the modernization school tend to emphasize internal constraints, while dependency theorists, including those of the world-system approach, stress historical processes and international structures. Though usually argued as antithetical, both positions can be defended.

Internal Constraints on Development

History cannot be denied, yet once certain structures take hold, they assume a life of their own. It is true that many of the structures put in place by colonialism persist, but in changed form; export dependency, for example, is no longer based on direct ownership of resources by a foreign power. Nearly all countries adopted import substitution policies, which many are abandoning only now. Import substitution was designed to break reliance on imports from the industrialized countries; even if unsuccessful, it certainly transformed the nature of dependency.

Countries that turn outward now do so by choice or as part of a "structural adjustment" arrangement with the International Monetary Fund. Illogical as they were, most of the borders imposed in Africa by European powers have stood the test of time and have become truly national borders of independent states. Contemporary modernization theorists can also point to Third World states as significant actors both domestically and internationally. Even in the most recently decolonized countries, there have been several leaders since independence, so the direct link with the colonial powers has been broken. The smallest of states has asserted whatever sovereignty they could muster against the largest of world powers, as the dictators in Haiti and the warlords of Somalia showed in the 1990s.

If Third World states have become relatively autonomous of their former masters, many have also become capricious and corrupt. Human rights violations are normative, and the struggle for power often is based on ethnic loyalties or personal relations and may be aimed more at profit for the office holders than at governance or any particular vision of development. When ideology *is* a primary motive, as in Marxist Ethiopia or the national security states of Latin America, the results often have been dreadful.

"Culture" is another internal constraint that is difficult to deny. Although the term has no generally recognized meaning and the concept can be perverted to an easy explanation for just about anything, there are obvious national and regional differences that must be accounted. Just as the individualism and materialistic consumerism of the United States has to be considered as a factor in its capitalist productivity, so might the group ethic and spirituality of Islam help account for its relative lack of industrialization despite the oil wealth that permits some countries to choose whatever path to progress they want. Tribal cultures and cultures based on subsistence agriculture invariably have very different concepts of economy and leadership than do Western nations, with the result that they may well follow developmental paths that seem irrational or arbitrary to outsiders.

Internal influences on development are undeniable; the problem arises when these are considered the only influences or when equally undeniable external influences are ignored.

The New Dependency

Even the most prescient of early dependency theorists could not have foreseen the enormous power of debt. With forty countries under standby agreements at any given time, the power of the International Monetary Fund to impose a singular economic model throughout the Third World is unrivaled. The big-stick diplomats of the heyday of gunboat diplomacy would have been envious. The model of open trade, based on the idea of comparative advantage, is that which the

industrialized countries believe is the most beneficial, and it may be —
at least for the industrialized countries. With the demise of the Soviet
Union, and its foreign aid and its military protection, other models have
virtually ceased to exist. Outside of China (which is successfully
adopting several aspects of capitalism) and a small group of other
socialist nations, capitalism clearly is triumphant. The New World
Order is a capitalist order, and, thus, the world system described by
Immanuel Wallerstein has grown immeasurably stronger and more
integrated. Innovative, alternative models of development are desperately needed, but there is little likelihood, given the power of the
international system, that even if they are invented they will be
enacted.

From the Third World perspective, there are several problems with
this new dependency. The capitalist world system tends to favor those
with the most economic and political power to start with. Countries like
the United States and Japan will continue to have the biggest input on
international economic policy, and the smallest countries will have no
say at all. The First World is guaranteed its oil, bauxite, coffee, and
hamburger beef, but there is no guarantee that the needs of the poor
countries will be served correspondingly. As the United States
discovered in the latter nineteenth century, when antimonopoly laws
were first enacted, laissez-faire capitalism increases inequality. Terms
of trade continue to favor manufactured goods over primary exports,
with the result that those many countries trapped in exports of
agriculture or ores likely will remain poor. Within countries, inequality
will also be exacerbated as land and mineral resources are increasingly
concentrated in the hands of wealthy elites.

Foreign aid was designed to provide at least a stepping stone for
countries trying to pull themselves up by their bootstraps, but it has not
been very successful in doing so. The end of the Cold War should have
freed funds from ideological constraints, and this was indeed the effect
— at least to the extent that there is only one, not two, ideologies now.
However, there is no hint that increased funds will be available; the
shift of funds to the former Second World has already meant a dimin-
ishment in money for the Third World. Aid will continue to be politically
motivated, heavily influenced by commercial lobbies, and tied to
procurement of goods from the contributing country. Also, aid will
continue to be used as an inducement for Third World countries to
retain their proper places in the international system.

Within individual Third World countries, comprador elites — those
tied by culture and economic self-interest to the First World — maintain
a great deal of power over national economies. The expansion of the role
of multinational corporations brought about by increased world trade
and the privatization of state-run companies can only augment the
power and wealth of this group. In democratizing countries, increased
political participation may somewhat temper this power, but democracy

does not preclude oligarchy. With more outward directed economies, comprador elites may gain power at the expense of more traditional, inward-directed elites.

In short, although dependency theory may have to adjust to the New World Order, the international structures are as strong as ever — or stronger.

A FINAL NOTE

The national and international structures that have defined and maintained the Third World for the past forty years continue today. Although a few countries in Southeast Asia and South America will claim their places among industrial nations, as long as these structures exist, there will be a "Third World" — by whatever name is politically correct at the time. Some of the domestic causes of underdevelopment — excessive government control of the economy, overvalued currencies, and so forth — are being addressed by the World Bank, the International Monetary Fund, and development aid agencies. However, almost no serious attention is given to the *international* causes of poverty; in fact, such causes are largely unrecognized by policy makers. This does not mean that nothing will be done. It took the World Bank decades to realize that its efforts were not reaching the poor and to redirect a significant amount of funds to grass-roots development, and it took another decade or so before the World Bank recognized the need to inject environmental considerations into its projects. Change — even structural change — does occur. Few people could have predicted the breakup of the Soviet Union or the relatively peaceful transfer of power to majority rule in South Africa. Hope for the future of the Third World is justified, but the end of hunger, poverty, and repression is not just a Third World problem. Such change will not come without profound changes in the First World also.

Bibliography

Adelman, Irma, and Cynthia Taft Morris. 1984. "Economic Development and the Distribution of Income." In *The Gap Between the Rich and the Poor*, ed. Mitchell A. Seligson. Boulder, Colo.: Westview.

Agarwal, Bina. 1991. "Under the Cooking Pot: The Political Economy of the Domestic Fuel Crisis in Rural South Asia." In *Women and the Environment: A Reader*, ed. S. Sontheimer. New York: Monthly Review Press.

Ahluwalia, Montek S., and Nicholas G. Carter. 1979. "Growth and Poverty in Developing Countries." In *Structural Change and Development Policy*, ed. H. Chenery. New York: Oxford University Press.

Alexander, Robert J. 1987. "The Import Substitution Strategy of Economic Development." In *Latin America's Economic Development: Institutional and Structuralist Perspectives*, eds. J. L. Dietz and J. H. Street. Boulder, Colo.: Lynne Rienner.

Alexiev, Alexander A. 1989. *Marxism and Resistance in the Third World*. Washington, D.C.: Rand.

American Anthropological Association. 1947. "Statement on Human Rights." *American Anthropologist* 49 (4): 539–543.

Amnesty International. 1981. *Disappearances: A Workbook*. New York: Amnesty International USA.

____. 1984. *Torture in the Eighties*. London: Amnesty International.

____. 1986. *Voices for Freedom*. London: Amnesty International.

____. 1991. *Women in the Front Line: Human Rights Violations Against Women*. New York: Amnesty International USA.

____. 1992. *Human Rights Abuses Against the Indigenous Peoples of the Americas*. New York: Amnesty International USA.

____. 1993a. *Getting Away with Murder: Political Killings and Disappearances in the 1990s*. London: Amnesty International.

____. 1993b. *Human Rights and U.S. Security Assistance*. Washington, D.C.: Amnesty International USA.

Amuzegar, Jahangir. 1986. "The IMF Under Fire." *Foreign Policy*, 64 (Fall 1986): 98–119.

An-Na'im, Abdullahi Ahmed, ed. 1992. *Human Rights in Cross-Cultural Perspective*. Philadelphia: University of Pennsylvania Press.

Anderson, John Ward, and Molly Moore. 1993. "Born Oppressed: Women in the Developing World Face Cradle-to-Grave Discrimination." *Washington Post*, February 14, A1, A48–49.

Apter, David E. 1987. *Rethinking Development: Modernization, Dependency, and Postmodern Politics*. Newbury Park, Calif.: Sage.

Bairoch, Paul. 1981. "The Main Trends in National Economic Disparities since the Industrial Revolution." In *Disparities in Economic Development since the Industrial Revolution*, eds. P. Bairoch and M. Lévy-Leboyer. New York: St. Martin's.

Barbier, Edward, Joshua Bishop, Bruce Aylward, and Joanne Burgess. 1992. "Economic Policy and Sustainable Natural Resource Management." In *Making Development Sustainable*, ed. J. Holmberg. Washington, D.C.: Island Press.

Barnet, Richard, and Ronald E. Müller. 1974. *Global Reach: The Power of Multinational Corporations*. New York: Simon and Schuster.

Baxter, Craig, Yogendra K. Malik, Charles H. Kennedy, and Robert C. Oberst. 1987. *Government and Politics in South Asia*. Boulder, Colo.: Westview.

Beaud, Michel. 1983. *A History of Capitalism: 1500–1980*. Trans. Tom Dickman and Anny Lefebvre. New York: Monthly Review Press.

Bienefeld, Manfred. 1994. "The New World Order: Echoes of a New Imperialism." *Third World Quarterly* 15 (1): 31–48.

Bissio, Roberto Remo, ed. 1984. *Third World Guide 86–87*. New York: Grove.

Bodley, John H. 1982. *Victims of Progress*, 2nd ed. Menlo Park, Calif.: Benjamin/Cummings.

Bornschier, Volker, and Christopher Chase-Dunn. 1983. "Reply to Symanski." *American Journal of Sociology* 89 (3): 694–699.

Bornschier, Volker, Christopher Chase-Dunn, and Richard Rubinson. 1978. "Cross-National Evidence on the Effects of Foreign Investment and Aid on Economic Growth and Inequality: A Survey of Findings and a Reanalysis." *American Journal of Sociology* 84 (3): 651–683.

Brandt, Willy. 1980. *North-South: A Program for Survival*. Cambridge, Mass.: MIT Press.

Bread for the World. 1992. *Hunger 1993: Uprooted People*. Washington, D.C.: Bread for the World Institute on Hunger and Development.

Brennen, Ellen. 1993. "Urban Land and Housing Issues Facing the Third World." In *Third World Cities: Problems, Policies, and Prospects*, eds. J. D. Kasarda and A. M. Parnell. Newbury Park, Calif.: Sage.

Brewer, Anthony. 1980. *Marxist Theories of Imperialism: A Critical Survey*. London: Routledge and Kegan Paul.

Brown, Donald E. 1991. *Human Universals*. New York: McGraw-Hill.

Bunch, Charlotte. 1990. "Women's Rights as Human Rights: Toward a Re-Vision of Human Rights." *Human Rights Quarterly* 12: 486–498.

Calverley, John. 1984. *Country Risk Analysis*. London: Butterworths.

Cammack, Paul, David Pool, and William Tordoff. 1988. *Third World Politics: A Comparative Introduction*. Baltimore, Md.: Johns Hopkins University Press.

Cassen, Robert. 1986. *Does Aid Work?* Oxford: Clarendon Press.

Castro, Fidel. 1983. *The World Economic and Social Crisis: Report to the Seventh Summit Conference of Non-Aligned Countries*. Havana: Office of Publications, Cuban Council of State.

Cawson, Alan. 1986. *Corporatism and Political Theory*. Oxford: Basil Blackwell.

Chenery, Hollis. 1979. *Structural Change and Development Policy*. New York: Oxford University Press.

Chenery, Hollis, and T. N. Srinivasan, eds. 1988. *Handbook of Development Economics*, vol. 1. Amsterdam: Elsevier Science Publishers B.V.

Chenery, Hollis, Montek Ahluwalia, C.L.G. Bell, John H. Duloy, and Richard Jolly. 1974. *Redistribution with Growth*. New York: Oxford University Press.

Chesnais, Jean-Claude. 1992. *The Demographic Transition: Stages, Patterns, and Economic Implications*. Oxford: Clarendon Press.

Chilcote, Ronald H. 1984. *Theories of Development and Underdevelopment*. Boulder, Colo.: Westview.

Chirot, Daniel. 1977. *Social Change in the Twentieth Century*. New York: Harcourt Brace Jovanovich.

Clapham, Christopher. 1985. *Third World Politics: An Introduction*. Madison: University of Wisconsin Press.

Clapham, Christopher, and George Philip. 1985. "The Political Dilemmas of Military Regimes." In *The Political Dilemmas of Military Regimes*, eds. C. Clapham and G. Philip. Totowa, N.J.: Barnes and Noble.

Clay, Jason W., and Bonnie K. Holcomb. 1985. *The Politics of the Ethiopian Famine 1984–1985*. Cambridge, Mass.: Cultural Survival.

Cohen, Abner. 1969. *Custom and Politics in Urban Africa: A Study of Hausa Migrants in a Yoruba Town*. Berkeley: University of California Press.

Cole, H.S.D., Christopher Freeman, Marie Jahoda, and K.L.R. Pavitt, eds. 1973. *Models of Doom*. New York: Universe Books.

Collier, David. 1979. "Overview of the Bureaucratic-Authoritarian Model." In *The New Authoritarianism in Latin America*, ed. D. Collier. Princeton, N.J.: Princeton University Press.

Dankleman, Irene, and Joan Davidson. 1991. "Land: Women at the Centre of the Food Crisis." In *Women and the Environment: A Reader*, ed. S. Sontheimer. New York: Monthly Review Press.

Davis, Shelton H. 1977. *Victims of the Miracle: Development and the Indians of Brazil*. Cambridge: Cambridge University Press.

De Soto, Hernando. 1989. *The Other Path: The Invisible Revolution in the Third World*. New York: Harper & Row.

Dell, Sidney. 1983. "Stabilization: The Political Economy of Overkill." In *IMF Conditionality*, ed. John Williamson. Washington, D.C.: Institute for International Economics.

____. 1991. *International Development Policies: Perspectives for Industrial Countries*. Durham, N.C.: Duke University Press.

Denoon, Donald. 1985. "Third World." In *The Social Science Encyclopedia*, eds. A. Kuper and J. Kuper. London: Routledge and Kegan Paul.

Diamond, Larry, Juan J. Linz, and Seymour Martin Lipset. 1990. "Introduction: Comparing Experiences with Democracy." In *Politics in Developing Countries: Comparing Experiences with Democracy*, eds. L. Diamond, J. J. Linz, and S. M. Lipset. Boulder, Colo.: Lynne Rienner.

Domínguez, Jorge I. 1987. "Political Change: Central America, South America, and the Caribbean." In *Understanding Political Development*, eds. M. Weiner and S. P. Huntington. Boston, Mass.: Little, Brown and Company.

Donahue, James P. 1994. "The Fat Cat Freeloaders." *Washington Post*, March 6, C1-C2.

Donnelly, Jack. 1985a. "Human Rights and Development: Complementary or Competing Concerns?" In *Human Rights and Third World Development*, eds. G. W. Shepherd, Jr. and V. P. Nanda. Westport, Conn.: Greenwood.

____. 1985b. *The Concept of Human Rights*. London: Croom Helm

____. 1988. "Human Rights at the United Nations 1955–85: The Question of Bias." *International Studies Quarterly* 32: 275–303.

____. 1993. *International Human Rights*. Boulder, Colo.: Westview.

Donnelly, Jack, and Rhoda E. Howard, eds. 1987. *International Handbook of Human Rights*. New York: Greenwood.

Drakakis-Smith, David. 1987. *The Third World City*. London: Methuen.

The Economist. 1993. "The World's Shame." *The Economist* 329 (November 13): 45.

Ehrlich, Paul R. 1968. *The Population Bomb.* New York: Ballantine.

Ehrlich, Paul R., and Anne H. Ehrlich. 1990. *The Population Explosion.* New York: Simon and Schuster.

Eisenhower, Dwight D. 1963. *Mandate for Change.* New York: Signet.

Eisenstadt, S. N. 1973a. "Social Change and Development." In *Readings in Social Evolution and Development,* ed. S. N. Eisenstadt. Oxford: Pergamon Press.

____. 1973b. "Varieties of Political Development." In *Building States and Nations,* ed. S. N. Eisenstadt and S. Rokkan. Beverly Hills, Calif.: Sage.

____. 1990. "Functional Analysis in Anthropology and Sociology: An Interpretive Essay." *Annual Review of Anthropology,* 19:243–260.

Evans, Peter B. 1987. "Foreign Capital and the Third World State." In *Understanding Political Development,* eds. M. Weiner and S. P. Huntington. Boston, Mass.: Little, Brown and Company.

Evans, Peter B., Deitrich Rueschemeyer, and Theda Skocpol. 1985. *Bringing the State Back In.* Cambridge: Cambridge University Press.

Farmer, B. H. 1983. *An Introduction to South Asia.* London: Methuen.

Fieldhouse, D. K. 1981. *Colonialism 1870–1945.* New York: St. Martin's Press.

Findley, Salley E. 1993. "The Third World City: Development Policy and Issues." In *Third World Cities: Problems, Policies, and Prospects,* eds. J. D. Kasarda and A. M. Parnell. Newbury Park, Calif.: Sage.

Firebaugh, Glenn. 1992. "Growth Effects of Foreign and Domestic Investment." *American Journal of Sociology* 98 (1): 105–130.

Fisher, Julie. 1993. *The Road from Rio: Sustainable Development and the Nongovernmental Movement in the Third World.* Westport, Conn.: Praeger.

Forsythe, David P. 1988. *Human Rights and U.S. Foreign Policy: Congress Reconsidered.* Gainesville: University of Florida Press.

____. 1990. "Human Rights in U.S. Foreign Policy: Retrospect and Prospect." *Political Science Quarterly* 105 (3): 435–454.

Foster, George M. 1973. *Traditional Societies and Technological Change,* 2nd ed. New York: Harper & Row.

Frank, Andre Gunder. 1969. *Latin America: Underdevelopment or Revolution.* New York: Monthly Review Press.

French, Hilary F. 1994. "Rebuilding the World Bank." In *State of the World 1994,* ed. L. Brown. New York: Norton.

Galtung, Johan. 1971. "A Structural Theory of Imperialism." *Journal of Peace Research* 2:81–116.

Garwood, Darrel. 1985. *Under Cover: Thirty-Five Years of CIA Deception.* New York: Grove Press.

Gavshon, Arthur. 1981. *Crisis in Africa: Battleground of East and West.* Middlesex: Penguin.

Gendell, M. 1986. "Population Growth and Labor Force Absorption in Latin America, 1970–2000." In *Population Growth in Latin America and U.S. National Security,* ed. J. Saunders. New York: Allen and Unwin.

George, Susan. 1977. *How the Other Half Dies: The Real Reasons for Human Hunger.* Montclair, N.J.: Allenheld, Osmun.

____. 1988. *A Fate Worse than Debt.* New York: Grove Weidenfield.

Gibbs, David N. 1991. *The Political Economy of Third World Intervention: Mines, Money, and U.S. Policy in the Congo Crisis.* Chicago: University of Chicago Press.

Gilbert, Alan. 1994. *The Third World City.* London: Latin American Bureau.

Gillis, Malcolm, Dwight H. Perkins, Michael Roemer, and Donald Snodgrass. 1987. *Economics of Development,* 2nd ed. New York: W. W. Norton.

Gordon, Donald L. 1992. "African Politics." In *Understanding Contemporary Africa*, eds. A. A. Gordon and D. L. Gordon. Boulder, Colo.: Lynne Reinner.

Graham, Carol. 1991. *From Emergency Employment to Social Investment: Alleviating Poverty in Chile*. Washington, D.C.: The Brookings Institution.

Graham, Evans, and Jeffrey Newnham. 1991. *Dictionary of World Politics*. New York: Simon and Schuster.

Grubb, Michael. 1993. *The "Earth Summit" Agreements: A Guide and Assessment*. London: Earthscan.

Gugler, Josef. 1993. "Third World Urbanization Reexamined." *International Journal of Contemporary Sociology* 30 (1): 21–38.

Gupta, Avijit. 1988. *Ecology and Development in the Third World*. London: Routledge.

Hagen, Everett E. 1986. *The Economics of Development*, 4th ed. Homewood, Ill.: Irwin.

Hardin, Garrett. 1974. "Living on a Lifeboat." *BioScience* 24 (10): 561–568.

Hardoy, Jorge, Diana Mitlin, and David Satterthwaite. 1992. *Environmental Problems in Third World Cities*. London: Earthscan.

Harff, Barbara, and Ted Robert Gurr. 1988. "Research Note: Toward Empirical Theory of Genocides and Politicides: Identification and Measurement of Cases since 1945." *International Studies Quarterly* 32: 359–371.

Harris, Nigel. 1986. *The End of the Third World*. London: Penguin.

Harrison, Paul. 1992. *The Third Revolution: Population, Environment and a Sustainable World*. London: Penguin.

Haya de la Torre, Victor Raúl. 1961 (orig. 1931). *El plan de acción*. Lima: Ediciones Pueblo.

Held, Colbert C. 1989. *Middle East Patterns: Places, Peoples, and Politics*. Boulder, Colo.: Westview.

Holmberg, Johan, and Richard Sandbrook. 1992. "Sustainable Development: What Is to Be Done?" In *Making Development Sustainable*, ed. J. Holmberg. Washington, D.C.: Island Press.

Holmes, Steven A. 1993. "A Foreign Aid of Words, Not Cash." *New York Times*, December 5, Sec. 4, p. 5.

Hooke, A. W. 1982. *The International Monetary Fund: Its Evolution, Organization and Activities*. Washington, D.C.: International Monetary Fund.

Hopkins, Terence K., and Immanuel Wallerstein. 1982. *World Systems Analysis: Theory and Methodology*. Beverly Hills, Calif.: Sage.

Horwitz, Tony. 1991. *Bagdad Without a Map*. New York: Plume Books.

Hourani, Albert. 1991. *A History of the Arab Peoples*. New York: Warner Books.

Howard, Rhoda, and Jack Donnelly. 1987. "Introduction." In *International Handbook of Human Rights*, eds. J. Donnelly and R. Howard. New York: Greenwood.

Huang, Mab. 1979. "Human Rights in a Revolutionary Society: The Case of the People's Republic of China." In *Human Rights: Cultural and Ideological Perspectives*, eds. A. Pollis and P. Schwab. New York: Praeger.

Huntington, Samuel P. 1985. "Will More Countries Become Democratic?" In *Global Dilemmas*, eds. S. P. Huntington and J. S. Nye, Jr. Boston, Mass.: University Press of America.

———. 1987. "The Goals of Development." In *Understanding Political Development*, eds. M. Weiner and S. P. Huntington. Boston, Mass.: Little, Brown and Company.

IDB. 1989. "Facts About the Informal Sector." *International Development Bank Newsletter*, March, p. 8.

Kadane, Kathy. 1990. "U.S. Officials' Lists Aided Indonesian Bloodbath in '60s." *Washington Post*, May 21, p. A5.

Kammeyer, Kenneth C. W., and Helen L. Ginn. 1986. *An Introduction to Population.* Chicago: Dorsey.

Kasarda, John D., and Alan M. Parnell, eds. 1993. *Third World Cities: Problems, Policies, and Prospects.* Newbury Park, Calif.: Sage.

Kats, Gregory. 1992. "Achieving Sustainability in Energy Use in Developing Countries." In *Making Development Sustainable,* ed. J. Holmberg. Washington, D.C.: Island Press.

Kaufman, Edy. 1991. "Prisoners of Conscience: The Shaping of a New Human Rights Concept." *Human Rights Quarterly* 13: 339–367.

Khan, M. S., and M. D. Knight. 1985. "Fund Supported Adjustment Programs and Economic Growth." IMF Occasional Paper No. 41, Washington, D.C., November.

Kidron, Michael, and Ronald Segal. 1991. *The New State of the World Atlas,* 4th ed. New York: Simon and Schuster.

Kinder, Hermann, and Werner Hilgemann. 1974. *The Anchor Atlas of World History,* 2 vols. Translated from the German by Ernest A. Menze. New York: Anchor/Doubleday.

Kirkpatrick, Jeane. 1979. "Dictatorships and Double Standards." *Commentary* 68: 34–45.

Kuznets, Simon. 1955. "Economic Growth and Income Inequality." *American Economic Review* 45 (March): 1–28.

Kwitny, Jonathan. 1984. *Endless Enemies: The Making of an Unfriendly World.* New York: Penguin.

Lenin, Vladimir Ilich. 1988 [orig. 1916]. *Imperialism: The Highest Stage of Capitalism.* New York: International Publishers.

Lewellen, Ted. 1978. *Peasants in Transition: The Changing Economy of the Peruvian Aymara.* Boulder, Colo.: Westview.

———. 1984. "The Missing Statistic: Income, Development and Basic Needs." In *Monograph Series on Global Development.* College Park, Md.: World Academy of Development and Cooperation.

———. 1988. "The U.S. and State Terrorism in the Third World." In *Terrible Beyond Endurance: The Foreign Policy of State Terrorism.* New York: Greenwood.

———. 1989. "APRA and Oligarchy: Building a 'Populist Elite' in a Proto-Democracy." Paper presented at the International Studies Association Annual Meeting, London, March.

———. 1990. "State Terror and the Disruption of Internal Adaptations by CIA Covert Actions." *Scandinavian Journal of Development Alternatives* 9 (2, 3): 47–66.

———. 1991. "Corporatist Assimilation of the Masses in Peru and Nicaragua: A Tale of Two Communities." Paper presented at the Annual Meeting of the American Anthropological Association, Chicago, November.

———. 1992. *Political Anthropology: An Introduction,* 2nd ed. Westport, Conn.: Bergin and Garvey.

Lobo, Susan. 1982. *A House of My Own: Social Organization in the Squatter Settlements of Lima, Peru.* Tucson: University of Arizona Press.

Loewenson, Rene. 1992. *Modern Plantation Agriculture: Corporate Wealth and Labour Squalor.* London: Zed.

London, Bruce, and Bruce A. Williams. 1988. "Multinational Corporate Penetration, Protest, and Basic Needs Provision in Non-core Nations: A Cross-national Analysis." *Social Forces* 66:747–773.

Mansfield, Peter. 1992. *The Arabs,* 3rd ed.. London: Penguin.

Mason, David. T., and Dale A. Krane. 1989. "The Political Economy of Death Squads: Toward a Theory of the Impact of State-Sanctioned Terror." *International Studies Quarterly* 33: 175–198.

Mathews, Jessica. 1994. "Population Control that Works." *Washington Post*, April 1, A21.

McCormick, James M., and Neil J. Mitchell. 1989. "Human Rights and Foreign Assistance: An Update." *Social Science Quarterly* 70 (4): 969–979.

McEvedy, Colin. 1980. *The Penguin Atlas of African History*. Middlesex: Penguin.

Meadows, Donella H., Dennis L. Meadows, and Jørgen Randers. 1992. *Beyond the Limits*. Post Hills, Vt.: Chelsea Green.

Meadows, Donella H., Dennis L. Meadows, Jørgen Rander, and William Behrens III. 1972. *The Limits to Growth*. New York: Universe Books.

Meller, Patricio. 1990. "Chile." In *Latin American Adjustment: How Much Has Happened*, ed. John Williamson. Washington, D.C.: Institute for International Economics.

____. 1991. "Adjustment and Social Costs in Chile During the 1980s." *World Development* 19 (11):1545–1561.

____. 1993. "A Review of the Chilean Privatization Experience." *Quarterly Review of Economics and Finance* 33 (Special Issue): 95–112.

Migdal, Joel S. 1987. "Strong States, Weak States: Power and Accommodation." In *Understanding Political Development*, eds. M. Weiner and S. P. Huntington. Boston, Mass.: Little, Brown and Company.

____. 1988. *Strong Societies and Weak States*. Princeton, N.J.: Princeton University Press.

Mikesell, Raymond F. 1983. "Appraising IMF Conditionality: Too Loose, Too Tight, or Just Right?" In *IMF Conditionality*, ed. John Williamson. Washington, D.C.: Institute for International Economics.

Monimart, Marie. 1991. "Women and the Fight Against Desertification." In *Women and the Environment: A Reader*, ed. S. Sontheimer. New York: Monthly Review Press.

Moorehead, Alan. 1960. *The White Nile*. New York: Dell.

Morawetz, David. 1977. *Twenty-five Years of Economic Development 1950 to 1975*. Baltimore, Md.: Johns Hopkins University Press.

____. 1984. "The Gap Between Rich and Poor Countries." In *The Gap Between the Rich and the Poor*, ed. Mitchell A. Seligson. Boulder, Colo.: Westview.

Morlino, Leonardo. 1990. "Authoritarianism." In *Contemporary Political Systems: Classifications and Typologies*, eds. A. Bebler and J. Seroka. Boulder, Colo.: Lynne Rienner.

Morris, Morris David. 1979. *Measuring the Condition of the World's Poor: The Physical Quality of Life Index*. New York: Pergamon Press.

Morris, Morris David, and Michelle B. McAlpin. 1982. *Measuring the Condition of India's Poor: The Physical Quality of Life Index*. New Delhi: Permillia and Co.

Morsink, Johannes. 1991. "Women's Rights in the Universal Declaration." *Human Rights Quarterly* 13: 229–256.

Muller, Edward N. 1984. "Financial Dependence in the Capitalist World Economy and the Distribution of Income Within Nations." In *The Gap Between the Rich and the Poor*, ed. Mitchell A. Seligson. Boulder, Colo.: Westview.

Murphy, Caryle. 1993. "Lowering the Veil: Muslim Women Struggle for Careers in a Society Ruled by Men and Religion." *Washington Post*, February 17, A1, A32–33.

Myrdal, Gunnar. 1970. *The Challenge of World Poverty*. New York: Vintage.

Nafziger, Wayne E. 1984. *The Economics of Developing Countries*. Belmont, Calif.: Wadsworth.

Nasar, Sylvia. 1994. "Economics of Equality: A New View." *New York Times*, January 8, pp. 39, 48.

Nordlinger, Eric A. 1987. "Taking the State Seriously." In *Understanding Political Development*, eds. M. Weiner and S. P. Huntington. Boston, Mass.: Little, Brown and Company.

O'Donnell, Guillermo A. 1979. *Modernization and Bureaucratic-Authoritarianism: Studies in South American Politics*. Berkeley, Calif.: Institute of International Studies.

Oliver, Roland, and J. D. Fage. 1962. *A Short History of Africa*. Middlesex: Penguin.

Open University. 1983. *Third World Atlas*. Philadelphia, Pa.: Open University Press.

Orubuloye, I. O. 1991. "The Implications of Demographic Transition Theory for Fertility Change in Nigeria." *International Journal of Sociology of the Family* 21 (Autumn): 161–174.

Parnwell, Mike. 1993. *Population Movements in the Third World*. London: Routledge.

Pazos, Felipe. 1987. "Import Substitution Policies, Tariffs, and Competition." In *Latin America's Economic Development: Institutional and Structuralist Perspectives*, eds. J. L. Dietz and J. H. Street. Boulder, Colo.: Lynne Rienner.

Pearce, David, Edward Barbier, and Anil Markandya. 1990. *Sustainable Development: Economics and Environment in the Third World*. London: Earthscan.

Pierce, Jenny. 1981. *Under the Eagle: U.S. Intervention in Central America and the Caribbean*. Boston, Mass.: South End Press.

Poe, Steven C. 1990. "Human Rights and US Foreign Aid: A Review of Quantitative Studies and Suggestions for Future Research." *Human Rights Quarterly* 12: 499–512.

Pollis, Adamantia, and Peter Schwab. 1979. *Human Rights: Cultural and Ideological Perspectives*. New York: Praeger.

Postel, Sandra. 1990. "Saving the Water for Agriculture." In *The State of the World, 1990*, ed. L. Brown. Washington, D.C.: Worldwatch.

———. 1994. "Carrying Capacity: Earth's Bottom Line." In *State of the World, 1994*, ed. L. Brown. New York: Norton.

Prados, John. 1986. *Presidents' Secret Wars: CIA and Pentagon Covert Operations Since World War II*. New York: William Morrow.

Preston, Julia. 1993. "For Rural Women, a Millstone of Poverty." *Washington Post*, February 15, A1, A24–25.

Rabkin, Rhoda. 1993. "How Ideas Become Influential: Ideological Foundations of Export-Led Growth in Chile (1973–1990)." *World Affairs* 156 (Summer): 3–25.

Randall, Vicky. 1988. "Introduction." In *Political Parties in the Third World*, ed. V. Randall. London: Sage.

Randall, Vicky, and Robin Theobold. 1985. *Political Change and Underdevelopment: A Critical Introduction to Third World Politics*. Durham, N.C.: Duke University Press.

Ranis, Gustav. 1987. "Challenges and Opportunities Posed by Asia's Superexporters: Implications for Manufactured Exports from Latin America." In *Latin America's Economic Development: Institutional and Structuralist Perspectives*, eds. J. L. Dietz and J. H. Street. Boulder, Colo.: Lynne Rienner.

Reanda, Laura. 1991. "Prostitution as a Human Rights Question: Problems and Prospects of United Nations Action." *Human Rights Quarterly* 13: 202–228.

Reitsma, H. A., and J. M. G. Kleinpenning. 1989. *The Third World in Perspective*. Assen: Van Gorcum.

Renteln, Alison Dundes. 1990. *International Human Rights: Universalism Versus Relativism*. Newbury Park, Calif.: Sage.

Richardson, Harry W. 1993. "Efficiency and Welfare in LDC Mega-Cities." In *Third World Cities: Problems, Policies, and Prospects*, eds. J. D. Kasarda and A. M. Parnell. Newbury Park, Calif.: Sage.

Robertson, A. H. 1979. "Human Rights: A Global Assessment." In *Human Rights and American Foreign Policy*, eds. D. P. Kommers and G. D. Loescher. Notre Dame, Ind.: University of Notre Dame Press.

Rodney, Walter. 1972. *How Europe Underdeveloped Africa*. Washington, D.C.: Howard University Press.

Rohr, Janelle ed. 1989 *The Third World: Opposing Viewpoints*. San Diego, Calif.: Greenhaven.

Rostow, W. W. 1960. *The Stages of Economic Growth*. London: Cambridge University Press.

Roxborough, Ian. 1979. *Theories of Underdevelopment*. London: Macmillan.

Ruchwarger, Gary. 1987. *People in Power: Forging a Grassroots Democracy in Nicaragua*. South Hadley, Mass.: Bergin and Garvey.

Schmitter, Phillipe C. 1974. "Still the Century of Corporatism?" In *The New Corporatism: Social-Political Structures in the Iberian World*, eds. F. Pike and T. Stritch. Notre Dame, Ind.: University of Notre Dame Press.

Schoultz, Lars. 1981. "U.S. Policy Toward Human Rights in Latin America: A Comparative Analysis of Two Administrations." In *Global Human Rights: Public Policies, Comparative Measures, and NGO Strategies*, eds. V. P. Nanda, J. R. Scarrit, and G. W. Shepherd, Jr. Boulder, Colo.: Westview.

Seligson, Mitchell L., ed. 1984. *The Gap Between the Rich and the Poor*. Boulder, Colo.: Westview.

Service, Elman R. 1962. *Primitive Social Organization: An Evolutionary Perspective*. New York: Random House.

Shannon, Richard Thomas. 1989. *An Introduction to World Systems Theory*. Boulder, Colo.: Westview.

Shepherd, Jack. 1986. "When Foreign Aid Fails." *The Atlantic Monthly* 255 (April):41–46.

Simon, Julian L. 1977. *The Politics of Population Growth*. Princeton, N.J.: Princeton University Press.

___. 1981. *The Ultimate Resource*. Princeton, N.J.: Princeton University Press.

Singletary, Michelle. 1994. "African Currency Devaluation Cheers Bankers but Few Others." *Washington Post*, June 2, A27.

Sivard, Ruth Leger. 1987. *World Military and Social Expenditures 1987–88*, 12th ed. Washington, D.C.: World Priorities.

Sklar, Holly. 1980. *Trilateralism*. Boston, Mass.: South End Press.

Smith, Adam. 1937 [orig. 1776]. *An Inquiry into the Nature and Causes of the Wealth of Nations*. New York: The Modern Library.

Smyser, W. R. 1987. *Refugees: Extended Exile*. New York: Praeger.

Snyder, Louis L. 1990. *Encyclopedia of Nationalism*. New York: Paragon House.

Sontheimer, Sally, ed. 1991. *Women and the Environment: A Reader*. New York: Monthly Review Press.

Soroos, Marvin S. 1987. *Beyond Sovereignty: The Challenge of Global Policy*. Colombia: University of South Carolina Press.

Spindler, George, and Louise Spindler. 1990. *The American Cultural Dialogue and Its Transmission*. London: The Falmer Press.

Stamatopoulou, Elsa. 1994. "Indigenous Peoples and the United Nations: Human Rights as a Developing Dynamic." *Human Rights Quarterly* 16: 58–81.

Stavrianos, L. S. 1981. *Global Rift: The Third World Comes of Age*. New York: William Morrow.

Sun, Lena H. 1994. "China's Social Changes Spur More Executions." *Washington Post*, March 27, A1, A22.

Szymanski, Albert. 1983. "Comment on Bornschier, Chase-Dunn, and Rubinson." *American Journal of Sociology* 89 (3): 690–694.

Taylor, Paul. 1993. "Apartheid Leaves a Legacy of Hunger." *Washington Post*, August 8, A1, A22.

Tennant, Chris. 1994. "Indigenous Peoples: International Institutions, and the International Legal Literature from 1945–1993." *Human Rights Quarterly* 16: 1–57.

Timerman, Jacobo. 1981. *Prisoner Without Name, Cell Without Number*. New York: Vintage.

Todaro, Michael P. 1985. *Economic Development in the Third World*, 2nd ed. New York: Longman.

Toulmin, Camilla, Ian Scoones, and Joshua Bishop. 1992. "The Future of Africa's Drylands: Is Local Resource Management the Answer?" In *Making Development Sustainable*, ed. J. Holmberg. Washington, D.C.: Island Press.

Turner, Louis. 1973. *Multinational Companies and the Third World*. New York: Hill and Wang.

UNCED (United Nations Conference on Environment and Development). 1992. *The Global Partnership for Environment and Development: A Guide to Agenda 21*. Geneva: UNCED.

UNDP (United Nations Development Programme). 1993. *Human Development Report 1993*. New York: United Nations.

United Nations. 1983. *Human Rights: A Compilation of International Instruments*. New York: United Nations.

Utting, Peter. 1992. *Economic Reform and Third-World Socialism*. New York: St. Martin's Press.

Wai, Dunstan M. 1979. "Human Rights in Sub-Saharan Africa." In *Human Rights: Cultural and Ideological Perspectives*, eds. A. Pollis and P. Schwab. New York: Praeger.

Wallerstein, Immanuel. 1974. *The Modern World System: Capitalist Agriculture and The Origins of the European World Economy in the Sixteenth Century*. New York: Academic Press.

Watkins, Alfred J. 1986. *Till Debt Do Us Part: Who Wins, Who Loses, and Who Pays for the International Debt Crisis*. Lanham, Md.: Roosevelt Center for American Policy Studies.

Weber, Max. 1964. *The Theory of Social and Economic Organization*, ed. T. Parsons. New York: Free Press.

Weiner, Myron. 1987a. "Introduction." In *Understanding Political Development*, eds. M. Weiner and S. P. Huntington. Boston, Mass.: Little, Brown and Company.

____. 1987b. "Political Change: Asia, Africa, and the Middle East." In *Understanding Political Development*, eds. M. Weiner and S. P. Huntington. Boston, Mass.: Little, Brown and Company.

Weissman, Stephen. 1979. "The CIA Covert Action in Zaire and Angola." *Political Science Quarterly* 2:263–276.

Wetzel, Janice Wood. 1993. *The World of Women: In Pursuit of Human Rights*. New York: New York University Press.

Wight, Jonathan B. 1994. "Developing Nations." In *Principles of Economics*, ed. R. W. Tresch. Minneapolis, Minn.: West.

Williams, Walter. 1991. *Javanese Lives: Women and Men in Modern Indonesian Society*. New Brunswick, N.J.: Rutgers University Press.

Williamson, John. 1987. "What Washington Means by Policy Reform." In *Latin American Adjustment: How Much Has Happened?*, ed. John Williamson. Washington, D.C.: Institute for International Economics.

Wimberly, Dale W. 1991. "Transnational Corporate Investment and Food Consumption in the Third World: A Cross-national Analysis." *Rural Sociology* 56:406–431.

Winston, Morton E., ed. 1989. *The Philosophy of Human Rights*. Belmont, Calif.: Wadsworth.

Wiseberg, Laurie S., and Harry M. Scoble. 1979. "Monitoring Human Rights Violations: The Role of Nongovernmental Organizations." In *Human Rights and American Foreign Policy*, eds. D. P. Kommers and G. D. Loescher. Notre Dame, Ind.: University of Notre Dame Press.

Wolf, Eric R. 1982. *Europe and the People Without History*. Berkeley: University of California Press.

World Commission on Environment and Development. 1987. *Our Common Future*. New York: Oxford University Press.

World Bank. 1984. *World Development Report 1984*. Oxford: Oxford University Press.

____. 1989. *Sub-Saharan Africa: From Crisis to Sustainable Growth*. Washington, D.C.: World Bank.

____. 1992. *World Development Report 1992*. Oxford: Oxford University Press.

____. 1993. *Trends in Developing Countries*. Washington, D.C.: World Bank.

Worsley, Peter. 1984. *The Three Worlds: Culture and World Development*. Chicago: University of Chicago Press.

Wright, John T. 1979. "Human Rights in the West: Political Liberties and the Rule of Law." In *Human Rights: Cultural and Ideological Perspectives*, eds. A. Pollis and P. Schwab. New York: Praeger.

Wyn, Grant, ed. 1985. *The Political Economy of Corporatism*. New York: St. Martin's Press.

Wynia, Gary W. 1978. *The Politics of Latin American Development*. Cambridge: Cambridge University Press.

Young, Crawford, and Thomas Turner. 1985. *The Rise and Decline of the Zairian State*. Madison: University of Wisconsin Press.

Zlotnik, Hania. 1993. "Women as Migrants and Workers in Developing Countries." *International Journal of Contemporary Sociology* 30 (1): 39–62.

Zvobgo, Eddison Jonas Mudadirwa. 1979. "The Third World View." In *Human Rights and American Foreign Policy*, eds. D. P. Kommers and G. D. Loescher. Notre Dame, Ind.: University of Notre Dame Press.

Index

ABOUT THE AUTHOR

TED C. LEWELLEN is Professor of Anthropology at the University of Richmond. He is the author of *Peasants in Transition* (1976) and *Political Anthropology*, now in its second edition (Bergin & Garvey, 1992).

ISBN 0-89789-399-9

HARDCOVER BAR CODE

DATE DUE